STRUTTING AND FRETTING

So You Think You Want To Start a Theatre Company?

Cecil Hayter

With contributions from Terry Hawes, Neil Cloake and members of
LOST Theatre and Southgate Opera Company

Edited by Drs Beverley and Dana Chalmers

**Grosvenor House
Publishing Limited**

The right of Cecil Hayter to be identified as the author of this
work has been asserted by him in accordance with Section 78
of the Copyright, Designs and Patents Act 1988

The book cover and interior images are copyright to Cecil Hayter

This book is published by
Grosvenor House Publishing Ltd
28-30 High Street, Guildford, Surrey, GU1 3EL.
www.grosvenorhousepublishing.co.uk

A CIP record for this book
is available from the British Library

ISBN 978-1-78148-718-1

TABLE OF CONTENTS

ACKNOWLEDGEMENTS

I would like to thank Bev and Dana Chalmers, Lynne O'Connor and Marek Oravec, without whom this book would not have been possible.

I would also like to thank Fay Davies for always being there when I needed her.

PREFACE

R ather than include a formal preface by a single LOST or Southgate Opera Company member, it seemed more in keeping with the spirit of these companies to preface this book with the words of many individuals who have all taken their LOST and Southgate experiences out into the world.

I know for sure that without being part of LOST - and learning from Cecil's unpretentious and ballsy direction, I would not have had the confidence to audition for any drama school (Ralph Feinnes, Actor).

...and happily we still survive...funds have been maintained...performances continue to be of a very high standard (Colin Davis, Chairman of the Southgate Opera Company).

I owe a great debt of gratitude to LOST for giving me such wonderful experiences, introducing me to lifelong friends and for instilling in me the confidence to pursue my dream of becoming a professional actor (Jamie Ballard, Actor).

LOST was never about being perfect. It was about rejoicing in the imperfections that occasionally make great art and always make extraordinary learning experiences (Dana Lori Chalmers, PhD).

...there were many parts of the jigsaw which made up the continued development of the opera company (Barry Golding, Member of the Southgate Opera Company).

Every single day I use talents, skills and techniques I learned at LOST (Stephen Lee, Actor and Director).

...numerous ups and downs with the establishment and maintenance of the Lost Theatre read like an unimaginable novel...at times heart-warming at others tragically disappointing (Beverley Chalmers, DSc(Med); PhD)

I am still heavily involved with SOUTHGATE OPERA teaching some of the membership (Jenny Lillystone, Soloist: Covent Garden Opera).

...a journey I can only now look back on with envy and appreciation of what LOST gave me (Simon Da Costa, Playwright).

LOST has given young people of all ages a love and understanding of theatre that has never really left them (Jenny Runnacre, Actress).

LOST was a unique and remarkable feat (Greg Mandry, Film Director).

Most of the young people working at LOST were not stardom seekers. They were serious and passionate about doing plays (The Nolan Sisters, LOST members).

I am so grateful to LOST for helping me to find my feet (Matt Ian Kelly, Playwright and Theatre Director).

Many of my friends from LOST have followed me into the profession (Matthew Hebden, Actor).

Thank you to all I worked and played with. It was a fantastic time of my life (Paul Rogan, Stand Up Comedian).

A number of the actors and actresses discovered at the LOST Theatre... have made their way into the professional theatre...while others will have settled back into their ...lives, all the better for the confidence-raising and friendship building experience. (Adrian Brown, Television Director).

PART 1

Cecil

The start of it all

I always wanted to visit London. On my piano stood a large poster of Big Ben and the Houses of Parliament and I knew beyond doubt that one day I would see them. I was born in East London, a seaside town in South Africa (SA), but I was now living in Durban where by pure circumstances I had become the manager/ artistic director of the Lyric Theatre.

Durban had one theatre only, which came about when a syndicate believed it would be a good business venture. Obviously this would not work by taking the best local amateur thespians and calling them professionals. Instead, a delegate was sent to London and a cast of ten plus a director and scenic artist were collected together and shipped to Durban where a cinema had been converted and the Lyric Theatre was born.

What impression these poor actors had of South African theatre we do not know. The scenic artist, Liz Mcleish, had been told to bring everything possible with her as SA never knew what stage paints were. Now Liz had always mixed her paint in bed chamber pots. A nice size to fit a large brush with a convenient handle to hold them. She had to explain to customs why she carried twelve piss pots when she arrived.

A piano technician by trade but the chairman of the local amateur-dramatic society, I rushed to get a job in this exciting new venture. I was taken on as a general stage hand plus dogsbody, learning this new trade by doing everything from sweeping the stage, serving the actors tea to servicing the air conditioning plant, washing dishes, making props, making costumes, painting scenery, ushering, cleaning the theatre, prompting, silk screening posters and yes, I even appeared on-stage once as an actor with a single line to deliver, "Put up your pipes and begone" in Rattigan's play *Harlequin*. There were no unions in SA, let alone Equity. A glorious four years passed doing two weekly rep. It was hard work and low pay, but who cared? We all loved the theatre.

Besides doing a new production every two weeks, rehearsing during the day, and performing at night, we occasionally hosted visiting companies from Johannesburg which, I believe, was the only other professional theatre in South Africa. It was run by Brian Brook. I guess there must have been another professional company in Cape Town, but I didn't know of it.

While visiting companies were in the theatre we, the resident company, toured, doing one night stands in small towns with large distances between them. We, the crew, would arrive in the town in a large pantechnicon with sets, costumes, furniture and props and set up shop. Straight after the performance each night we started the whole procedure again, loading sets, props etc. and driving through the night to the next town. We took driving and sleeping on the truck in turns usually reaching the next town at six in the morning to find an open café for breakfast then on to the theatre, school, or hall in which we were booked, to set up shop again for the evening performance.

Oh for a bed and a hot shower....And the cast? Well after each performance, a cocktail party was given by the hosts for the evening, then to a hotel for bed and breakfast to catch a train to the next town fresh and ready for the next performance. Oddly enough, as crew, we never thought to envy them. After all they were ACTORS and we loved our jobs.

One of our crew, Norman, an excellent stage manager and exceptionally hard worker, was black and although among us there was no difference, when we arrived at a café for breakfast or lunch he was not allowed in to join us. At least one of us always stayed outside with him to keep him company.

Today I cannot believe that we just accepted this as normal. I also found in later years that his pay, even though he did exactly the same work as the rest of us, was under half of what we received and God knows ours was low enough.

Four years had passed since the inauguration of the theatre. Needless to say we were a tightly knit unit both cast and crew, but all good things end. We had struggled hard to fill the seats with bums by doing many farces and murder mysteries, occasionally throwing in something more serious such as *Taste of Honey*, *Lower Depths* or a Chekhov etc. desperately hoping that South Africa would eventually learn that there was more to theatre. Remember that at that time the government would not allow television in the country just in case we could see what was going on in the rest of the world. The film of *Othello* was banned until such an outcry from the public caused the ban to be lifted on the grounds that Laurence Olivier was really a white man just painted black and therefore there were no restrictions about falling in love with a white Desdemona. The film of the musical *South Pacific* was so badly censored and cut that it no longer made sense. It did cause much laughter in the cinema though. Even the book *Black Beauty* about a horse was banned. However, although a full book could be written about the life of the Lyric theatre in Durban, this is not the object of this book.

Money was not coming in and the inevitable day arrived when, on the Monday for the first rehearsal of the next show, instead of the next cast list being pinned up on the board, notices informed us that the theatre would have to close, in other words we were all sacked. This was not quite true---- everyone but me. I was not sacked. Remember I was the only one who knew how the air conditioning worked or how to fix any fuses that blew or where the water mains turned off in case of burst pipes etc. I was retained as a sort of handymen come manager.

We still had two shows to do, one of them being a farce called *Reluctant Heroes*. Perhaps word had got round that the theatre was about to close or maybe it was just a very funny farce, but it hit....HARD.... and played to capacity houses. The money rolled in on this one. The management relented and decided to continue for another year. And so, as a two weekly rep company, the Lyric lived for another year. Sadly to no avail. The end of the year was a repeat performance and once more I was the sole survivor. No need to relate the emotions on the final performance.

I suppose everyone working in the theatre has a roller-coaster life, sometimes hitting the highs and sometimes the lows and this was a low. Come Monday morning, which was normally the first rehearsal of the next show, as usual I opened the front door, walked through the foyer and switched on the auditorium working lights and entered. I sat. There would be no rehearsal. The theatre was empty, very empty, and I knew it would remain so. Five years of memories flooded back. I felt I should write a book about them, but writing is not my forte. I wondered if anyone would, after all it was the first and only fully professional company in Durban. One memory burned bright in my brain. My main function in the theatre had become lighting. While operating the lighting board I watched every performance. We had recently done a performance of *The Entertainer*. We knew that like Archie Rice in the play our position was precarious. Archie fails to keep his theatre going and on his final performance he addresses the audience "You've been a lovely audience. Tell me where you're working tomorrow, I will come and see you."

Each night the audience (what there were of them) laughed. I cried.

We were to find.....correction, I was to find as there was no longer a WE; that the theatre had been bought by a Mr Pearson, interested in opera and knowing nothing about the running of a theatre. No longer a rep company. Large musicals with freelance actors and importing leads from overseas came into vogue. Also intrigues, jealousy, sabotage, lies, slander, the lot seemed to abound.

For fear of being sued I will not go into all this. In brief a Mr M for reasons of his own tried to destroy Mr Pearson or The Lyric by spreading false rumours about antisemitism, stealing lighting equipment from the theatre, destroying parts of the stage revolve to sabotage visiting shows, even to bugging my flat where a meeting regarding the theatre was to be held. He even went so far as to tell a 14 year old Dorothy (in the *Wizard of Oz*) in the middle of a show, in the middle of the run, that that would be her last performance (because she was Jewish). Fortunately, the wrong was quickly righted and she continued to spellbind the audience for another few weeks. However we'll skip all the details. I'm sure it would make a perfect B movie all of its own but that's where we'll leave it

Kathy and I shared a flat on the Berea. We had both talked of going to London but never had the money so always put it off. Finance was not our strong point. Many were the times we pooled our last pennies to buy food for the cat. We could starve but we couldn't see the cat go hungry. Kathy had an amazing sense of logic.

We returned home from the theatre one night cold and hungry. As Kathy put the percolator on for coffee, she asked,

"Would you like a sandwich?"
"Yes please." There followed a small rummaging around followed with
"Oh damn. No luck. We're out of bread......... Never mind I'll make some toast instead."

I think it was this logic of making toast instead of sandwiches when there is no bread that helped her to get the money together for, one night she came home and informed me that she had booked on the *Southern Cross* to go to London. I congratulated her and secretly decided that I would join her. By doing a lot of odd jobs I somehow managed to save enough to buy a boat ticket and also booked on the *Southern Cross*.

I had discovered that passengers were expected to board the ship on the Saturday afternoon but that it only departed on the Sunday. The intention was to see Kathy off on the Saturday then sneak in late Saturday night and see if I could book a seat at her table on board to meet her out at sea. All our friends somehow managed to keep it secret .....but I made one mistake. The Wednesday before sailing we came home from work, both tired and hungry as usual. That day at the theatre Kathy had been in a bad mood and was still grumpy.

"O.K. Kathy, what's wrong?"
"You're glad I'm going overseas. You just want to get rid of me."

I realized that I had not made a fuss over her going or said that I would miss her, etc. I tried talking my way out but nothing would appease her. It grew into an argument until after one more of her.

"You're glad to get rid of me."

I lost control and shouted back,

"That's why I'm coming with you" as I threw my boat ticket and passport on the table in front of her. It was all supposed to be a big surprise.

Silence for a second and, still angry.

"Then why are you telling me?"

By the Saturday we had both calmed down, happily boarding the ship together. About eleven that night all friends had said their goodbyes and left. Kathy and I decided to take a walk round the harbour. We were, of course, as usual, broke. Or at least I had five pounds in my pocket. I don't know how much Kathy had. We contemplated a cup of coffee.

"You know, when we're in London and we have no money left and we're dying for a cup of coffee we'll be saying 'If we hadn't spent the money on that coffee in Durban we could have a cup now.'"

We skipped the coffee.

Kathy's sister and brother-in-law were to meet her in London. She would be staying with them until she found work. On the other hand I had five pounds. I had heard about Hyde Park and was convinced that I would be able to sleep on a bench there until I found a job. We had been warned all about the fact that we must not tell customs this and that we must have enough money in the bank to pay for our trip back home again plus sufficient money to live for the duration of our stay. Mr Pearson (the now owner of the Lyric in Durban) had lent me sufficient funds to cover this. I had promised to return it as soon as possible.

After leaving Durban, the boat had stopped for one day in Cape Town and we were now at sea on our way. I had been extremely busy right to the last moment with extra jobs to pay the fare and everyone kept reminding me of the glorious luxury I would have sitting in the sun on a deck chair during a two and half weeks cruise. I had really been looking forward to it. Just think, over two weeks of pure luxury.

I was BORED. One day of deckchairs and table tennis was all I could take. After that I hated every moment of it. Somebody please, please, invent intercontinental flights. BORED> BORED> BORED>

I did enjoy the day's respite when we stopped on the Canary Isles.

Arriving in London

At long last Southampton arrived and I had to face customs. My passport also stated that I worked in the theatre. Not very encouraging for immigration.

"Just on holiday?"

"Yes."

"How long will you be staying?"

"I don't know. It depends on when my money runs out."

"How much have you got?" I produced the bank statements.

"Two separate amounts?" He was quite calm.

"Yes," I said with all confidence.

"One is my spending money and the other is to pay my fare back home."

"Why did you not get a return ticket?"

"Well, I hope to get as far as Greece but if my money runs out before then I will have to return from where ever I am at the time."

"You work in the theatre?"

"Yes."

"So how long do you think you'll need?"

"Well put it this way. We have a production opening in Durban on (I gave them a date about three months ahead) and I have to be back by then."

"Right. Three months," he said, and stamped my passport.

I had not been one bit nervous. I never even dreamed that there was a possibility that I could be refused. Oh! The daring of the young. Kathy and I met up again and took the boat train to London. Memory fails me but we must have paid this all in advance as it did not come out of my budget. The thing I remember most about the ride to London was that I had never seen countryside so vividly green. Very different from South Africa. On seeing Lambeth Palace I thought it was the Tower Of London.

John and Christen were at the station to meet Kathy. I suppose it's inevitable but on hearing that I intended to sleep in Hyde Park .... I don't know whether shocked or amused, but they insisted I stay with them until I found a job. So sad for my memoirs if ever I wrote them as I would now never sleep in Hyde Park on a park bench. So my first week in London was spent in Chipstead. Until Marlene, a friend from South Africa now living in London phoned me and invited me to stay with her in Montague Square which was right in the centre of London.... Baker Street. With many thanks to John and Christen I moved to where I thought it would be easier to find a job. I found I was now living in the flat next to Ringo Star and across the road from Peter Sellers. It was the week that Zack (Ringo's son) was born so each morning as I opened the front door to the street I was met by a sea of cameras, reporters etc. They didn't seem interested in me.

I came across an ad needing a piano technician in Fulham. I phoned, went for an interview, found that the firm of Fulham Pianos was owned by a Mr Shakespeare, got the job and started work the next day. Despite the fact that I was now working for a Mr Shakespeare and the first piano I was asked to work on, was for the Lyric Theatre in Hammersmith and that on the radio that day the music was from *Sound of Music*, one of the last shows I had done in Durban, I dared not mention that I had worked in the theatre for fear that I would not be kept on.

I had a job. Thanks to John, Christen and Marlene feeding me, my five pounds had seen me through.

Les Shakespeare was very soon to become a sort of father figure to me. First of all just down the road from the workshop in Lillie Road, he owned a rather derelict house which stood empty. He offered it to me free of rent if I wanted it. I took it. This was completely alien to me. A house without a bathroom and an outside toilet. I was informed the public baths were in North End Road. I spent some days cleaning and trying to get rid of the smell of cats which had inhabited it, before I moved in.

It was April 1st. It was freezing cold with the snow still coming down. The glass of water next to my bed was frozen solid. I got out of bed, or should I say I got up taking the bed with me and went through to the kitchen. There was a jug of water. It was frozen. I turned to switch on the tap. It was frozen. I went outside to the loo. It was frozen. Eventually I arrived downstairs at the front door to go to work. The post had arrived. I picked up a letter from South Africa and with frozen fingers managed to open it.

"Dear Cecil, Oh to be in England now that April's there".

In the meantime I had come to London to study theatre. Knowing nothing of drama schools, and not having an equity card, I discovered evening institute classes which seemed to cover just about any subject imaginable for just two shillings and sixpence per class. A big rush to the City Lit to sign up for everything I could, managing to fit in theory of music, modern dance, theatre design and drama. I was allowed to enter the advanced modern dance after owning up to the fact that

I was a professional ballroom dancer. The timetable did not allow me to join the beginners' class. Tremendous excitement and much nervousness, knowing the standard of theatre in England to be so far above that in South Africa. I was scared of proving myself an idiot.

The music theory... I was correct. It was far above me and I soon gracefully retired with the excuse that I was finding the timetable of fitting everything in impossible.

The scenic design.... a waste of time. I found I was being asked to explain to the class the use of gauzes, scrims, flies, lighting etc. I had worked on all this in the theatre.

The modern dance.... a complete waste of time. Again no teaching of technique or exercises to develop stretching, jumping, moving etc... just giving simple routines to follow.

The drama.... mostly just doing improvisations. Again no real training but I suppose useful.

A bit later I was able to join another modern dance class on recommendation which was brilliant and where I really had to work hard to keep up. I had found that although the opportunity to sign up for all these classes so cheaply was a wonderful idea which we certainly did not have in SA, it did depend largely on the expertise of the teacher.

Four of us had now teamed up. Kathy, who had managed to get a job as an au pair and who was also accepted as a student at the Drama Centre, Tony, a friend of mine from South Africa and Pip Donaghy whom I had met at the City Lit and who was eventually to succeed as a lead in TV and on the West End stage. We all moved into the house in Lillie Road where we had one bed between the four of us. A bit complicated but we managed.

In the bedroom, the one room we had so far opened up, there was a fireplace. I found a place down the road and ordered a sack of coal. It arrived.

"Where do you want it mate?" I loved what I considered to be a Cockney accent.

We were now on the first landing of the stairs. I summed up the sack of coal and thought I could easily carry it the rest of the way up when I had the fireplace cleaned out.

"Put it here."
"Wot...'ere?" I got an odd look. ("What... here?" My version of Cockney.)
"Yes."
"Wot...'ERE????"
"Yes."
"WOT....'ERE??????" A third time.
"Yes," now very puzzled.
"O.K., mate," and with a shrug he emptied out the sack. I can still see lumps of coal bouncing down the stairs.
"You don't leave the sack?" when I got my breath back.
"No mate."

Doing theatre again

I had come to London to do theatre and didn't know where to start. First of all I was spending every night possible in the cheapest seats or standing at the back at Covent Garden after queuing all night, or in the Gods at the Old Vic. My brain was seething with all the new ideas and types of theatre and ballet. I had never actually seen an opera or a large ballet. I never believed that Shakespeare could be funny.

Les (Shakespeare) eventually gave me a start by organising for me to direct three one-act plays at his club in Parsons Green. I then managed to join and direct at the Harlequin Rep Company in Fulham and finally after picking up courage I was able to direct at Questors theatre. In the meantime I had managed to get an evening job on the lighting board at the Haymarket Theatre. It was a huge lighting board about twenty feet long with banks of levers and wheels to turn. It took three of us to manage it.

I think the first show I worked on was *The Glass Menagerie* with Gwen Ffrangcon-Davies. I watched the dress rehearsal from up on the lighting board and observed Ffrangcon Davis just sitting on the stage not acting but sort of quietly reciting lines. I thought not to worry she will give a great performance that night. The curtain went up and I watched Ffrangcon Davis just sitting on the stage sort of quietly reciting lines. I think it was the first time in my life that I began to understand that great acting consisted of not acting.

My next big surprise was the first time I saw Ralph Richardson. I knew he was in the next play and my excitement at actually seeing a god in the flesh was barely containable. At last my fellow lighting man tapped me on the shoulder and said Richardson had just come through the stage door, which was on the reverse side of the stage. I peered down from the lighting box. My disappointment was great. He was just an ordinary man. I had only ever seen him on the big screen and somehow imagined he would be at least fifteen feet high and float in the air about five feet above the ground but no....he was mortal like anyone else. While I found over time that some of the lesser stars would barely greet us mere stage hands the big ones like Margaret Rutherford and Richardson, would make a point of talking to us and thanking us for the work we did.

I had just come from South Africa where there were no unions. When a show ended there the pay stopped until the next one opened. As a result the crew would work extra hard to change shows over getting one out and the next in. When the first change over came at the Haymarket I was brought to task by a fellow stage hand saying that I was working too fast and must slow down. I did not understand. It was explained to me that on the get out if we kept working after midnight we would then get double pay until 2am. If only five minutes work was left undone triple time for the entire Sunday would be paid. It was not only the money grabbing that got me but I could not see that these people could have any love whatsoever for the theatre which was practically my religion.

Another incident-- I was sitting down under the stage before curtain up. The conductor of the orchestra came through to check the pit.

"Oh Cecil, Do you have a spare chair? I need an extra one in the orchestra."
"Yes, I think there's one in the office."
He stepped into the orchestra pit and I stood up to get him a chair. From behind me a hand pushed down on my shoulder.
"No."
"No????"
"No, you don't get him a chair." I didn't understand.
"He is Musician's union. You are Electrician's union. You don't get him a chair."
I smiled sheepishly thinking he was joking and tried again to stand up. I was forcefully pushed back into the chair.
"Get him a chair, I'll call a strike and there'll be no show tonight."
"Can I tell him?"
"No."

This was my first brush with unions and as a result, the birth of a long hate of unions. I could not offer a man a chair and I could not be polite about it. In the meantime I dared not say I was not a member of any union or that would have meant a strike.

School For Scandal: To design the lighting John, who had lit large shows such as musicals on the West End, had been brought in as lighting designer. The Haymarket, at the time still used this very large antiquated board with rows of levers and wheels to turn. John did not use follow spots to highlight actors around the stage. Instead, the stage was divided into sections each of which had a separate lighting plot to itself so as actors moved around areas could imperceptibly grow darker or lighter as required. To do this, six extra subsidiary lighting boards were hired and placed under the stage, each with its own operator. For this show I was put on one of these boards. From under the stage there was no possibility of seeing any action so we naturally responded to cues from the stage manager's board.

The lighting rehearsal ....

"Board five take dimmer six to seven and a half......... no make it seven and a quarter..... no just a little up on that... Fine, plot that."

This went on for hours until the entire show was plotted for all six boards. On the opening night sat six lighting operators, mostly students, petrified of missing a cue or having something a quarter of a degree out. The curtain went up and cues started furiously, non-stop. Nerves were running high struggling to sort out cues, not getting anything the least bit too high or low. Fifteen to twenty minutes with no mishaps when the operator on the first board suddenly sat back, folded his arms and sat with a grin on his face. Panic.

"Hey folks, relax. The mains have not been switched on."

It slowly dawned on us that not one light from our boards was alive on stage. None of this extremely delicate lighting was showing or more to the point had been missed by the stage manager, the main board lighting operator, the director, or more to the point, by the lighting designer who was in the audience. At the first blackout we switched on the mains and continued with no more thoughts of nerves. We never ever owned up.

Starting the Fulham Arts Centre

I was beginning to settle in to life in London. As a piano technician Les had managed to get me a work permit so there was no fear of me being sent back to S.A. I was now directing plays at both Harlequin Reps and at Questors. We had by now cleaned out the house and Kathy, Pip and I all had our own rooms so we no longer had four in a bed. Tony had returned to SA. And we had cleaned the coal from the stairs. I still wanted to do opera.

Now living in Chesilton Road I had started organizing small home concerts in my front living room never dreaming that these would rapidly grow until hosting what were to become world renowned musicians Also, Les had retired and I had a piano shop in Fulham Road, 512. On the corner of North End Road and Fulham Road to be exact. One morning I noticed that the Granville theatre just down the road from me was being pulled down. I got very angry and decided, out of the blue, to phone the council. I didn't really know what I intended to say to them. I was put through to Barry Stead and started a tirade about the arts etc. and this beautiful theatre being demolished. Barry allowed me to continue for a short while and then interrupted with

"Hold on, Hold on. I'm on your side. Now what do you want to do?" I was a bit nonplussed and said, "Start an arts centre in Fulham."
"Good idea." said Barry.

I felt a bit trapped and my hesitation must have been obvious.

"Well," said Barry, "the first thing you need to do is to get a committee together. Once you have done that come back to us and we will help."

He then gave me some encouragement and thanked me for phoning. I'm sure he must then have thought to himself

"Well that's that. We won't hear from him again."

I sat there thinking what the hell have I done? How the hell do I get a committee together? I never thought to quietly run away and forget I had ever phoned. However, I sat to think it out. I don't think I even seriously planned exactly how or where the centre was to be situated. Still as I have no understanding of money or how it works, I decided the most important person would be someone who did..... A bank manager. I don't believe I even had a bank account so I went into the nearest bank and asked to see the manager. I explained to him about the Granville etc. and the idea of an arts centre and asked if he would come onto the committee. He said yes.

Walking out into the sunlight in Fulham Road and thinking 'Shouldn't he have said NO? Shouldn't I have to approach five or six banks and get five or six refusals and then eventually give up?' But he had said yes and I was now under an obligation. Now what? I again sat to think it out. What about the principal of the evening institute at Beaufort College. At least I knew him as we had been rehearsing operas in the college. He said yes.

This is too easy I thought while getting more and more nervous about what I had, or was doing.

A week or too earlier a man had come into my shop and noticed a model of the set of Carmen, the opera I was rehearsing at the time. We had got talking and he since attended one or two of the music evenings which I had going in my home in Chesilton Road. He was a retired diplomat. I wonder?? His name was Murry McMullen. He said yes.

WOW! A retired diplomat. That's three out of three.

I was now beginning to feel very confident. I had a friend Stuart who was a solicitor. He said yes, but I expected that as he was a friend.

It would be good to have a local businessman of repute. Well there was my ex boss Mr Les Shakespeare (What a good name to have on an arts centre). He said yes.

Only now did I start to think about practicalities. It was to be an arts centre so I needed someone to deal with art, dance, drama and music. Well I could manage the art and drama. Dance? Hold on. Sheila. Sheila Wartski who had just choreographed *Ipi Tombi* on the West End was a friend from South Africa who had also choreo-graphed a musical for me. Would she?? She said yes.

That left music.

Now I was friendly with Peter Katin but Peter is a world celebrated concert pianist. No chance he would say yes. So I approached him and asked if he would suggest someone. He said he would do it. WHAT? He said yes.

I now sat bewildered with a very strong committee, no premises, no money, no plans. I phoned Barry who I think was a little surprised to hear from me again as I really was a nobody. However he arranged a meeting with the Council. A week or two later I faced a meeting of councillors feeling like a fish out of water. I presented them with the proposed committee. They looked a bit surprised.

"Peter Katin, you mean THE Peter Katin?" they asked.

I said yes. This obviously threw them.

"But he doesn't live in Fulham."
"No, but if you can find somebody better than Peter Katin who lives in Fulham I'll gladly accept them".
"No, no, no, He's all right."

There was a bit of an awkward pause, and then,

"Mr Hayter, what would you do if we flatly turned you down?"

I didn't stop to think.

> "No don't do that" I said "'cause if you do I will just
> have to start protest marches and slinging mud at
> you in the papers."

There was no malice or anger or hurt in it. It was just as
if I was playing a game. 'Your move next,' I thought.

> "No no, it's quite all right Mr Hayter. We are going to
> help you. We just wanted to know what your answer
> would be."

It was decided that they would put two members of the
council on to the committee and get started by drawing
up a constitution to be registered as a charity. This was
all Chinese to me. I just wanted to get started with the
arts. The two Council members turned out to be Barry
Stead and councillor X.[1]

The meetings started, held in my house in Chesilton
Road. I got my first taste of red tape and bureaucracy.
The constitution went from us to the council to the
charities committee and each section wanted to change
something always needing yet another meeting. In the
meantime the music evenings on Friday nights were
going from strength to strength as more artists heard
about them and wished to try out their programmes
before recitals etc.

---

[1] Mr X's name has been omitted for reasons that will become
apparent.

Opera as well

I developed a kidney stone. Very painful. While I was in hospital it turned out that the man in the bed next to me was an opera singer. I wanted to do opera. He gave me the number of Pearl Butcher who directed opera in the north of London. On getting out of hospital I phoned.

"Well yes. I have nothing to offer you but come up and have a chat and I'll see what I can do."

Pearl lived in the North of London, Bush Hill I think. I found my way there and spent a Saturday afternoon talking to Pearl in her kitchen as she baked cakes and prepared for some do for the next day. At the end as I said goodbye she once more stated that she had nothing to offer me but would let me know if anything came up. I went back to Fulham and after about a month I had almost forgotten her when I received a phone call.

"Is that Cecil Hayter?"
"Yes."
"It's Terry Hawes here from the Southgate Opera Company."
"Yes".....?????????
"I wanted to know if you would direct our next opera." I was bewildered.
"You wish to interview me?"
"No. We'd like you to do it."
"Don't you want to meet me first?"
"No. Pearl Butcher has already talked to you and we'd like you to do it."

I was completely taken aback. I gratefully accepted and arranged to see their current production *The Merry Wives Of Windsor* and to meet Terry after the performance.

"Oh, and can you choose an opera you'd like to do?"

Complete panic. I had accepted. I must have really impressed Pearl. But I had lied to her...... well not EXACTLY lied. When she asked me what I'd done, I just said "Well, quite a lot" but I never mentioned that it was all straight theatre and I had never directed an opera in my life and now I was committed to do so. Not only that, but to choose one as well. All this with a company I had never even seen.

I rushed to the Fulham music library and started to hunt for an opera. I don't think I had even seen an opera score before but found that there existed complete piano scores with words and of course, librettos, a word I knew not of. It was also possible to borrow an LP. On the shelves I found something called *Louisa Miller*. I had never heard of it although I had heard of Verdi. The LP was also available. This choice was in complete ignorance. It just happened to be on the shelf. Gosh!! Was I grateful to Fulham Library? At least I need not look completely ignorant.

I found my way to Southgate and the Southgate Technical College. The theatre was one of those school hall theatres with a flat floor, not too big a stage and the inevitable balcony. It was a small orchestra and when the curtain opened there was hardly any set but....... a big surprise to me ..... real opera voices. This may sound odd to you, but in South Africa there were no opera companies at all, at least not in Durban. I had once seen an opera when the La Scala opera visited but I had never met anyone at all who could sing opera, so opera singers were those mythical creatures that appeared on Covent Garden Stage for short moments and then mysteriously disappeared until the next performance. After the show I met Terry for the first time. I was extremely nervous and expected him to see through me in the first few minutes.

I can't say I received a nice warm welcome. He seemed a bit distant and certainly did not give me the impression that I had convinced Pearl that I was the best thing since white bread, but then he had just finished conducting a complete opera. I mentioned *Louisa Miller* as though it was a brilliant idea but all I got was a very non-committal promise that he would look it over.

Getting going on the Arts Centre

In Fulham, after about six months of meetings doing nothing but discussing the drawing up of a constitution for an arts centre, I got very impatient.

"Can we do something, anything to get started?"

I didn't know what.

"Cecil, if we give you £500 (I can't remember the exact amount) would you do something to get some publicity so that Fulham gets to hear about the Arts Centre?"

I immediately said yes. I never seem to think before I open my mouth. Now what? I decided to make contact with one of the Youth Clubs and see what we could come up with. Pure serendipity... I went to the Methodist youth club under the church in Fulham Road where I met the leader who turned out to be Ian Clerk the ex-drummer from *Uriah Heep*.

At the height of his career, Ian had one day entered some big dinner do in some foreign country or other and, when passing all the screaming fans in the street, decided that they looked hungry while he was rolling in luxury. He gave up his entire career to become a youth worker. Ian suggested what he termed a "Happy Walk." I didn't exactly know what this was but the first thing was to collect together all the youth clubs in Fulham. This is how I came to meet Roy Hickman from the Brunswick Club.

The idea snowballed and just kept growing until it turned into a full scale festival preceded by a parade of floats through the streets of Fulham. Although I was chairman I cannot take the credit for all of it even if at times I did feel I had the world on my shoulders. But with the help of Roy, Ian Murry and Fulvia (his wife) and others we ended up with 10 to 15 thousand people (according to Police records) on Eelbrook common. There was everything, fairground rides, stalls, army displays, athletic competitions...you name it. It was a wonderful sunny day. I remember Ian and me grabbing onto each other and saying "What have we done?" I also remember having a dreadful headache and going into the first aid tent to be refused an aspirin. It was not allowed without permission from my doctor. As I was about to walk out one of the nurses called me quietly and said she had some aspirins in her bag and would I like one? In the evening Ian had organized a gig from some famous pop group (It may have been *Uriah Heep* - I don't know one from the other) so the festival went on well into the night. Fulham now certainly knew we existed.

The home based concerts had rapidly snowballed to once a week instead of once a month. I was now getting phone calls from pianists about to enter music festivals (mostly Leeds) wishing to try out their recitals before entering the contests or even performing in public. They were unknown then but quite a few of them such as Antony Peebles, Christopher Kite, Jaun Martin (Guitar), Tessa Uys, and Mitsuko Uchida, are now world famous.

One day at work, the phone rang.

"Is that Cecil Hayter?" a voice asked.
"Yes." I said.
"It's Martin Stevens here," said the voice.

Martin Stevens was then the Conservative MP for Fulham. I knew of him of course and was baffled, surprised and bewildered as to why on earth an MP would be phoning me.

"Well" he continued, "I've read so much about you in the papers that I think it's about time I met you."

This threw me completely. An MP wants to meet me??? Shouldn't MPs be running the world, making new laws, fighting wars? And he wants to meet me? Instinctively my hackles rose. I had seen his pictures in the paper and knew he was a big fat Conservative and I was staunchly Labour. No way was I going to put myself out for him. I was surprised to hear myself saying,

"Well you had better come round then."
"I'd like to do that" he said. I had to think quickly. Safety in numbers.
"Would you like to come to the recital on Friday night at my house?"

He said he would and I gave him all the details. I put the phone down. PANIC. I know, phone Murry, he's an ex diplomat. He'll know how to treat an MP. Murry was most amused.

"Cecil, he's just a man like any other but don't worry I'll look after him on Friday.

Friday was packed. Mark Raubenheimer was due to play for us that night. Martin arrived and Murry took over. I remember feeling very smug as I saw both Murry and Martin awkwardly sitting on the floor with the rest of us. 'Just where a diplomat and a fat MP ought to be.' How smug of me, but then I had no idea of how much Martin would help and support us in the future.

My first opera

I do not remember one minute of the auditions of *Luisa Miller* but of course I must have been there. I had agreed to design the set and make a model to present at the first rehearsal which, much to my relief, was to be music only. It was explained that there would be a month or two of just music rehearsals before I started putting it on the stage. Thank God. I could sit in on these and get to know the opera.

Terry Hawes had suggested that at the first rehearsal he would introduce me and I could then talk to the cast about my concept of the production. Again in terror, I suggested I don't talk yet until I had got to know them a bit better.

In the mean time I had designed, drawn up plans and made a model of the set. I was extremely nervous that this would all not be up to the standard required and was even more petrified when I was informed that before I could present it to the company I would have to show it to the head of the drama section for his approval. It was a big college and I had never met the head of drama whoever he was, but apparently he was therefore responsible for anything that went on in the theatre.

In much trepidation I presented the model and plans expecting a stern look and possibly a reprimand that it was not really up to the standard required or at least that changes would have to be made. Instead of which.... a long look ....and,

"It's wonderful."

I remained taken aback and silent. Mr "M" (I will tactfully refer to him as such) spent more time examining it from different angles and then asked,

"But how do you know it will fit the stage?"

Total disbelief from me. This was the head of drama in a huge college in London, England, where I honestly believed that the standard of the lowest of amateur theatre companies was above the highest of professionals in South Africa.... and he had obviously never seen a model of a stage set in his life. It was hate at first sight. What on earth was this man teaching the students??? I quietly answered,

"It's built to scale."

I doubt he understood what this meant but I handed over both the model and plans to him being told that he would present them to Terry and more than that, they would be built by the technical staff and painted by the arts department so I need have no worries. My offer to help with both the building and painting was turned down as totally unnecessary.

Thank the Lord that contrary to Mr "M," Terry had proved to be extremely popular. Rehearsals were a pleasure to watch starting on time with no time wasted. The atmosphere was always pleasant with no shouting or tantrums and above all Terry was a supremely competent musician.

His knowledge was incredible.

Time for me to address the cast. I had now spent many hours in the reference library.... (No computers available in those days)... studying up on Verdi, Schiller, on whose play the opera was based and of course Louise Miller. Although I had attended every music rehearsal I had never had time to spend talking to Terry and was now convinced that at this rehearsal I would be found out as the complete fraud I was. I got away with it, actually convincing a number of members that I was knowledgeable.

Rehearsals started for me. I treated them exactly as if it had been a straight play where the words were sung instead of spoken finding that although singers had the difficulty of the problems of breath control, timing, following beats and bars and all the other problems of singing more than an actor, the huge advantage of opera is that in advance the composer has already determined the sense of dramatic timing, pace and above all emotional interpretation with the music. A tremendous advantage which actors and directors of straight theatre need to discover for themselves.

On stage right was the dock door leading through to a small scenic workshop where the set was to be built. Mr M had assured me that my help with building the set was entirely unnecessary and it would be better if I kept out of it leading me to believe that the college had a professional team on the job.

I received a phone call to tell me very apologetically that the plans of the set had gone astray. Needless to say this did not please me as I had spent some time doing perfect tracings while trying to impress.

"It's all right." I answered as calmly as possible.
"I will let you have the original drawings to save time instead of doing another set of tracings."

Photocopiers were still unknown to me. I brought them up to the college and again handed them to Mr M imploring him that there were no other copies so please take special care. I had still seen no sight of set building. And then I received another call, the drawings had mysteriously vanished. Again I kept cool and offered to help in the workshop and we could build them referring to the model.

I was informed that someone had accidentally sat on the model. Realizing that I was still on probation and could be sacked at any time I managed to keep absolutely calm and again offered help in the workshop to do the best we could. This offer was accepted and I was introduced to the person in charge of the workshop who turned out to be the general school handyman and who had probably never seen a set in his life. A couple of students came in to help. There were a few old flats around but all amid utter chaos. Painting had been done on the stage where spilt oil paint was to be found everywhere even on the front tabs. Apparently sets had previously been painted in oil paint and no-one had ever washed a brush. I was given a budget to get new brushes and invest in some stage paints. There was of course no wash basin or water supply in the workshop so this had to be fetched from the dressing rooms.

Building began and, while everyone was being very helpful and pleasant no one had any experience whatsoever, at least of set building. The handyman (I name him Bill as I cannot remember his real name) was very good with a hammer and a saw but that is where it ended. We had built the flats for the church which in reverse would be the interior of the farm cottage and I kept asking if it was going to be trucked. I always received the answer "Yes, we're getting to that."

At last when it was getting nearer the performance I once more mentioned the truck.

"Cecil," was whispered in my ear..... "What's a truck?"

I couldn't help laughing and explained that it was a platform on casters on which the scenery was built to be able to revolve it on stage. Enough was now built for the painting to begin. I was reminded by Mr M that I was not to lift a brush as it would all be painted by the art students under the guidance of the art teacher.

Ann, the arts teacher, and her students arrived. I had already mixed some paints for them. It was very obvious in the first few minutes that again there was complete inexperience. I hesitated, took my heart in my hands, and approached Ann.

"Ann, do you mind if I show them what to do?"

Ann appeared completely competent and her students seemed to like and trust her so I was rather afraid that I would be told in no uncertain terms to keep out of it. Instead of which...

"Oh please do. I would be so grateful. I know nothing about stage painting and it would be good for them to learn."

In my books any teacher who can openly admit in front of their whole class ignorance of something, is an exceptionally good teacher, and of course over the years Anne proved to be exactly this, a talented artist herself, a great help to the opera company and of course to me.

I had now managed to get the set together despite the problems, and what's more, to survive rehearsals without appearing too much of an idiot. I had of course gained more confidence at each rehearsal and Terry in his quiet way had been a great help. The dress rehearsal arrived and before it started I was standing in the audience when Mr M approached me proudly announcing...

"Mr Hayter, this is the finest set we have ever had on this stage."
"Who is in charge of the stage?" I asked.
"I am."
"Then Mr M, you should be kicked out the college immediately."

I had blurted this out again without thinking, a sort of Pavlov's dog response.

I can't say that *Louisa Miller* was the greatest opera the school had seen or even that it was great, but it passed thanks to Terry and the singers, and I had not been found out. Terry must have been at least satisfied as

I was immediately asked to do the next one. I learned later Terry had quite a job to get me re-accepted by the principal of the college, as I had been reported by Mr M for insubordination and as head of drama, he did not want me on the staff.

It was only about a year later that I learned all this from Terry and, of course, I also learned the truth about the great impression I had made on Pearl. Mr M had previously been quite successful as a professional actor and in view of this had been employed as drama teacher at the college. Unfortunately, as good as an actor he may have been he proved enormously unsuccessful with the students who finally refused to work with him. He could at the time not be dismissed without a union strike and there was no provision for a second drama teacher. This opening could therefore only be made if M was promoted to head of drama leaving a vacancy for another teacher.

Pearl who had directed the last three operas at the college suddenly had to withdraw and unless a director could be found within three days M as head of drama had insisted that he would direct the opera. Terry and Pearl were prepared to take on ANYBODY when Pearl suddenly remembered that chap in her kitchen..... ME.

I was that "ANYBODY"

Meanwhile, back in Chesilton road...

I can't help telling a bit about these concerts, or at least some of them. First Christofer Kite:

Chris was a brilliant pianist who played as a repetiteur at some of the rehearsals and who had already given one or two recitals for me in Chesilton Road. When he arrived to play I would put him in a private room where he sat quietly wearing a dinner suit before playing. At 8pm I would call him and he would come upstairs where everyone was already seated. He would take a bow, sit at the piano and begin. At the interval, Chris would again retire to the room and then reappear for the second half. In other words the format was exactly as if he were performing at the South Bank. He was after all doing a dry run for a performance either at Wigmore or Purcell Room or similar.

One day he phoned me to say he was due to play the Brahms first concerto .....I don't remember where, but could he have a dry run at no 12 and did I have a pianist who would play the second piano for him. I said

"Sure. Mark is staying with me at the time and I'm sure he would do it."

The afternoon of the concert Chris arrived to have a trial run with Mark. They obviously knew of each other but had never met. I introduced them and led them to the pianos. As they sat down, each at his own piano, and Mark opened the music Chris asked,

"Mark do you want to play the orchestral tutti to start or should we leave it for just before the entry of the piano?"
"I don't know, I'll see how I feel tonight."

I could foresee trouble. Chris wanted everything perfect and Mark was very easy going. I retired to make the tea.

Now Mark was another very brilliant pianist who would stay with me whenever passing through London, and who had played a number of times for me. When Mark was due to play there would naturally be a packed house. I should have explained that I had two pianos which allowed the orchestral part to be played on the second piano and that most of us had to sit on the floor. With two giants of the keyboard playing, there was a naturally completely packed house with people not only on the floor but in the passageway and halfway up the stairs.

Chris was in his room composing himself. Mark was sitting on the floor in the noisiest corner of the room dressed in jeans and T-shirt. How could I get them both to the pianos together? I thought 'an orchestra is always there waiting for the soloist' so I 'dragged' Mark to his piano first and then went to fetch Chris. Chris made his usual entrance took a bow and sat at the piano. All went quiet and Mark very seriously opened the music score. The Brahms first opened with a full orchestra so the page was covered in notes.

Mark looked into the crowd on the floor and said,

> "Hey, Tamar" (a friend of his and another pianist) "come here. You play these notes and I'll play these."

They bunched together on one stool. By this time there was loud laughter with Mark and Tamar crossing hands and leaning over each other. I looked across to Chris, petrified that there would be a scene but on his face was a gentle smile.

"Thank God," I thought "He's got a sense of humour."

The orchestral tutti over, Tamar returned to her seat on the floor and Mark worked his magic. It was almost as if he had said 'OK that was just a bit of fun but now we listen to Chris and Brahms.' I had also worried a little that, as brilliant as Chris was, Mark may outshine him. But in no way. Mark followed Chris's every mood handing it to him on a silver platter. In turn, Chris seemed to have caught a little of Marks ease at the piano. He was Brilliant.[2]

Then there was Tessa. Tessa Uys, sister to the South African comic Pieter Dirk Uys. Tessa phoned to say she was booked for a tour of South Africa where among other things she would be playing the Mozart D minor and the Beethoven third concertos and again.... a dry run. I knew she had just played the Saint Saens second at the Queen Elizabeth Hall and as I particularly liked it said, yes, if she would play that as well. I really was only joking but she laughed and said yes, so we got three concertos in one night. I can't remember who was on the second piano but it was remarked afterwards

---

[2] Chris went on to become an international concert pianist specializing in period music on the harpsichord. He also became a professor of music at the Royal College of Music. Sadly Chris died of cancer at a young age.

that after that retreads on their fingers would surely be needed.

La Bohème at Southgate

At Southgate the next opera was to be *La Bohème*. With my vast experience of doing opera.... after all I had already done one complete opera, I decided I would modernize it and bring it into the Hippy period. It's amazing what confidence, youth and inexperience can produce. We had virtually no chorus which imposed a problem in presenting a passing parade plus a full chorus in act two. Easy, I thought. Instead of a passing band I can get the students to do a protest march through the audience and up onto the stage. Were there protest marches in the Hippy period? Oh, that didn't matter...poetic licence - and as we had one or two of Terry's music students singing in the opera I asked them to round up a few more from the college, they need not be music students, just students and virtually no rehearsal would be necessary.

Two or three turned up for a rehearsal, a very short rehearsal, in which they were shown to start in the foyer on a given cue, enter the back of the auditorium, march down the aisle, up onto the stage and off into the wings. Just dress as you would for a real protest (pure Stanislavsky). Yes they could get more students together and make some banners. This solved the problem of a full military band being employed.

After the fiasco of the set building for *Louisa Miller*, I had not wanted or designed another full set. I had however insisted on four beds on the stage for the four residents of the attic. Two sets of bunk beds that allowed the upper bunks to fold down and become market stalls in the second act.

The opening arrived. Act one went well. The singers were good, and who can fail with Puccini? Act two neared the end when the protest march was to begin. A large number of students had collected in the Foyer and I cued them in.

"Just follow the ones in front of you"

A chanting of "OUT...OUT...OUT" started in the foyer. The auditorium doors burst open and it seemed like a million students came down the aisle chanting... louder than the orchestra and not in time with it. Terry conducting, swung round to face the audience with a look of complete horror and panic on his face still conducting the orchestra with one hand while trying to silence the march with the other.

To no avail. The march continued. The chanting continued even louder. The singers went on singing, the orchestra kept playing and the audience still sat. I was thrilled. .....over the moon. This was REAL theatre. This all occurs at the end of the act....... and the curtain closed.

I rushed round the back stage to congratulate the kids. Terry rushed round.... I don't think to congratulate them. Confusing for them with Terry on one side looking a bit like thunder and me on the other looking like bright sunlight. However, a compromise was reached and the following performances were presented with much more decorum although the principal of the college did receive a number of letters from members of the public complaining about the students doing a protest march in the middle of an opera. Wonderful theatre, I thought but is this really what Puccini wanted? However Terry, Puccini and some good singers won the day in the end.

The Brunswick Theatre

Roy Hickman approached me saying that he wished to start drama at the Brunswick in Fulham club and would I direct *Oliver* for them. I didn't know it then but the Brunswick was considered one of the tougher clubs in London. Anarchy among the boys reigned supreme. Roy was determined to bring the level of the club up. He had already succeeded in getting the football and boxing section into some order and decided drama would be very useful. His management committee did not believe that drama would ever be successful and had refused to back it. Roy decided to finance it himself.

I arrived for the first audition/rehearsal - whatever. Unfortunately Roy had had to attend some meeting somewhere and was not there that night. The sub leader was in charge.

That night the rehearsal lasted about ten to fifteen minutes. About thirty kids had turned up either out of curiosity or just to take the mickey out of me. I think the trouble had started in the boxing section but eventually the police were called to close the club down. I really did wonder what I had got myself into. As the kids were leaving I said half to myself "O.K. Kids. Round one up to you."

The next night, order had been restored and Roy was back. Roy was a remarkable leader. He NEVER raised his voice and certainly never swore but somehow he was able to keep order. This night there were about six to ten kids who came back interested. We started to read and got some sort of casting. One or two seemed genuinely interested but because of peer pressure didn't want to show it. At the end of the evening one of the youngsters asked me. "O.K. Sir. Who won that round?"

Roy was determined to push on, so I kept going. Each night walking into the club was like running the gauntlet. To them I must have appeared like a "theatre type Toff" or whatever, but I was horribly sent up. I sort of wore imaginary blinkers and earplugs 'till I got to the rehearsal room. Rehearsals continued with half a cast and odd kids dropping in and out, sometimes half way through a rehearsal when we were trying to get a chorus together. I think they came in more for a laugh than a desire to sing. Still we pushed on. A close friend Val was wonderful. They would not misbehave in front of her and she was one of those marvellously organized people who had records of who came or didn't, etc. She also organized costumes, make-up, etc.

One particular rehearsal, the kids were being decidedly unruly. Roy was strong on no swearing in the club.... from anybody. Suddenly I had had enough. I normally do not swear but I let rip. I remember trying hard to remember every swear word I could. My voice was loud and my shouting stopped all other activities in the club as they watched in wonder. I believe the remarks passed between them at each new swear word were things like "Nice one Hayter...Good on you Hayter.....Keep going... Well done Hayter... don't stop" etc. I eventually stopped to suddenly become aware of faces staring through all the doorways, including Roy and the staff. Roy had not tried to interfere. There was an awkward silence before people at doorways went back to their sections. Roy and staff also retired without comment. Rehearsal now continued rather subdued but without trouble. It seems that on that night I had won the respect of the entire club, including the cast and possibly the staff. I think Roy was aware of what was happening and that was why he never commented. I felt that in the club I was now accepted.

The opening was getting nearer. I decided that we would do a major sized set almost right round the gym. As the set got bigger so the kids that had decided that drama was not for them, started to come back right up until almost the opening night. Val was starting to do a panic.

"Cecil, you can't just let them on the stage. It will ruin the production."

"Get them on," I said, "They'll sing something."

Poor Ricardo... the music director who had shown so much patience during rehearsals.

The opening night..... The audience was packed. Roy had invited a couple of celebrities (I can only remember

Sandy Shore) Lionel Bart was there and oh yes... the television..... and on the stage were about 50 to 60 kids who didn't have a clue what they were doing but were having the time of their lives. The show was a tremendous HIT. With a chorus of frogs... Nobody even tried to say that it was a tremendous theatrical success. Even Lionel Bart looked happy as he gave a speech among the kids on stage at the end.

I don't remember how many nights it ran and I think they had to add an extra night as it had been completely sold out. The trustees now, of course, were only too pleased to meet the press and celebrities and claim credit. I am being unfair to the trustees (management committee) as although they never believed it would happen they had, when it got going, been very support- ive. I am also being unfair to the cast as with all young people there were some very talented performances among the soloists.

Establishing The Southgate Opera Company

It took about two years for me to begin to understand how the company was run. As it was really an evening class under the wing of the Southgate College, I took it for granted that it was completely run by the college. After all it was the college who paid my salary. But I was to find that the Principal, Mr Easton, was a music lover and singer and had suggested to Terry that the college should try to present opera. Terry had therefore started the opera class, found someone to direct and had presented three operas before I arrived on the scene. In fact it was a solo effort.

Terry was on his own having to book rehearsal times and space, to acquire music scores for the cast, to find someone to do lighting, to book a stage manager, to organize dates for shows, to get together an orchestra, to re-orchestrate the opera parts to fit the orchestra, to do the publicity, to organize costumes, front of house, ticket sales, programmes etc. etc. etc.

I had slowly begun to realize this and was getting increasingly annoyed when I heard moans because this or that had not been seen to, particularly when their remarks were aimed at Terry.

Eventually I suggested to Terry that we form a committee of the members and let them take the responsibility. At first Terry was a bit reluctant, but with persuasion that it would not be breaking the rules of the college, he agreed. The company was still being run as an opera class. The members were approached..... a committee was voted in, a chairman was elected and I guess the company was born in its present form.

The company was rapidly growing. Music students from the college were now joining the chorus or even taking minor leads, one or two of whom eventually were to become professionals of a high calibre. We would drag in members from wherever we could find them.

Finding premises for the Fulham Arts Centre

In Fulham the battle with the constitution had continued to be waged and at last was accepted by all and we were now a registered charity. Thus began the first

search for premises in which to run the arts centre.
I never dreamed that this would be the start of a thirty
year search. I have, through reading old newspaper
cuttings, remembered that my first thought was the
basement of my shop where I had wanted to start a
small theatre. This was more than completely impracti-
cal. I had no idea where to start so I just began riding
around in the car looking for possible buildings. Among
the ones I remember getting excited about were a small
church hall near Barons Court another at the top end of
Fulham Road. Another on the corner of Fulham road
and Lillie Road, and another in Kelvedon which was an
empty scout hall, that I begged the council to buy for us,
to no avail. At the time, as I discovered each new building in my mind it became the absolute ideal place to
start so each time was a huge disappointment when
there was always a reason why this or that was not
available. I had also started to approach the churches
about their halls and again lovely halls but always
already in use. The same went for the clubs. I just kept
looking knowing that one day it would turn up.

Each day I parked my car in a small road (Cassidy
Road) opposite my shop. Because it was so close to me
I had somehow missed looking, but suddenly I became
aware of the fact that the building I was parking outside
of was in fact an empty hall. It appeared to be in the
grounds of the post office (sorting office). I approached
the post office who also had not noticed it and they
told me it must belong to the Gas board next door.
I approached the Gas board. They said it must belong to
the post office. I went back to the post office and they
then said well it must belong to the council. I approached

the council who again said it must belong to the post office. Once again I went to the post office and told them the council suggested it did belong to them. They looked up their records and discovered that although it was in the grounds of the sorting office, it did belong to the council. I went back to the council. They looked up their records. Surprise.... It did belong to them even though it was in the grounds of the post office. It was an ex scout hall.

Since nobody had known it existed,

"Could I use it?"
"Yes," was the answer.
"Could I have a key?" I asked.
"That, you would have to get from the post office."

Back to the post office.

"No, we don't have a key. You will need to get this from the council."
Back to the council.
"We don't have a key. We will have to fit a new lock"
"I'll fit a new lock."
"NO, it's got to be done by the council."

They promised to do this within a week. True to their word I received a phone call from the council saying they had fitted the lock and they would send a man round to me with the keys. He arrived in my shop and together we crossed the road to the hall. There was no new lock. He looked bewildered and said but I've got the keys.

"Wait a bit," I said. "Cassidy Road used to be a crescent and returns back on itself."

They had put a new lock on a small church hall in the next road. The keys were donated to the church.

The building was absolutely ideal. Downstairs was a small hall, an office and a toilet. Upstairs was another hall. I couldn't believe my eyes. Although it had been empty for so long it seemed to be in good condition with no leakages. The committee all came round to inspect it with great approval. Peter (Katin) of course was interested in the acoustics for recitals and also gave it his approval. Obviously there would have to be a certain amount of work on it to comply with all safety rules etc. A friend of one of the trustees was an architect. (I wish I could remember names). He offered to draw up plans and we set about budgeting for what would be needed.

We started writing letters to every possible charity for help. I am a poor typist and had great difficulty as Murry would not pass a letter with a single corrected mistake. It had to be perfect, so they were very slowly and carefully written. If anyone has done this you will know the impossibility of getting money from charities, no matter how good your cause. I was however in contact with the Greater London Arts Council (GLA) through the music evenings going on in my house, which were doing better and better. By now we had had a great deal of publicity in the press.

Since the festival and *Oliver* I had been asked to do a production of *Wizard of Oz* at the Methodist Youth club. Getting this production started was not half as hard as *Oliver*. I did have the same problems at the start; I mean being sent up as gay or "upper class." I seemed to get over this a lot quicker than at the Brunswick. Although I was naturally trying for the best possible standard of performance from everyone, these productions were more community events rather than serious theatre, one of the youth workers just going out into the streets and collecting children into the production. One or two stayed while one or two didn't. Of the cast, three of the 'ring leaders,' I don't know what else to call them, were the Twins, so identical that we just referred to either of them as Twin, and the other was Brendan. I guess they were about sixteen to seventeen years old. Brendan played the lion, his sister played Dorothy and one of the twins played the straw man. I mention this as it was roughly two weeks before the opening that Brendan, one of the twins and another member of the cast stole a motor car, and took a joy ride to Croydon, were spotted there by the police but managing to get away, they stole a second car to come back to Fulham. This time they were caught but did manage to beat up a policeman or two. Ian had to bail them out for them to be in the production. After each rehearsal someone had to accompany Brendan home as he was not allowed on the street without the presence of an adult. Again the production was an enormous success, with lots of publicity.

Collecting members in the streets was not reserved just for children at the youth club. I was choreographing a ballet for a small dance company. Rehearsals were being held in a studio directly opposite Leicester Square Tube

Station. After rehearsal it was raining and a group of us went into the pub during which time Pip had had a drink or two and was now a bit merry. Closing time for the pub so we moved across the road to an all-night café for coffee. Pip had an umbrella and as we entered the coffee shop he bumped into a young guy in the street. We went in for coffee but Pip and this young guy remained outside under the umbrella talking. I said hello to the guy he had been talking to and apologized that he had been cornered by Pip but he seemed perfectly happy about this. As Pip had kept him out in the rain for some time I offered him a lift home. He accepted. On the way he asked about the ballet we were doing. I invited him to join us at the next rehearsal. He seemed pleased and asked if it would be O.K. if he brought his brother with him. His name was Phil and his brother's Barry. Over the years Phil and Barry became two of the mainstays in building the opera company not only with their tireless work and involvement but also singing many leads in the performances. I don't know how many other members may have also been picked up in the streets.

With all this going on hardly a week passed without write-ups of some sort in the local papers. As a result our name was exceptionally good with GLA and to my utter amazement and joy, we were offered a grant of twenty five thousand pounds to refurbish the hall in Cassidy Road. It all seemed too easy. I don't know why I say that when without all the work of the productions and recitals while still doing Operas with Beaufort opera performing in the Fulham town hall it would never have happened. But it had and it had been worth all the work.

Southgate was growing

Southgate Opera Company was obviously showing signs of growing and the Principal had decided to have a big scenic workshop built onto the side of the stage and also to take on a full-time stage carpenter come manager. Although I cannot claim to be the instigator of the building of the workshop, it is easy to imagine my elation at the thought of a new scenic workshop in Southgate and a new theatre in Fulham. Talk of being on top of the world.

Adverts were to be put out for the position of stage carpenter. Terry approached the head to suggest that as I was the only person who knew anything about building scenery that I be invited to the interviews of prospective candidates. Unfortunately relations between myself and Mr M had never improved and as the head of drama he refused, insisting the he alone would be the person to decide.

I had been told that this was in the offing and I was only too pleased to have the chance of again designing a full set. On approaching M to suggest that if he could give me a list of whatever flats and materials were in stock, I could then design accordingly. I was informed that we were to get this new employee, (he didn't know that I was already aware of that) and as a result I could design whatsoever I wished and it would be made. M showed no signs of the slightest understanding that existing flats could be used saving time and money. I'm afraid his superior attitude got to me and the devil appeared.

The opera was to be *Elixir Of Love*. Good. This meant a composite set could be used. Setting it in a small Italian village it would have three practical houses. One for the pub, one for Nemorino and one for Adina. Easy... these could all be built from standard flats. No. As stated the devil had appeared and I decided to design everything without a single right angle. This meant tapering walls giving a good effect but it also meant that every flat would have to be individually built from scratch. I had also specified that sawdust was to be mixed into the paint to give a rough finish. This would make it difficult to use the flats again.

The model and plans were handed in, not to the opera company, but directly to M as were his strict instructions. I almost expected him to call me back and insist that they be altered but I suspect he was incapable of reading them.

The new theatre technician was duly appointed and I was informed that I was to meet him in our brand new workshop to discuss the building of the set. I headed out to Southgate. It turned out to be someone I knew and had worked with on other shows in the past. This made me really happy as I knew his work was exceptionally good. It was perhaps just as well I had not been present at the interviews as I would strongly have recommended him and just perhaps because of this M may have turned him down.

We said hello both surprised to find who we were working with. John had the model and plans in front of him.

"Any problems?" I asked.

"No, none. It seems pretty straight forward."

I headed back to Fulham. This meant I had had a three hour round trip just for that. I got on very well with John. He informed me that at his interview for the job Mr M had promptly consulted him with my model and plans and asked,

"Can you build that?"

He looked at the plans and as it was a fairly simple set on a small stage he answered,

"Yes."

And that ended the interview. I was now virtually banned from the workshop being informed that everything was now in professional hands and I would only be in the way. In fact, I spent many hours there working happily with John. Whenever he knew or saw M coming he would warn me and I would disappear into the next room.

Elixir marked the beginning of many more Southgate productions which now boasted full chorus, sets, costumes and soloists. Memory fails as to how many operas John spent with us but I think M was a bit much for him to take and a new technician was taken on.... Donald Mc Donald.

Donald and I got on exceptionally well together, in fact Donald got on well with everyone and soon not only was the company attracting better class soloists and singers in general but a solid stage crew now existed. Derek Basham was now a regular in the workshop and Alan Legget had joined to take over the lighting, both very competent people.

As a director designer I was completely spoilt. I was encouraged to design bigger and better sets to challenge the competence of the crew and helpers. Hence I could now design whatever I wanted, make a model, present it to Donald and then sit back and wait for it to be built. A rough layout of a lighting plan was handed to Alan and I could then leave him to perform his magic...... last of all, the entire responsibility for the music was in the hands of Terry. Now with a full committee to look after publicity, costumes etc. It's impossible to mention all the names.....When after a successful production audience members come up to you and congratulate you on your wonderful production, it's just so easy to believe that you did it all when in fact, you weren't even on the stage and had to rely on everyone already mentioned right up to the smallest chorus member.....AND of course I was the best and most experienced opera director in the world who knew exactly what was needed in every incident.

Ahh!!! There's the rub. I wasn't. I thought I was, but I wasn't. Fifty years later, no doubt like many others of my age, I now look back and wonder---how did I have the nerve to take on opera with no training and no experience? I could hardly tell the difference between Mozart and Verdi. Perhaps I should now be grateful to M and especially to Terry for his faith in me. Still after fifty years of doing operas, not just for Southgate but also with a number of other companies in London besides been given the chance to work in Wales, Spain and as far afield as New York, I must have learned something. But with experience comes insecurity, and every time I face a full chorus at a first rehearsal, that feeling of terror and 'what am I doing here?' overcomes me. They are going to find me out. A throw back to that very first rehearsal with *Luisa Miller*.

Intrigue over the Fulham Arts Centre

It was a Friday. I was at work and the phone rang. It was Prescilla from the GLA.

> "Cecil, I just want to check with you about the grant. Everything is passed and the cheque will be written out on Monday. Are you sure you have included everything because once the cheque is written you will not be able to change the amount. Don't phone me on Tuesday and say 'we forgot the toilets' or anything else."
> "I'm sure we haven't. But I'll just check that all is O.K. And phone you back."

I then phoned X and told him it was all going through on the Monday. A small hesitation and...

> "Cecil, I want you to withdraw."

I didn't understand and said so.

> "I can't tell you on the phone. I'll come and see you."

I sat and waited, very bewildered. At length he arrived. After preliminaries....

"I couldn't tell you on the phone as if you mention a word of this to anyone it will cost the council hundreds of thousands of pounds."

I was now even more bewildered.

"The council intends to buy Riverside Studios. It belongs to the T.V. Company and we have told them that the building is to be pulled down and turned into flats. As such we get it at the price of the land only. In fact, we want to turn it into an arts centre and if they know that, we will have to pay for the building as well. Now if you accept this twenty five thousand from GLA it means that when the council applies to GLA for funds they will claim that Hammersmith and Fulham have already had that amount and it will be subtracted from anything they intend to give to Riverside Studios and there is no way that the council will be able to fund Fulham Arts Centre in any way as every penny is to be used on Riverside. On the other hand, if you withdraw, when Riverside opens it is huge and we will be able to house you there with all the support you need. You can still remain as the Fulham Arts Centre."

He left me with it. I phoned Murry and explained the whole lot to him. Murry thought it over.

"Cecil, if they are to start a true community arts centre [which is how X had put it to me] then after all the publicity we have had, they will need people like us. I think it is a good idea to withdraw and take up their offer."

I had to decide. Murry is a retired diplomat, he must know what he is talking about. I phoned Prescilla. I can't possibly recall the exact conversation but when I told her I didn't want the money and I couldn't tell her why, she eventually became very angry, saying they had done everything to help us and this is how I treat them. She put the phone down on me. I realized now that I had closed the door to GLA forever more.

Now we just had to wait.

The One Act Festival at Brunswick

In the interim Brunswick had now been bitten by the theatre bug and had decided to enter a play in the Federations one-act festival. I was busy directing an opera at Southgate so suggested someone else direct it. About a week before the festival was on I got a phone call from Val who I think had been directing asking if I would please come down and give some tips or whatever before they went on. I agreed. I came down on the Wednesday. It was due to be performed on the Saturday. It was a children's one-act written by Bill Owen, with a cast of about fifteen, all about a football team in the dressing room and a stolen purse. The culprit gets caught but they find he needs the money for medicine for his sick mother so all ends happily. I started a run through. I stopped them. It was all very correct and very slow and dead.

"Now come on, that's not how you behave among yourselves when there's no one listening. First of all I want you to try and put it into your own language which would mean the odd swear word here and there, and talk over each other"

They looked worried. Remember no swearing was allowed in the club. Roy had certainly turned it into a VERY successful club. They started again with hesitation nervously trying to add a bit of swearing. Roy had been watching the rehearsal tactfully and quietly left. A bit more hard pushing from me and they were soon going hell for leather with every second word starting with F.

I stopped them again.

"Hold it. I'm sure that's not how you behave in the dressing rooms."

A bit more work and it started to come right. The next night they were obviously enjoying the freedom of being allowed to half improvise and not worry about correct pronunciation etc. Like all rehearsals at clubs there was always at least one member of the cast missing with whatever excuse.

Friday night was to be the last rehearsal. I had warned, NO missing cast and NO stops not even for a prompt which I would not allow anyhow. Roy, Val and a few friends were there to watch the final run through.

"Now remember NO STOPS."

They got off to a good start and suddenly there was silence.

"What's the matter?"

"We haven't got a Johnny."

"Where is Johnny?"

I rather exasperatingly asked after making so sure no one would be missing.

"We've never had a Johnny."

The room went silent with everyone now thinking the performance would have to be cancelled. Even Roy looked a bit lost. I laughed, almost wanting to get the giggles.

"Don't worry. There are three things we can do. One, we can say that the boy who was playing Johnny has broken his leg and so someone will read it in for him.... or 2, the prompt would read it in for him or 3, you can improvise your way through it and fool everyone like you fooled me that there never was a Johnny."

We opted for plan 3. The next run went well without anyone missing 'Johnny.'

The following night we met at the Brunswick, loaded up the club bus and were ready to leave when we noticed one of the cast was missing. He had apparently decided not to be in it and had gone for a swim. Due to go on first, Roy phoned the organizers and asked if it would be possible to go on third. (There were three plays). They agreed, while Roy went to the swimming baths to collect the errant boy.

Arriving at the club which was in the East end of London, with a motley crew, one short in the cast, intending to improvise our way with a couple of swear words thrown in and who do we find is the adjudicator: Bill Owen. I saw Bill, whom I happened to know, just before the evening started and rather sheepishly just said,

"Bill it really isn't your play."

We had arrived in time to see the first two plays. I can't remember what the first play was. It was something classical done by what must have been a much more upper class club than the Brunswick. Beautifully set and costumed in period. Well-spoken but a bit slow. The second play was rather similar.....and then came Brunswick. I stood in the wings and just said 'Go for it' and they did. I thought if they could just get through it I would be proud of them. Just forget the other two plays.

The adjudication came. Prizes were not awarded as first, second and third. Awarded was a gold, silver, bronze or nothing. The first play received a silver, the second also a silver.

Bill spoke well of them both. He then came to Brunswick. I wasn't too concerned about what he would say as I was just proud of them pulling it off.

"Well,"..... he hesitated...

"This is not exactly the play I wrote," ......pause, "but it is what theatre is all about and I have awarded it a Gold." ....

. ...continuing then to talk about what theatre should do, especially youth theatre in clubs etc., but I don't think our lot heard any of it.

The trip home was especially noisy and a bit embarrassing when we pulled up at a red light and a rather buxom young lady stopped on the corner also waiting for the lights. One of the lads leant out the window and in a loud voice,

"Nice pair of tits you got there girl" I pulled him back in and tried to disappear under the seat.

Singers

Now I talk a lot of the mounting of a production almost forgetting that after the musical director the people most relied on to carry the production are the singers. While some singers can be brilliant actors there is always that one proverbial tenor who has a block of wood for a head. Very good to resonate perfect sounds but rather devoid of brains. *La Bohème* (I have done three productions of this so will not mention which one to avoid insulting the tenor). In the last act using a terrible translation at which time I was too inexperienced to dare to alter, the tenor sings,

"Your cheeks are the colour of sunrise."

Soprano's answer,

"Nay the simile fits not. Rather the colour of sunset."

The tenor delivered this beautifully all with an encouraging smile.

"CUT … Rudolpho what have you just sung to Mimi?"
"Your cheeks are the colour of sunrise."
"YEEES. And what does she answer?"

Confused look from the tenor.

"I don't know."

A confused look from me. A tenor who doesn't even listen to his soprano.

"Nay, the colour of SUNSET."
"OOOh," he answered, as if this were some big revelation.
I didn't think any further explanation was necessary.
"Do it again."

A complete repeat of his first performance...smile and all.

"CUT."

A repeat of our first conversation only this time he knew what her answer was.

"So what does it mean?"

Some hard thinking and…

> "Well I think the colour of her cheeks are like sunrise and she thinks they are a different colour."
> "No Tony. She's telling you that she is dying."
> "Oh."
> "Right again please."

Exaggerated sad look from Tony.

> "CUT. Now what's the matter?"
> "She's dying."
> "Tony, she hasn't told you yet...........I tell you what, just smile 'till the c sharp and then look sad."

He was a very good singer, but I could not help thinking of Anna Russell saying about a singer: 'You have resonance where your brains ought to be.'

In all fairness, it's not only tenors and I must admit that although we pick on tenors I have been fortunate to work with some very talented and highly intelligent ones, so let's look at bass and baritone. A production of Boito's *Mephistopheles*........

First rehearsal ....the character playing Mephistopheles insists that the part requires a complete devil's make-up and costume to the point of even having horns on his head and of course giving the most evil performance possible. Whoops!! My interpretation is that he should be a young good-looking extremely friendly and lovable character. I will spare you the ensuing problems of trying to convince him of this. I do not believe that a director impose an interpretation on a character but must convince the actor/singer, and this I thought I had eventually done until the opening night. The opera begins in heaven with beautiful projected clouds and a huge chorus of angels. A trap door in the stage opens and up pops Mephistopheles with a complete devils make-up. I suppose this did appear as a nice dramatic moment but what of the next two hours? I think this does prove that the final performance is only as good as the cast.

I must add that not all singers are like that but a singer goes to music school and spends three to five years learning to sing. An actor goes to a drama school and spends three to five years learning to act. No actor would just presume that without training he could sing opera but somehow many singers take it for granted that without training they can act. As this is on the history of Southgate Opera I am referring to fifty years ago since when, acting has become an integral part of a singer's training.

Fulham Arts Centre falls through

Time was running by. Hammersmith Council had bought Riverside Studios and was giving out all the publicity of turning it into a community arts centre. X and Barry Stead both resigned from our committee, X now joining Riverside studios. After many requests it was made very clear to us that there was to be no place whatsoever for us in Riverside Studios. I had given up the scout hall which had now been reclaimed by the council and turned into offices. I had given up the offer of the grant of £25,000 with GLA. So I was back on the streets with nothing.

And then I remembered........ When we were doing the Youth Festival, the council had given me the use of the old Fulham wash house as a base for storage for the festival. This was a large almost derelict hall below the level of the street in Dawes Road almost on the corner of Fulham Road. I still had a key so I decided to squat. I called a meeting of the trustees plus anyone from the council who wished to come plus any interested members of the public, and the local papers.

There was quite a good turnout with everyone sitting on scaffolding planks placed on cool drink boxes. I opened with the bland statement

"Welcome to the new Fulham Arts Centre."

Representing the council was Alderman Sondergaard. I had no idea what an alderman was but was told it was something important on the council. Someone warned me.... 'be careful. She is a very tough lady and will close you down in a week.' After some discussion with ideas thrown in by everyone I turned directly to Sondergaard and said,

"This is the new Fulham Arts Centre. Should the council wish to help us, all help will be gratefully accepted. If not, will they please just leave us alone to get on with it, just ignore us completely."

Sondergaard got up and made a glowing speech about how the council had decided to back us to the hilt, not because of what we said we were going to do, but as a result of what we had already done.

It was just on a year since the loss of the scout hall. The trustees had since disbanded, as besides the house concerts in Chesilton Road, there had been nothing to do but wait for results from Riverside studios. We agreed to form a new committee there and then. Sondergaard put herself forward and was voted on as chairman. I was again warned, I think by Tim Godfrey, who had stood beside me all the way. With a huge hall (however derelict) no rent and an alderman as chairman I was too euphoric to hear.

The first committee meeting was held. Sondergaard's first proposal was that since the council was going to support us we could stop all fund-raising. Tim, who was our treasurer and had already raised a bit of money was flabbergasted. He did not believe it. A rather heated discussion ensued with Sondergaard insisting that money raising would be a waste of time as it would only mean that the council would give us less. Tim was obdurate and eventually offered his resignation. I pleaded.

> "Please Tim. She's on the council so must know what she is talking about."
> "Cecil, we've been friends for too long for us to fall out over this. I do wish you all the best."

Tim left the meeting, although not the company, as he and Sondergaard were both around helping to clean the hall. I must here mention Fay who although not on the committee, throughout the years was always there to help with whatever was needed. We were getting pretty excited over the opening as Peter Katin had offered to open with a recital. What a start! A recital by a world famous concert pianist.

Peter had organized with Steinway to deliver a Steinway for that night and had asked me what I wanted on the programme. Roy had organized seating to be sent over from the Brunswick. I had had to fix up some light fittings above the piano which were just light bulbs in tins painted black. This could not be happening to the likes of me... but it was. I think we only charged about fifty pence for a ticket although there were a lot of comps.

The opening arrived. The house was packed, the entire front row being filled with councillors including the mayor. I got my very first inkling as to the workings of the council when Sondergaard started organizing a standing ovation at the end for Katin. This baffled me. Surely that would be a spontaneous thing from an audience and should not be 'organized.'

Needless to say the evening was a huge success. Katin got his standing ovation which turned out to be perfectly genuine without any help from Sondergaard. She got up and made a glowing speech pointing out all our successes so far and saying what we intended in the future. The Mayor then got up and reiterated this saying that the council was going to back us all the way and to prove it they would immediately give us £7000 to get started and we were to apply for more as it was needed.

Champagne was served afterwards during which the mayor instructed me to write in to the council the following day and we would receive the £7000 within the week.

All my fears that Tim had inspired or that I had been told by X about us not getting a penny as everything would be channelled to Riverside Studios, had now abated. The promises had been publicly made and had been reported in the press. In jubilation I wrote to the council.

So the opera company was on its way and the Arts Centre was about to get a helping hand with its launching. As requested I wrote to the council'. No reply. I wrote again. Still no reply. I wrote again and this time received a reply saying nothing was known about this £7000?????? I phoned. I do not know who I spoke to but when I referred to the mayor and his promises I was told that the night of Katin's concert had been the last night of his office and that there was now a new mayor. There was NO £7000, nor anything to follow. My life long war with the council had begun.

More about singers, Southgate and opera

I have an extremely bad ear for music. I cannot tell if a singer is singing flat, or sharp, or off key. At auditions we have a panel of five. Four of whom are musicians and me, which means I am vastly outnumbered when I feel someone is perfect for the part and the rest of the panel are completely shocked as the particular singer was singing flat and there is no way that anyone could sit through an opera with that.... (I could.) "But she sounds marvellous to me." (Nearly all singers sound marvellous to me.)

"Yes, but she's flat."

Sadly, or maybe fortunately, I am outvoted. Now, how does this affect the final production? I tell the story of an incident at a rehearsal of *La Bohème*. At a certain point in the last act I called cut to give a note. Having done so......

"Terry can we pick it up from the weird chord?"
"What 'weird' chord, Cecil?"
"Terry, there's a weird sounding chord. You can't miss it."
"Puccini did not write any weird chords."
"Well, there's a weird chord as Mimi dies."
"Oh, you mean this, "as he played the chord........ C minor"
"That's it."

Rehearsal continued.

Afterwards Terry patiently explained to me that Puccini never wrote 'weird' chords. It was just the extremely clever way in which he used them. I pondered for days over this and came to the conclusion that, where musicians heard C minor very cleverly used, I heard some wild, mysterious, exotic chord that thrilled me to the boots. I have never been able to decide who gets the greater pleasure from music, the trained musician with a perfect ear who appreciated the genius of composers or me in my ignorance......but I ask, can you imagine what I experience when listening to works such as *The Rite of Spring*?

The opera was Faust, with a small professional company *Arena Opera*. Sitting on the audition panel with me was Marion, very much a professional with whom I had had the pleasure of working on many occasions. In came a soprano to audition for Margarita.

One look at her and I thought she was perfect for the part. She opened her mouth to sing and I heard the voice of an angel. She could also act.

As she left the room I turned to Marion. She's gorgeous and perfect for the part. Marion did not show the same enthusiasm. I was completely bewildered.

"The voice is tired. I want to hear her again when she's had a rest."

I didn't know what she meant, but Marion asked for her to be called back. Sure enough, it turned out that at the moment she was singing in *Opera for All* having had performances every night that week. As a true professional she had made no excuses at her audition. Happy ending... she got the part and gave me a perfect Marguerita.

Now I know that this was not with Southgate Opera but it did prove to me that these musicians really could tell about voices and I really should listen to them. Perhaps in production the combination of their ears and mine gave us the best of both worlds.

Even among musicians disagreements happen. Five of us were on the panel for the opera *Cavaleria Rusticana*. I cannot remember how many Santuzas we had already heard when on came Fabien. This voice and performance sent me to heaven. At the end of the auditions when the five of us got together to discuss the casting, first on the agenda was to sort out any obvious castings. Immediately four of us said Fabien. Neil disagreed. Neil was the musical director. We were all flabbergasted. Quite some discussion followed trying to understand why Neil disagreed. At length Neil was directly asked,

"What don't you like about her?"

Rather fearing it may be something personal.

"Well...................... she sounds too much like Renata Scotto."

The four of us collapsed with laughter...

"We'll settle for Scotto any day."

We won the day and Fabien gave us a marvellous Santuza. I have been lucky with *Cavaleria* as the next time I was to do it I had another voice that "sends me to heaven" in one of our home grown products, Shirley. But more of Shirley later.

The Derelict Arts Centre

Trying to describe the Arts Centre is a problem. It was behind a corrugated fence along Dawes Road, down some steps and into a large virtually derelict hall. There were two toilets, one unusable, and two offices. It leaked and there was no heating. The Evening Standard reported Katin's concert under the heading of "World famous concert pianist plays in wash-house." From this you may gather that it was the old wash-house which had been left empty for many years. Steinway had supplied a piano for Katin but that was the only bit of luxury in the place. There was electricity but no light fittings necessitating the light bulbs suspended in tin cans that were used for the concert.

Yes it was a cold, damp, dirty, derelict hall, but I saw none of that. It was Fulham's brand new art centre and in my eyes it was all gilt and velvet. There was work to be done. I closed the piano shop in Fulham Road. I was never any good at business anyhow and brought my personal Steinway down to the centre with the idea of bringing the concerts down here. This would be a start.

A number of the artists who had played for me at Chesilton Road offered to play again free of charge at the Centre. Tickets to these concerts were 25p. which meant that some of the same artists who a week later would be playing at the Albert Hall or Wigmore Hall or even at the now opened Riverside Studios could be heard for 25p at the Fulham Arts Centre. Yes Riverside studios was open and our friend X had deserted us to join them. We had charged 50p for the Peter Katin concert.

This obviously did not go down well with Hammersmith Council as they had now spent very large amounts on launching Riverside Studios. We applied again and again for help from the council but were consistently refused. The Arts Centre was growing in popularity and letters were beginning to appear in the papers from the public urging the council to support us. Each time there was a public performance I had to borrow chairs from either Brunswick or the Methodist youth club which meant transporting them back and forth.

The phone rang. It was Martin. I had met him once or twice since the concert and was no longer afraid of MPs and now knew him as 'Martin.' Hammersmith at the moment was Labour and Martin had explained to me that even if Conservative got into power they would not be able to help us financially as there just wasn't the money but they would support us in every way possible. I was too naive at the time to realize that for the only time I can remember, even since, I was hearing the truth from a politician. Remember Labour had promised to 'Back us to the hilt.' (Their words).

"Cecil, you said you needed some chairs. Is this still the case?"
"Yes."
"Well, there's a conservative club closing down. I can send you about two hundred."
"One hundred will be ample."

And so no longer did I have to fetch and carry chairs. At the same time he gave me a roneo machine, which meant that by typing a stencil on a typewriter, putting it into the roneo and getting ink all over my hands I could then turn a handle and feed in paper to print off programmes or leaflets, at least until the stencil tore, and then start all over again. And so I began printing leaflets for each week's programme and distributing them by walking down North End Road on Saturday morning handing them out. I had no knowledge or experience of how to run an arts centre. I had no big plan in mind, in fact no plan at all, just blind faith and one or two very good and supportive friends.

Word seemed to spread very quickly that there was a performance space available in Fulham. It was the late sixties/early seventies when fringe theatres were springing up in every small space available. The arts laboratory (rather similar to the Arts Centre) was presenting things like Andy Warhol films on a sheet hung on the wall with a single noisy projector in the middle of the audience, stopping the film at the end of each reel. I still feel this is the best way to see a Warhol film.

Experimental theatre had just been invented and every small group in London believed that what they were doing was entirely original and their own secret invention, only to find whatever.....had been done by someone before.

"Happenings" were the thing. A Happening was an event when an audience congregated and waited for something to happen. Usually someone would try to start it by perhaps switching out the lights and passing a watering can or some such meaningless article round the audience in the dark to discuss the reaction afterwards. This of course defeated the aim, as by instigating it, it didn't just happen. Usually audiences would just get bored and slowly disintegrate until only one or two die-hards were left who would then discuss it saying what a tremendous success it had been watching how people got bored and the different ways in which they left.

"Tube Theatre" had been born. I was at the time running the experimental group at Questors theatre. At the end of sessions a plan would be hatched to do a bit of Tube Theatre on the way home. Example: Two members, one wearing black shoes, the other brown would swap just one shoe so each would now be wearing one black and one brown shoe. Each gets on at either end of a carriage. After a while one would get up and start going down the carriage examining everybody's shoes until at last reaching his plant at the other end of the carriage with matching one brown, one black. Shoes would be swapped back with the two of them becoming great buddies. The idea was just to give people something to talk about when they arrived home. Some of it was very funny and very inventive. We never did a repeat. It had to be something different every night.

As I said word soon got round about space at the centre. The rules were very simple. Book a space with me, do your publicity, present your event and go home. If it made money, give a donation to the centre. If it didn't, book another date and have another go. I didn't ask or even think about vetoing work. There were no rules about what could or could not be done.

I did have a few very good musicians to get the Sunday evening concerts going. And of course that grew very quickly extending into chamber concerts, lieder recitals, and jazz groups. Even opera.

The Greater London Arts Council (GLA) was now taking an interest and would sponsor young musicians. So now we included people like the young musicians of the year or the young jazz groups of the year. I remember one jazz group specifying that there had to be a good piano. I asked how they defined a 'good' piano. The answer was 'Any piano on which all the notes play.'

On the theatre side the first few ventures were kiddies' shows and of course the inevitable budding young rock groups who wanted rehearsal space where noise was no problem. One in particular under the name of *Scruff* started doing gigs and collected quite a following.

By today's standards the centre would have been shut down before even opening by health and safety regulations, but laws were very vague. Clubs only admitting members were not liable for safety regulations. This meant that all groups and fringe theatres signed up any patrons as members. The question arose as to how much would have to be paid to be a member and for how long before buying a ticket. Buying a ticket meant running a business so an entry charge was not allowed.

The clubs' answer to this …..entry was free but a programme had to be bought in advance. The "Almost Free" theatre club took up the challenge and announced that membership had to be obtained ten minutes before buying a ticket, ticket and membership amount being decided by the purchaser. It was a very open challenge to the law to get their act straight. "Almost Free" was never sued so we all followed suit.

Next came Equity. Members of Equity were not allowed to perform for under the minimum wage set by Equity. There was no way in which fringe venues were able to pay that amount for visiting companies and there was no way in which the companies could pay that to their actors. Now as these venues were the only ones in which budding young professionals could display their wares to be seen by agents it meant that they could not perform at all and therefore earned nothing. Equity had to back down.

Very quickly the Arts Centre settled into a routine. With the offer from people like Neil Immelman, Tessa Uys, Marion Bryfdir and other professionals who had performed in Chesilton Road and who were now willing to play for nothing to get the centre going, plus young pianists recommended by Peter Katin, the Sunday evenings were doing very well.

Week days were rapidly filling with youth clubs, young rock groups and a few amateur companies who did not have homes. Added to this both the inner London Education Association (ILEA) and the GLA were now recommending us as a venue. The GLA offered grants to small professional companies for particular performances which now meant that there was an even cross section between kiddies, youth clubs amateur groups and professionals. It had become quite common to do nine different shows in one week, seven plus two matinees.

The place was still dirty, cold, wet, with no heating, inadequate toilets and no proper lighting but it still managed to attract anything from totally empty houses to completely sold out performances depending on who dared to use it. Oh, and the roof leaked.

On one occasion Christopher Kite had offered to give a harpsichord recital arriving with his own very valuable harpsichord and of course attracting a large audience. The concert started and so did the rain. Suddenly Chris stopped playing. Panic. The roof was leaking directly over the harpsichord. A mad rush as we moved the harpsichord to a different spot and the concert continued ignoring the dripping water.

On another occasion, although the piano was a five foot Steinway it was not in tip top condition and during a recital by Antony Peebles who was the winner of the BBC piano competition, suddenly a note in the middle register stopped working. A small delay in the recital while the action of the piano was dismantled to do a quick repair. The concert then continued and came to its triumphant finale.

I continued to beg the council for support but to no avail. As I have noted, Barry Stead and X had left us to concentrate on Riverside studios. By now we were a complete thorn in the side of Hammersmith council as we were presenting exactly the same artists and companies in Fulham as Riverside Studios were doing. Only it cost a quarter as much in Fulham while Fulham was receiving no support and thousands of pounds were being given to Riverside. Letters from the public were beginning to appear in the papers.

Financial woes

Financially I was struggling. My only income was now from Opera productions I did for various companies, and this hardly covered my living expenses let alone any money I spent on the Centre. An exceptionally good friend of mine, Francis (Fay) who had stood beside me through everything would visit every day and bring me a plate of food, jokingly saying,

"I know if I don't feed you, you will forget to eat"...

And, of course, she was right but it wasn't forget, it was that I had no money for food.

With the help of Murry, I started writing to every possible charity asking for help. I was a bad typist and Murry checked every letter. If there was a single error in the letter I would have to type it again. Murry would not allow mistakes, typing errors or otherwise. The answer, if we received one was always the same except for one, "The Gulbenkian Society."

In one or two letters I had innocently stated that we had written to the Gulbenkian and were hoping for help. The Gulbenkian were very put out and wrote a rather scathing letter to me accusing me of falsely stating that they had offered some help and we were using this as leverage to obtain funds from other society s. OOPS!!!!

It was quite right. We were desperately hoping that somebody, anybody would help.

Tim, who was our "money man" had managed to get a donation from some large firm (I forget which) and an offer to match pound for pound anything we could raise from other sources...but of course after the row with Sondergaard all this had stopped as we were convinced the council would help. I had by now accepted that there was no help at all coming from that direction. The council (X) had already taken twenty five thousand pounds from us and had no intention of giving a single penny back. I approached GLA who as I said were giving grants to companies to perform in the centre but their answer was that they could help the companies but not a venue. I couldn't understand this.

I had approached ILEA for a grant for lighting equipment. At last... a positive answer. Yes they would give me a grant provided I did some work with the schools. I had still continued doing productions for the youth clubs but would I now include the schools. My heart sank. I just could not handle any more. Winter was approaching. The place was cold and damp. I was already working with the youth clubs and presenting sometimes nine shows a week in the centre with only Faye to help me keep the place in something vaguely resembling cleanliness. I was not eating properly nor getting enough sleep and my health was beginning to show signs of weakness. A true sob story, only I didn't realise all this at the time and said, "Yes, OK." I approached the London Oratory School.

In the meantime my fights with the council continued. On the surface if anyone spoke to them about me they always sang my praises but all money still went to Riverside. The wash house was connected to the old Fulham baths where there had been a removable floor built over the swimming bath. This floor was now to be disbanded and was stored in part of the wash house to which I had access.

Unbeknown to me they were offering it to all the clubs around. I had not been included. The Townmead Archers, another youth club I had been working with, told me of it and that they had been offered as much as they wanted.

I phoned the council to put in a request.

"Oh Cecil......We're so sorry but it's all gone already."
"Why was none offered to me?"
"Cecil we are really sorry about this but we forgot all about you as you're not registered as a club. We're really sorry."

I phoned back Townmead.

"You say you've been offered as much as you want?"
"Yes."
"Do me a favour. Ask for an extra lot for me."
"Sure," they said.

And that was how I ended up getting a stage built in the centre. In the meantime there was still a lot more left over in the wash house. I asked about that but was told that that particular lot was not to be given away as it was still in use. I was now completely convinced that I was definitely not wanted by the council, especially when after being told this, one of the councillors came down to collect some more to put a floor in his attic and I helped him to load it.

Brunswick again

A year before, the Brunswick had won the one-act trophy and they were now keen to win it again. They approached me help them do it but like the year before I was involved with the Southgate Opera and the London Oratory School so it was just impossible. I suggested a couple of plays for them. They chose one and with the help of Val, another friend who had supported me through thick and thin, started rehearsals. I had agreed to help in the last week before the performance.

I managed to attend a few of their rehearsals. The final Friday night came when it was to be a full dress. Like the year before, a small group from the club including a number of the management attended to give moral support. It was a very good little one-act called "*Toys In The Attic*" in which four actors emerged from a box and acted out the history of a Victorian family. The rehearsal went very well: I was proud of them. Roy got up to speak and after saying how good it was came out with the news that they would be unable to perform as the Federation had banned the play. One of the toys was a Golliwog and within the play there were references to religion through the eyes of native tribes in Africa.

The kids were dumbfounded. I say 'kids' but the ages were roughly fifteen to sixteen. The remark from one of them was:

"They keep telling us to act like adults and when we do, they ban us."

Roy went on to say that although we could not win our trophy again he had organised for them to give a performance to a private audience on the Sunday and that the adjudicator of this year's festival would attend and give a crit.

The performance was quite a success with a good audience. I cannot remember who the adjudicator was but at the end she got up to mention her surprise at such a high standard. She mentioned that on the previous night the highest award had been a silver but here she had no hesitation in awarding a gold which was officially recognised. Of course the trophy had already been awarded the night before. As the opera I had been working on was now over I agreed to do the next major production for them which was to be *Dracular Spectacular*.

The London Oratory School

At the London Oratory school I had met their club leader and after some time it was agreed to do *West Side Story* to be presented in the Fulham Arts Centre. As theirs was a full time registered club, finance would be no problem. ILEA would support it. This meant enough money to get a musical director, a band, good sets and good costumes. I arrived at the auditions with that dreaded sinking feeling knowing that once more I would have to face being sent up in the usual way. Somehow I had conquered both the Methodist Club and the Brunswick so at least I did not feel the fear that I had originally endured.

I entered the school room where the auditions were to be held. To my disbelief the kids all stood up and waited for me to speak.

"Good evening," I said.
"Evening Sir," came the reply.

SIR????? Was this real? They were well behaved. Was I really in Fulham?

I plucked up the courage to look straight round the room. There were twenty three girls and one sixteen year old boy, Paddy. OUCH ... What do I do?

We sat and chatted and of course it was agreed that the boys had to be brought in. I don't know if it was bribery or corruption but at the next meeting the boys were there and believe it or not also very well behaved, although they were no angels, thank God. Auditions over, rehearsals began.

Pressure on the Arts Centre

It was about two in the afternoon when I received a visit from two council members. From their attitude I immediately sensed trouble. They took a look at the stage I had built and asked where I had got the wooden flooring from. I told them Townmead Archers.

They then said that there was a new lot missing from next door and they believed this was it. I denied this. After some discussion where they were now openly accusing me of theft they said:

"Well Mr Hayter. There is nothing we can do but bring in the police."
"Yes. Please do and I'll tell them exactly which councillor took it and where it is."

This was met with dead silence. I heard nothing more from them and to this day I still feel a satisfied smirk come over me when I remember that moment.

Winter had now come. Patrons who knew, came prepared with blankets, and more letters started to appear in the papers. I'm afraid that by now I so distrusted councillors that I began to wonder if the letters were all genuine or if one or two of them could have been written by Opposition councillors who had objected to the money spent on Riverside Studios, trying to win Brownie Points. I quote as best as my memory allows me, an editorial from the Fulham Chronicle.

"The good Lord helps those who help themselves but it seems that Hammersmith council does not wish to emulate divine providence. Next time they are handing out a feast of £50,000 to Riverside Studios won't they throw a few crumbs to the Fulham Arts Centre."

By now The Arts Centre was pretty well known by Fringe companies, musicians, both jazz and classical, amateur groups, youth clubs, solo artists and even opera companies. It had truly become a centre where performances of any and every sort could be tried without the fear of failure. In the interim I had been privileged in being able to meet some exceptionally talented people who really did do some crazy stunts for me.

Christmas was coming and I decided to organize singing *Songs from the Shows* in the streets. Members of the Southgate opera company offered and Mark (Raubenheimer) always ready for fun, said he would play the piano, so we put an upright piano on a piano trolley and wheeled it through the streets of Fulham with Mark walking along beside it and playing at the same time. I doubt if anyone ever realized that they were listening to opera singers, one or two who had sung in Covent Garden plus an international concert pianist. I believe that just recently (nearly forty years later) the same experiment has been tried in New York subways.

Besides the cold and lack of solid funding the Centre was now proving enormously successful. I had no trouble getting bookings and everyone who performed here knew just what they were coming to and appeared very happy to do so. I had been offered the very first grant from ILEA for the lighting which had now been ordered and was due to arrive any day. Of course I would have liked a salary of some sorts and because of the constant cold and wet I can't say I was in the best of health but I was extremely happy.

It was Monday morning. I was sitting in the office and the phone rang.

> "Hello."
> "Is that Cecil Hayter?"
> "Yes."
> "It's the ILEA here. You have an order with Strand Electric for some lighting equipment."
> "Yes," I said pleased that it was about to arrive.
> "Can you cancel it?"

I didn't quite take this in and said,

> "How do you mean?"
> "The council have told us that they are about to close you down permanently and that we must stop any grants or money of any sort going to you."

I was completely bewildered and said,

> "But I have heard nothing from them."
> "Well, we've just had the phone-call now and they said they were closing you down."

I paused to think then:

> "The lighting has been delivered already." I said.

Whoever she was she must have just been a secretary who never knew the ins and outs as there was no personal emotion of any sort expressed. It seemed a normal thing to her.

I sat for a second and sort of moved into automatic gear.

I picked up the phone and dialled.

"Strand Electric," said a voice.
"You have an order for lighting for the Fulham Arts Centre to be delivered this week."
"Yes."
"Is it at all possible to deliver it today and back date it for last week?"

He knew who I was and all about the grant and that IlEA was paying for it.

"If so we get the order. If not, you lose the sale and I don't get my lighting."

I really can't remember if I explained any more to him or not but he said he would be able to get it to me the following morning and he would back date it. I then sat in limbo waiting to see what would happen. That afternoon the council rang. I don't think I asked who I was speaking to but they knew me.

"Cecil, we've got to ask you to close down. Don't worry it will just be for a week. We have found that the building is unsafe and we will be spending £7000 on it and you can move back again. Really sorry about this but it will just be for a week"

Seven thousand pounds!!!!!!!! Where had I heard that figure before?

I was running on automatic. I went straight over to the district surveyor who had his office just down the road from me. I don't remember how I knew there was such a thing as a district surveyor or how I knew where his office was. I guess it must have been from when we, at the very first, had to check the building to store things for the festival.

I didn't tell him that I had heard from the council. I could be almost sure that one department of the council never ever knew what another was doing. But I did tell him that someone had mentioned that the building looked a bit unsafe (The council had mentioned the skylight in the ceiling) so I wanted it checked. He said he would be able to do it in a day or two. I mentioned that we had a performance that night and I couldn't take a chance. He came straight over with me. After getting on the roof, which was not difficult, he assured me that it was quite safe. I stayed open. The lighting was delivered the next morning.

It was an odd week, but then every week was an odd week, but this week I remember well. On the Sunday night a quartet (classical) had booked in, arriving in the afternoon, to have a run through. That night they appeared in full evening dress. Faye and I had cleaned the place and set out all the coffee cups etc. for interval.

Not one audience member turned up. Not an auntie or an uncle or anyone at all. This was a new experience even for me. They were so disappointed and came over to me to apologise. I just laughed offered them some coffee and said, "Don't worry. This is what the centre is for. Book another date and have another try but now you know you need more publicity." They began to see the funny side and had a practice instead.

The Tuesday night was a young jazz group who had just won the young musicians of the year award and were sponsored by GLA. It was a fairly successful evening with not too big a crowd. It was quite cold that night.

Wednesday was *Shared Experience*, that had booked in at fairly short notice but the place was packed so full that physically we could not get another person in. I hated turning people away but just said if you could get in, go in.

Thursday night was a regular poetry reading night which got its usual audience.

Friday night was to be the *Incubus Theatre*.

That afternoon two council members had turned up with official papers closing me down saying that they were sorry they had got it wrong. It wasn't the building but it was the electricity that was unsafe. I knew that I would not be able to get around this one.

Somehow I suddenly switched off. I seemed to just go blank. I knew it was the end. I don't even remember wanting to cry. I just stood at the door telling people that the show was cancelled and sending them home. Incubus was a popular company and there was quite a large number to turn away. I think perhaps I was still running on automatic.

Losing the Christadelphian Hall (Cassidy Road) and the £25,000 grant had been a slow occurrence happening over time. This had all happened in one week not really giving me time to think. I should have stayed. I should have fought. I had the public and the newspapers on my side so why did I just give in? It's so easy now thinking 'I should have done this, or I should have done that' but somehow I was suddenly hit with a total despair. I knew the council were once more lying and that there would be no £7000. I knew the Arts Centre would never open again. I felt I had already exhausted every possible chance of finding suitable premises.

Trying to carry on...and New York! New York!

A production of *Dracula Spectacular* with the Brunswick had been agreed, but rehearsals had not yet started. I couldn't do it. This made me feel worse. How could I tell Roy? I had gone home to virtually bury myself. I wouldn't go out and I wouldn't answer the phone. Roughly thirty five to forty years have now passed and it's hard for me to remember exactly what I did. I say I would not answer the phone but I must have made a lot of calls cancelling things. I must have organized getting my piano back home and for that matter, clearing the Centre. I do know I gave all that brand new lighting equipment still in its unopened boxes to the Brunswick Club, but those few weeks after closing have really disappeared from my memory.

One thing I do remember is going down to the Brunswick to tell Roy. Roy was away at the time and the sub leader (I don't remember who he was) was in charge. I went into the office to tell him and promptly broke into tears. It would have been easier if Roy had been there. I just said that I could not do the *Dracula*, and I didn't know how to tell Roy. I was told not to worry as he was sure Tim would do the show and that he would explain to Roy.

BUT... I had started rehearsals at the London Oratory School and I couldn't bring myself to just go in and tell the kids it was all off. I went to talk to the youth leader and we discussed performing it in the youth club which was part of the school. I did suggest that it could go into the main hall of the school where there was a stage but was told that the principal of the school was very strict and he did not think it would be allowed. I thought I would chance my arm and booked an appointment to see the principal who was John McIntosh.

John turned out to be very friendly, very co-operative and thought it would be a great idea. Between the school and the ILEA, finance would be no problem. This meant that besides having money for scenery and costumes we could afford to pay a musical director and also have an orchestra. On writing this I now realise how much I actually needed *West Side Story*. However, even though it proved to be very successful, I had vowed that I would never work in Fulham again.

I returned once more to directing wherever I could, excluding Fulham. It was during this period that I was lucky enough to work all over England, Scotland and Wales with different opera and theatre companies including such theatres as The Young Vic and in

Stratford at the Swan Theatre. I also travelled to New York where I was fortunate enough to direct and design *South Pacific* and on another trip to do the scenery for an off Broadway production. During this time John McIntosh kept trying to persuade me to do another production at the London Oratory School. I consistently, but politely, declined.

At the time Mark Raubenheimer, was staying with me while on a concert tour. He was due in one week's time to return to New York and was trying to persuade me to come back with him to spend a week or two. Of course I couldn't afford it. On the Sunday afternoon I came back from rehearsal of *Turandot* at Southgate and Mark excitedly told me New York had phoned and wanted me over there the following day. I naturally took it that he was joking but he kept insisting telling me that Helen had phoned and that she had left her number. I sort of began to wonder as I didn't know how he knew that I knew a Helen in New York.

In fact a month or so back Helen and her opera company had come across to the Edinburgh Festival and had asked me to go up there and paint their set for them.

I had taken a train to Edinburgh, reading the libretto on the way and found that all that was needed was a simple living room set with doors and skirting boards etc. Having allowed myself three days to paint, I realized that this would only take a half a day, so as a joke, since it was a romantic little opera of Offenbach's, I started painting garlands of flowers and little cherubs all over the walls while they were out. AMERICANS!!!!.....

They did not see the joke and thought it was all wonderful and would I paint the whole set only,

"... leave out the little drunk cherub with the glass of champagne in his hand as that might offend." I thought they were turning the joke on me but no, they were deadly serious. So I did it, and that's who Helen was. Eventually after lots of Mark's persuasion I phoned the number.
"Hello............. Helen?"
"Cecil, hello.... did Mark tell you? We're doing the opera again Off Broadway and we want you to paint the set again. Can you come over here tomorrow?"

I explained that I had no money but Helen said, "Borrow the money, we will pay it all back."

Monday morning.....the Bank manager said I was mad but he allowed me the overdraft. I went to the airport and on the Freddie Laker system, bought a ticket and got on the plane, trusting Helen to meet me when I arrived.

At Kennedy Airport I was confronted by customs. I dared not say I was over to paint scenery but told them that I had painted the set for the group in Edinburgh and I had now been invited over by Helen to do it in New York.

...."You have no money on you?"
"No they are paying everything."
"And your plane ticket back home?"
"That too."

"Where are you staying?"

"With Helen."

"Where does she live?"

"I don't know."

"Helen who?"

I could not remember her surname.

"I don't know."

"You have no money....you do not know where you will be staying and you don't know who Helen is?????"

"Well...if you come outside and Helen is not waiting for me, I am in big trouble."

He shook his head, sighed, stamped my passport and said,

"Go through."

I'm sure he was thinking .... ENGLISH!!!

I only spent one week in New York as I had to get back to rehearsals of *Turandot* where Jenny Lilliestone was singing the title role. Jenny is tiny, which incidentally Puccini had asked for. There had been some concern about getting a soprano strong enough for the part, but no problem, one of the critics complained that Jenny's voice was too strong for the size of hall. Hard to win when doing opera.

This was all during the rehearsals of *West Side Story*. Paddy was interested to know what an opera was so

I offered to take him with me to a rehearsal of *Turandot*. At the moment when Nessun Dorma came up, Paddy lit up, after rehearsal telling me that he knew that piece of music. It was the start of Paddy's great love of opera. Years later he was eventually to direct *La Gioconda* for the company.

The London Oratory School Theatre: the birth of LOST

About a year had now passed and I guess I was beginning to get over the bitterness of losing the Arts Centre. While walking down North End Road, I bumped into Paddy. Paddy, besides being a brilliant little actor, had played Riff in *West Side Story*, had also proved a very hard worker spending many hours helping build the sets and also spending a night in Fulham jail for trying to put posters up for his school play in North End Road. Had the police nothing better to do than to arrest a sixteen year old kid for putting up posters for his school play? Paddy was very persuasive in asking me to please do another show at the school..... I weakened and said yes.

John Mc. appeared very pleased to hear this and immediately booked another date for us while asking me to start a company especially for the group as a number would soon be leaving school. The thought of starting another company terrified me having just burnt my fingers so badly. I said, if I did, it would be under the strict understanding that no adult would have anything whatsoever to do with it. It would have to be run by the students themselves with their own committee, under their own chairman and if a single councillor tried to put his foot in the door I would immediately close the thing down and resign. John thought this was a brilliant idea and so we went about preparing to do a musical, *Comedy Of Errors*, written by Terry Hawes under the new committee of school members.

The committee was duly elected. Paddy, captain of the school rugby team, was elected chairman and the company was officially born under the name of "The London Oratory School Youth Theatre" or, for short, "LOSYT" Theatre. This being awkward to say soon metamorphosed to the "LOST" Theatre. Although I sat in on all meetings I never had a vote so if I disagreed with any policy or proposal I had to convince the committee against their decision. Trying to run a theatre company through a committee of sixteen year olds with no experience whatsoever of procedure or experience of theatre in general proved a very exciting and rewarding venture. Rehearsals were going pretty well even with the usual troubles of people missing to play rugby, or whatever, and the problem of getting the cast to learn lines. In the end it turned out to be another great success.

Between shows, drama classes were held. These were in the evenings. John was exceptionally pleased with the reaction of the students and allowed us the hall or if that was in use a classroom was always provided. Conditions were vastly different from working in the cold, damp Arts Centre with very unruly kids. I remember in one of the earlier rehearsals when someone came into the rehearsal with a radio playing, albeit softly but I turned.

"Please switch the radio off."

"Sorry sir," said a voice and it was switched off.

I had braced myself for the usual response of "Why?" and an argument, and strong words before it was done. I was surprised to find that I was forgetting how to respond to good manners.

Classes were going exceptionally well with some members now working really hard and beginning to take drama much more seriously despite the continual late comers.

"New rules: Class now begins at seven sharp and the doors are locked. Late comers will not be admitted."

This worked ....after one or two people had found themselves locked out.

We were now ready for our first public performance of work done at the classes. This was when experimental theatre was the "thing" so the performance was very much the same as the now popular *Whose Line Is It Anyway*. I was at the time, running the experimental sessions at Questors Theatre so was able to keep up with the times. The evening proved almost as successful as the full length shows.

Terry and Southgate opera

Besides the operas, Terry Hawes was a very accomplished composer and writer of both reviews and musicals. Of course one of the great advantages of having the composer as musical director was that parts could be written to suit specific singers. During the chase scene of *Italian Straw Hat*, written by Terry, Terry announced that at this moment he had added a tenor solo for David as David did not have enough to sing in the musical. I was horrified.

"Terry, you can't possibly put an aria in at this point, for it will hold up the entire action at a peak moment."

I didn't add that I also thought that writing in an extra aria just to give a singer more to sing was a crime.

"I'm sorry Cecil, but there it is,"
"Well I suppose we had better hear it" ...as I sat back a bit deflated ....UNTIL...

On came the tenor to sing,

"...that no matter what the action, or how much the disruption to the play, a tenor had to have his aria every day."

I roared with laughter, apologised to Terry and admitted that it was the exact right aria in the exact right place. The action froze, the tenor sang, the action continued. For those who remember it (how could we forget) there was also *Whispering Zephyr* specifically written for Alex.

More Terry musicals followed. Everyone a huge hit with audiences demanding, and getting, repeated performances at later dates. The LOST theatre presented

Terry's *To The Woods* a musical version of *Mid-Summer Night's Dream* at the Edinburgh festival to great critical claim.

I also had the honour of doing another of Terry's works, *Sweeney Todd* a melodrama for young and old with the kids at the Brunswick Club in Fulham (the same kids who did *Kick Off At Three*) with Christopher Kite (The same pianist who played the Brahms with Mark Raubenheimer) in the middle of which, Chris was laughing so much at some business of the kid playing Sweeney that he missed a music cue. 'Sweeney' stopped, looked at Chris and demanded "Fingers man, fingers."

There must be some reason why Southgate Opera has not repeated Terry's musicals and offered at least one performance for Terry to conduct, to celebrate the 50 years anniversary.

Patience and LOST

The next show in Fulham was to be *Dark Of The Moon* which had a large cast with an equal number of parts for both male and female. It was getting close to the opening night when we had a visit from Patience Mostyn. I had met Patience at one or two meetings during the organisation of the Youth Festival. She was always immaculately dressed with every hair in place and always sat bolt upright with a bright smile on her face even when she about to slaughter a slacking worker. She took an immense interest in all youth work. If she believed in the work being done she would bend every rule in the book to help. If she thought there was incompetence or slacking that same book would be thrown at the perpetrator with some considerable force.

Somehow she was also a bit frightening. I had been warned not to get on the wrong side of Patience. She was the area head of ILEA and as such was in charge of all the youth clubs in Fulham.

Patience quietly entered the rehearsal and sat, bolt upright, next to me to watch the rehearsal. It was the revival scene where Barbara Allen is virtually raped in the middle of the church in the name of religion.

At the end of the scene Patience looked at me, still with a smile, and ....

"Are you being paid for this?"

I was rather relieved to be able to answer...

"No, but the play is on the school's syllabus" hoping to retrieve the situation. Patience smiled, said a few words about unfortunately not being able to stay to see more but she had to see John. She left. I could foresee trouble.

As expected the following day I was called in to see the club leader.

"Patience was in to see your rehearsal last night."
"Yes."
"Apparently you are not being paid."

Completely bewildered, I remained silent.

"She has now put you on the payroll and has organized seven weeks back pay for you."

I still said nothing.

..."so I will need you to sign some forms. You will, of course, now have to keep a register of attendance at all classes and rehearsals and fill in a claim form for your pay at the end of each month." I was completely taken off guard but was pleased at the pay cheque which came at the end of the month.

It was a full year, after I had gotten to know John a lot better that I found what had really happened. Patience had gone straight to John and started by asking if the LOST members were behaving strangely in any way whatsoever when at school. John answered not that he knew of. She asked if he had seen any of the rehearsals. Again he said no. She then explained that in the play was a revival scene and that the cast were getting carried away and really living it and not acting. John assured her that it was just a play and they were obviously doing it very well. She then set about getting me paid. Over the years Patience proved to be a rock of support for LOST.

Dark Of The Moon was again well received. Classes were thriving. A real sense of belonging and being a LOST Member had set in. There was some real talent among this lot and I was keen to extend it. We had by now done one or two more improvised shows with some success but of course audiences still just consisted of parents, relatives and friends, who of course are always sympathetic.

Time passed and we were now becoming quite proficient. We had included two more musicals, *Pyjama Game* and *Cabaret*. Ricardo had remained with us as our musical director. In the mean time I still had this longing to have our own theatre. Patience had become extremely supportive of the company and like John (McIntosch), was always ready to back us in any way she could. She was particularly enamoured with the idea that the company was to be run by the members without adults but was a bit perturbed when she found that in fact I had no official standing with the company remarking that as such in due course it would be possible for the company to be taken over by someone else. She asked to come to a committee meeting and after advising on committee procedure then suggested that I be voted in as Life Artistic Director. To avoid any possibility of anyone else ever trying to take over the company. This was thought a good idea and I was duly elected as such.

I had by then become very familiar to the staff of the ILEA resources centre and their costume department. I continually begged ILEA to find us a home of our own. Through Patience we were able to borrow costumes free of charge from ILEA, and John had now allowed us £500 to spend on each production while we were permitted to keep all the door takings. The costumes were mostly ex-television or film costumes so shows were exceptionally well dressed. The resources centre helped with the printing of posters, getting props etc.

My dream continues

And yet with all this, my persistent dream was to have our own theatre. My almost daily greeting to ILEA and to Patience was "Have you bought us the Coliseum yet," until one day when I was offered the ex-scout hall in Broomhouse Lane attached to the Castle Club. Apparently the Castle Club was empty. The scout hall was in bad repair and needed a new floor.

The Castle club was an ex-school but now belonged to the council who were allowing ILEA to use it. We jumped at the idea. Weekend rehearsals at the school were difficult and space for performances was not always possible at the school. We begged the council to give us the Castle Club as a home but the usual answer came from the council. NO.

However, in the meantime we were allowed to store costumes and props there and after much begging and delays, a new floor was completed in the scout hall with electricity and heating installed. The extra space proved a godsend. We installed a couple of spotlights so that it was now possible to have performance evenings, which proved a godsend to the idea of members thinking up their own ideas. This idea became very popular and soon time had to be booked in advance.

With this as encouragement I instigated the One Act Festival. In my younger days entering one act festivals was a large part of my learning process. The rules meant the performance was to last no longer than forty-five minutes. Participants were allowed ten minutes to set the stage and five minutes to strike. No more than five pounds was to be spent on the production. Rights, if there were any, would be paid by the company and of course a strong emphasis was placed on doing original material. The one act festival was a hit from the start and I was thrilled when Seamus, a young member wrote the first one act play called *Jesus Saves* This proved such a success that he extended it and it was later performed as a full length play.

Auditions for *Romeo and Juliet* were now in progress. A new young lad arrived to audition. I took his name,

"Have you done any acting before?"
"No, not really."

He got to auditioning and began to read. He had hardly done two lines when I turned to the person sitting next to me and said:

"Wow. We've got a Romeo. He is brilliant."

I called him over.

"What did you say your name was?"
"Ralph Fiennes."

I had purposely held the auditions just before Christmas telling the cast to please read the play over the Xmas break so they would at least have in inkling of what it was about at the start of rehearsals. The first rehearsal arrived and we were about to start a read through. I noticed that Ralph did not open his script.

"Ralph... your script"
"No, I've learnt it. I don't need it."

Of course when associated with the stage there are always embarrassing moments. After a performance of *Turandot* I was in the foyer and a little old lady singled me out.

"Are you the director?"
"Yes."
"I wanted to speak to you."

She was tiny and looked rather frail but full of life and enthusiasm and, as I thought, feeling thrilled to meet the 'director.'

"I wanted to tell you I so enjoyed it and it was so well directed."

Knowing full well that little old ladies hardly know what a director does I smiled and in my most patronizing voice.

"Thank you so much. So nice of you to say so."
"I know about these things, you know. I used to be a singer."

With her obvious enthusiasm, I imagined her singing her heart out in the local church choir.

"Thank you again."

I repeated trying to look really honoured, and off she went no doubt hoping to meet one of the "stars" of tonight.

A tap on my shoulder.

"Do you know who you have just been talking to?"
"No."
"That was Dame Eva Turner."

My heart leapt and had a cadenza. I should have been on my knees begging for her autograph. Dame Eve Turner, a living legend recognized as probably the world's greatest Turandot, in fact also the world's first Turandot under the baton of Toscanini, besides being considered one of the world's greatest Wagnerian singers. When into her eighties, she was still a professor of singing at the Royal Academy, training singers such as Kiri Te Kanawa and Dame Gwyneth Jones. Into her nineties she remained an avid opera goer very alive and with a great sense of humour. But.... what was she doing at an amateur production even if the company did use professional leads? Well, apparently our Turandot was one of her pupils. Little old lady from church choir?????

At the time despite the fact that I was completely overawed at actually meeting a living legend of the theatre I was completely unconscious of the charmed life I was beginning to live associating with living legends and unknown schoolboys who were later to become world famous.

I would like to say that *Romeo and Juliet* was a brilliant production, but it wasn't. Ralph was of course outstanding and through him a lot of people did think it was, but in truth, I really did not know enough about Shakespeare and, since I had been their only drama coach, nor did the cast. Yes there were one or two pass-able performances as there genuinely was some talent in the group. I remember afterwards talking to Ralph and saying that he really should be playing this with a professional company with a professional director. I was also sure that someday he would. However Ralph stayed with us for about a year during which time I was lucky enough to direct him in what was a much better production: *Five Finger Exercise*. Needless to say that in that year he won the cup for the best performance in the One Act Festival and also the Tim Godfrey Trophy for memorising the complete script before the first rehearsal. And also needless to say, we then lost him to RADA. He is now a patron of LOST.

The time spent at the London Oratory School was almost idyllic. We had no money problems whatsoever. The best of costumes were available free of charge from the very large costume department belonging to ILEA. The music recitals continued on the Sunday evenings, although not so well attended which was sad as people like Antony Peebles, Hugh Tinney and Joanna Mc Greggor, etc. who in the same month would fill Wigmore Hall, only attracted audiences of ten to twenty at the school.

Besides, there were occasional blinks, such as the night Joanna MacGregor was to give a second recital. We arrived at the school to find no caretaker, so no key to get in. Phone calls to John Mac were of no help as he was not home. The result, standing out in Seagrave Road with a brilliant, soon to be international, concert pianist, an audience and nowhere to go. To this day

I wonder if Joanna McGregor has forgiven us. I forgot to mention that at the time Joanna was our rehearsal pianist for *Threepenny Opera*.

The LOST Theatre

And yet, despite the successes we were having with audiences growing larger, no longer just consisting of friends and relations, I still kept up my plea to ILEA and now Patience who had proved a tower of support,

"Have you bought the Coliseum for us yet?"

Why this longing for our own theatre when here we had such ideal conditions?

The phone rang. It was Patience.

"Cecil, the Methodist Youth club has closed down. Would you be interested in taking over the premises for the LOST theatre?"

WOW!!! Would I be interested? This was where I had done *The Wizard Of Oz* so I knew the building well. It was a huge Gym with dressing rooms, offices, toilets, space for a restaurant and a flat upstairs for the Youth Leader...... and what's more it was right next door to Fulham Broadway Tube and across the road from Fulham Town Hall. A meeting was arranged with the vicar and the church wardens. The church remembered *Oz* and the other things I had done there and seemed particularly keen to have us as the new youth centre.

The meeting went well, with discussions of sharing responsibilities with the church. A small hiccup when I insisted there was to be no form of censorship whatsoever. The church had to trust in the integrity of the company. After a short discussion this was agreed and then the big problem. It had to be called the Methodist Youth Theatre. I could not agree to this as I did not believe a theatre company would ever be taken seriously or disassociated from religion under this name. I reluctantly said no. We would have to remain "The LOST Theatre." The meeting came to an end.

Two sleepless nights passed dreaming of these wonderful premises being turned down because of a title. On the third day I could resist no longer and decided to phone the vicar and suggest a possible combination of Methodist and LOST. However the vicar beat me to it and phoned me. Fortunately I waited for him to speak first:

"We've had a discussion and have agreed to the name LOST."

I could hardly contain my excitement at the next meeting with the LOST committee. The premises were then seen and the idea was met with great enthusiasm. I then suggested that we now planned our next production to be at the Club-- big objections from the committee. The club was not yet equipped. No seating, no lighting, no stage, no curtains. When it was fully equipped we would move. Until then we could remain at the school. This stumped me. I knew if I could get them just to do one show there they would never want to return to the school. A visit to John.

"John, do me a favour. Book a date for our next show in the hall and just two days before we are due to open find an excuse to cancel it."

I told him the whole story and explained that if he cancelled we would have no choice but to move to the club. Of course, John would have to lend us some seating and stage lighting.

The next thing scheduled was a solo reading from one of our more talented members, easy to move as there was no scenery. Of course a whole lot of chairs and a few spotlights would need to be carried with us. It worked.....the feeling of being in what was to be our very own theatre where we did not have to get out at any specific time after a performance triumphed. Even though it had just been a one man show it proved the possibility of performing without a stage, etc.

More meetings with the church. Obviously separate funds were now needed as the school would not be there to pay all our expenses. Combined with the church, we agreed on a fête to be held at a pub at the end of Fulham Road. It would be possible to present a couple of one-act plays there as part of the event. All the usual entertainments were laid on such as coconut shy, stocks with wet sponges, tombola, etc., and I believe the pub had agreed to give us a commission from drink sales. The weather was great and the whole thing turned out to be a huge success. The agreement was to pool all money with whatever the church had brought in and put it all towards starting to equip the hall.

Now I cannot remember the exact details, which is probably a good thing, but we were unable to get through to the vicar and organise a meeting for further discussions or to sort out the money. Eventually, news arrived that the vicar had caught his wife having an affair with one of the wardens of the church and had "up and left." There was now no vicar, so no church services, and nobody to run the ship, as it were. Whoever was left from the church, which at the time only had a congregation of about twelve and which, I should have explained, was above the gym, advised us to stay and just get on with it.

We found that the connection between ILEA and the church went back to the initial building of the premises when the church needed money and ILEA put in a certain amount to the building with the proviso that the church ran a youth club for ILEA in the gym, specially built for the purpose. Hence the full time leader of the club paid by ILEA and the flat above the church. I believe the lease was for thirty years.

So, we were in what was really an empty building seemingly belonging to no-one, and it was thus that with only the money from the fête, a bit in our funds from the school, and an empty hall with no stage, lights or seating, planning started for our grand opening which we decided would be the musical *Grease*. Somehow it felt a bit like an old black and white film where someone says "I know where there's an empty barn, let's do a show." Patience came to the rescue, sending down Irene Spencer, one of her workers.

Irene asked exactly how much we would need to open up. My hopes rose, thinking ILEA would supply it all. When adding up office equipment, including what to us was a godsend, a roneo, which would enable us to print our own programmes, newsletters etc., equipment to furbish the restaurant, darkroom materials for publicity photos etc. etc. it all added up to near on £1000.

It was explained that since we were a voluntary organization ILEA would supply half i.e. £500, if we could supply the other half. Had we been an official club they would supply the whole lot. My hopes sank again. Then Patience phoned again. "Cecil, just keep quiet. You will get your equipment.

About a week later I received a phone call from John.

Patience had ordered everything to be delivered to the School which was registered as a full time club. John or the youth leader at the time had signed for it on the understanding it was for the LOST Theatre. Patience apologised to us that she could not get it delivered directly to us and we would have to fetch it from the school. ILEA's computer did not have us registered on its books. And so we confidently began rehearsals of *Grease* in preparation for our grand opening. I should say my life was now complete. I had my theatre, but this was really only the beginning. I was fully aware of the struggle to get it up and running successfully.

ILEA loaned costumes, seats and rostra to build up a stage, free of charge with delivery and collection included........ The lighting equipment given to me by

ILEA and passed on to the Brunswick club, could I possibly ask for it to be returned? On approaching the new leaders at Brunswick to ask if we may BORROW it for the show, I and *Oliver* were well remembered and so this was gladly granted, but of course only on loan.

Grease was NOT one of our best productions but by virtue of the fact that it officially opened our new theatre optimism ran high resulting in a great success. There was now definitely no desire for anyone to go back to the school. The fact that we still had so very much work to do to furbish the premises only seemed to add to the enthusiasm. As to my own feelings, I thought of the hurt at losing the scout hall in Cassidy Road and again the despair at being evicted from the Arts Centre. At last I had indeed had a guardian angel for it to end up with better premises than the other two put together. I was once more on top of the world.

Sadly, after the performance that night, Stan had insisted on giving me a lift home and then coming in for a coffee. In fact it was to gently tell me that two planes had collided on the runway in Spain with no survivors and that Mark (Raubenheimer) had been in one of them.

Running LOST

Housed in the basement of the Methodist church; a huge gymnasium that had been run as a youth centre by the church with Ian Clerk as the youth leader, although very successful as far as being a youth theatre, finance was always a problem.

The company was still run by a committee of the members themselves. I did sit in on committee meetings but as I was over 25 years old, I did not have a vote. This policy of the theatre being run by the young members themselves was still foremost in my mind. Also, as I was completely hopeless at anything to do with finance or office work I had to rely on whoever was the chairman and treasurer to keep books straight, and this of course meant relying on the expertise of under 25's.

We now had to pay rent to the church, did not get the flat upstairs, nor did I get a salary. I did get to be paid by ILEA to do two drama classes per week, so to run the entire LOST my pay was roughly £200 per month, getting about the same from Southgate Opera Company for doing the operas. This meant I had to live on plus or minus £400 per month, doing both Southgate Opera and LOST.

Committees always came in with great enthusiasm but when it was found it meant real work and not just telling others what must be done enthusiasm soon waned. On one occasion when things were not getting done, one group of non-committee members walked in and did a takeover throwing the entire reigning committee out. The takeover committee lasted for about a month and then gave up. They were no better.

However we did have one or two excellent young chairmen and treasures. It seems sad but some of these names now elude me, but I must mention one or two outstanding ones. First there was Paddy who was the very first chairman of LOST right back when we were still in the school. Although with no knowledge of committee procedure, Paddy had the remarkable ability to bind people together, mostly in the pub after rehearsals where I did not go. Granted at the school we did not have to worry about finance but the company owes a lot to him for its solid foundation.

Then there was Nick Kapica. Nick was one of those quiet people who, while everyone else was getting into long debates as to how or whether a lighting gantry needed to be built, he was busy building it. One incident, when there were kids (not members) who were continually breaking into the theatre to smash windows. Nick caught one of them and although he knew the police could do nothing phoned them and got them down to speak to the kid.

Between Nick and the copper they hatched a plan and the cop told the kid that he wanted to arrest him but since Nick was such a nice guy Nick wouldn't press charges.

"BUT," said the copper, "if ever you or your friends break another window, I am coming down to arrest you personally as I know who you are." We had no more trouble after that.

"This would make you, the police, look like villains while we would appear the nice guys."

"The kids around there already considered cops as villains so we may as well make use of it," was the reply.

Next on the list is Steve Quinn. Steve was one of those faithful steady hard workers with his heart truly lodged in the company. We always had financial problems and I think it was about this time that an agreement was made with members of hot dog stands selling their goods to the football crowds on the church forecourt. They paid well and it was much needed.

Steve in despair would sometimes call me into the office ....

"Cecil, we're broke. We can't afford to do another show."

I would answer:

"You mean we can't afford to NOT do another show."

And would return to rehearsal or painting scenery or fixing the toilets. I know this would make Steve very angry and I now apologise but between him and his co-worker, Antony, they somehow pulled us through.

In 1989 Mark McGill had joined the company. He was at the time running a very successful company of his own winning awards on the London Fringe. Mark was an exceptionally hard worker, extremely organized with a very tidy mind and was very dedicated to LOST. He was exactly what LOST needed. Also he got on very well with Steve and the rest of the gang. LOST was situated directly between Fulham Broadway Station and the Chelsea Football Ground which meant that whenever there was a match on, thousands of people passed our front door enabling us to charge stallholders to use our forecourt. I think he and Steve at one time worked together and were able to negotiate with the stall holders and get them to pay for their sites. This money certainly kept the wolf at bay.

And, of course while mentioning people who helped, I cannot forget Patience Mostyn. Patience took a great interest in LOST.

The opera company was now well on its feet with a very competent committee looking after the various duties and problems of running a company. As at LOST, I had no idea how the finances of the company worked but unlike LOST, here there never seemed problems about enough lighting, printing of programmes, costumes and, of course, money. The opera company had the advantage of a beautiful scenic workshop with enough volunteers to build elaborate sets and although naturally expected to leave hall, dressing rooms etc. clean and tidy, the general cleaning of the premises was looked after by the college staff. A very different position at LOST where we had nothing, not even seats for the audience and as for cleaners, young people especially actors do not relish sweeping floors, cleaning toilets or washing dishes. All these problems had to be solved.

Just keeping the theatre in some state of cleanliness was a major operation. As wonderful as the members (all under 25) were at doing shows, at building scenery, or anything to do with performances; cleaning was not a strong point. I would end up at two or three in the morning on my own washing coffee cups, cleaning floors and toilets, etc. The committee tried everything from asking volunteers to forming rotas but there was always someone who refused as an "ACTOR" to do his share.

So all systems broke down until at last someone came up with a plan. Until the theatre, including toilets were clean, no rehearsal could begin. There was a choice. Clean the theatre, have a rehearsal and the following day beat the s..t out of whoever left the mess, OR miss a rehearsal and go home and the following day beat the s..t. out of whoever left the mess. This still didn't quite cure the slackers until at one particular final dress rehearsal before the start I walked onto the stage and demanded that the cleaning be done before the rehearsal, dress or no dress. There were objections but I stood firm defying them to rehearse around me. From then on a sort of cleaning was done.

Equipping LOST

Each month ILEA would supply rostra to build up the stage or audience and chairs, for the audience. Front curtains for the acting area were needed. I knew that the school had just renewed their front tabs on the stage. I approached John.

> "John, please can we have the old front curtains from the stage?"
> "I'm sorry," said John "I have promised them to someone else, but we can't find them."
> "If I can find them, can we have them?" I asked.

"Yes."

"Good. They're under the lighting box."

We got the curtains.

Now we needed a rail to hang them on....and this would cost about two hundred pounds. Back to Patience.

"Patience, we need two hundred and thirteen pounds for a set of curtain tracks."

"No" said Patience with her upright stance, perfect hairdo and bright smile.

I waited.

"I can give you two hundred to fix your toilets. I don't care what you do with the money but there it is."

The words 'Curtain Rail' do not exist on the ILEA's computer but the word 'toilet' does.

We now had front curtains with a curtain track.

On another occasion we needed a park bench as a prop in a play. Off went the kids to get one. The phone rang. It was the police.

"We caught some kids taking a bench from Eelbrook Common. They say it's for a play at LOST. Is this true?"

I apologised and said 'yes'....sheepishly.

"Well all you need is to ask. You can have it, but don't make this a habit."

We got the bench which remained outside the front for many years after, so we now had front curtains, a curtain track and a park bench.

Chris Watford had now taken over from Eileen Spencer, the ILEA worker. Chris became a great friend of LOST in liaising with Patience and helping with whatever funds he could get for us. Still being paid for two classes a week, I had wanted to become a full-time leader and had spoken to Patience about this. She was very anti the idea. First of all a course would have to be taken. I agreed, but she said this was ridiculous.

"The work you do is unique. You could train them!"

She really wanted LOST to retain its individuality and not just become another Youth Club under the rules of ILEA, who would then want to dictate policies to us.

To receive my pay it was necessary to fill in a register every week of each class of a minimum of twelve students or the classes would be cancelled. A monthly pay claim form was also necessary. This was the rule book which could have been thrown at me in no uncertain terms. I never ever filled in a register or a pay claim. Bookwork is not my forte. Patience soon discovered this and as a result had given Chris strict instructions to invent a register for me and once a month to get me to sign a pay claim already filled in by him without disturbing a rehearsal. Chris told me years later that if in the end, I had signed my own pay claims they would have been returned as forgeries as he had been signing for me for so long. The cheques kept coming. (Not a vast amount I must admit but they were very much appreciated.)

ILEA loaned us rostra and chairs once a month for each production. These were delivered and collected by them free of charge. I had requested that they be donated to us as this would certainly cost less than the continual deliveries. Like the curtain rail their computer never had a slot for this so it could not be done. This was all out of Patience's department.

One Easter when the collection day turned out to be Easter Monday, a holiday, nothing was collected. After a week or two I asked Chris if he would mention this to ILEA as everything was still standing outside the theatre waiting collection.

> "For God's sake, just Shut Up. They've obviously forgotten about them and you need them more than they do."

He was quite right. It had been forgotten and each month a new lot arrived as usual but now with the extra we were able to build up a permanent raked audience. Besides, we had the initial lot given to us by ILEA. I still wonder if perhaps Patience somehow had a hand in this.

We now had front curtains, a curtain track, a number of chairs and permanent raised seating and, oh yes, a park bench.

Next...... stage lighting. We had to hire lighting for each show... not good for our budget. I remembered the brand new lighting for the Arts centre which I had given to the Brunswick Club. Time had passed and the leaders of the club had all changed and would not remember where the lighting had come from. I approached Brunswick and without telling them of the history of the lights asked if we could borrow them on a sort of permanent basis. Brunswick hardly ever used them and we offered that if they did a show we would gladly install and operate it for them. I had to wait for them to have a committee meeting before I could get an answer. I eventually received the answer that I could borrow the lighting whenever I liked but it would have to remain the Brunswick's.

Chris Watford was also the ILEA rep for Brunswick and knew the history. He went straight to them and said

"That lighting belongs to Cecil. Give it back to him."

They did. (I doubt that Chris used those exact words).

We now had front curtains, a curtain track, a number of chairs, permanent raised seating, a park bench and stage lighting complete with lighting board.

The opera company had also just acquired a brand new portable lighting board. Of course they had had the money to pay for it themselves. Something that never entered my head...the vast difference in the way that each company was run.

Things at LOST, all in all though, were now running very well, or as well as could be expected with an under 25 committee, no money and with continual upsets with the church above us who gave every indication of wanting to get rid of us. Something I could never understand as they had been so unsuccessful at running a youth club themselves, even with a full time leader paid by ILEA and supplied with a flat on the premises to live in. Now we were running it without full time pay for a leader, paying them rent and their flat upstairs was free for them to rent out. In all fairness they did help us out when on one or two occasions we could not pay the rent. In fact the Church waived several hundred pounds of rent arrears and allowed LOST to pay the rest spread over several payments. On thinking back, the vicars seemed to like us a lot, but one of the wardens really gave us hassle.

Until Mark joined us, even on my small income from the money I got from ILEA, plus the pay I received from Southgate Opera and the money I received from one or two other productions, I had been generally financing the company. Yes I did get some of my money back from door takings when available but being as disorganized as I am, who knows what? I seemed to spend my life trying to get enough money to eat let alone pay the bills.

However between Steve, Mark, Antony, Matt and a few others, the books were now being kept as straight as possible and I no longer had to hand out money all over the place. I am also eternally grateful to another friend of mine, who saved me from bankruptcy by sorting out the tax man who wanted something like twenty five thousand pounds from me. I had not filled in a tax form for years. Lynne after hours of endless paper work and meetings, eventually convinced them that I was not cheating them, I don't know how, but it ended up at just owing about two hundred pounds odd. Thank you Lynne.

The problems of running the company

The company was now running as smoothly as could be expected, ignoring all usual blips that go with any theatre company....... twelve shows a year which included the One Act Festival, the Christmas Panto-mime and a musical. The other nine shows had to be varied and of course there was always the problem of organizing a balanced programme giving equal oppor-tunities for both sexes.

The problem of doing large cast plays had to be balanced against a small cast. As one show was being rehearsed while another was in production, no member was permitted in two consecutive plays. The twelve shows were selected by me; a thankless task and of course no-one was ever happy with the entire choice.

One year, after I had drawn up the year's programme, I was nervously approached by the committee and it was suggested that the committee drew up the plan. Contrary to their expectations, I was only too pleased; for two reasons. Drawing up the programme was a difficult and thankless task and of course my whole ambition was to get the members to do things for themselves.

A three hour meeting was held with those members who were interested. First, it was thought twelve shows a year was too much and at least one had to go. After three hours... no conclusion. Another meeting was called. Another three hours passed. I was not present but had purposely left them to it. At last after six hours in total, the programme was brought to me.

One show had been dropped and two had been added making it thirteen for that year otherwise the programme was exactly as I had presented it to them in the beginning. We were all amused at this as they had not realized it. The list was posted up on the board. Steve Requena one of our more brilliant actors was one of the first to read it.

After a quick scan his remark....

  "What a lousy programme."

Still from now on, it was no longer my problem although I could have vetoed anything I violently objected to. The result was of course that a few of the future shows would definitely not have been chosen by me, but as long as they were accepted good theatre I had no objections to subject matter. Some of the modern playwrights being a bit strong, I would attend the first ten minutes or so to see the standard, and then quietly leave.

After each show a discussion group to which the public was invited, was held. The intention of this was never to blame if things had gone wrong or if the standard was not high enough but to try to prevent the same problems in the future. A right to fail was gladly accepted and another chance was always offered.

The *Opus* shows...... one off evenings at which any member was allowed to do whatever, provided it was not too long. The evenings were given a title such as *Lost For Words* or *Lost In Space*, etc. Whatever the idea, it had to fit that title. Given no help with this, it was up to members to do their own lighting, costumes, props, whatever and either write it or devise it themselves, find their own cast and present it. Although open to the public, audiences were usually friends and relations. Still it was close to my heart as once more it encouraged people to think for themselves and openly encouraged experimentation. Tim Godfrey had now donated a trophy for anyone doing something entirely of their own, again to help encourage the idea.

I got my start as a director doing one act plays for the Salters Cup Festival in South Africa. So I had started the LOST One Act Festival based on the rules of the Salters Cup which meant no play was to be longer than 45 minutes. Directors had to find their own cast and rehearsal time. Professional actors or adjudicators were invited to give criticisms after each performance and to present awards to the best production, best male performance and best female performance.

Trophies

A note here on the trophies. After thinking long and hard for an idea for a LOST Oscar I eventually came across a statue by Gilbert, (the sculptor of *Eros* in

Piccadilly), as I thought a young actor carrying the comedy mask about to play the jester, a look of tragedy on his face and one foot awkwardly placed on the back of the other leg. It was titled Comedy and Tragedy. Perfect...... and, being a sculptor, I adopted this design as the LOST Trophy. Later I found it was not an actor but a stage hand who had been stung by a bee while carrying the mask to the actor........Perfect. So anyone reading this who may have one of those which, embarrassingly by some members were referred to as the *Cecils*, now knows the true source.

Probably the dearest thing to me at LOST was the student group. When any prospective new member auditioned for a part and did not get it, an offer was made to join the student group. This meant attending a series of at least five acting classes and then taking part in a production in the main theatre at which a guaranteed part, whatever his or her standard, was offered. New members were permitted to attend the student group as many times as wished, but after a part in a main production was awarded, were no longer eligible as a student. One or two of our top actors started this way.

The *Tim Godfrey* trophy was awarded once a year to any person who dreamt up and carried out the best idea, event, function or whatever. I believe Ralph Fiennes was the first to get it for arriving at the first rehearsal of *Romeo and Juliet* knowing all his lines. One student group, en mass, got it another year for getting together and repainting the foyer while the main group was at the Edinburgh festival, and Nick of course for building the lighting gantry. Another group for presenting a complete three act play in the studio theatre which then transferred to the main theatre.

Standards at LOST

At one general meeting it was put forward that LOST was too strict on members, too demanding. This was the social life of some of them and as such they just wanted to enjoy themselves. A red rag to a bull. I replied rather firmly that we were NOT a social club. We were a drama club aiming at high standards. There were plenty of social clubs or even social-drama clubs to join if so wished, but this was not one of them. Fortunately the vast majority strongly agreed. This meeting was brought to mind much later when I heard that Hanna Eidenow, now doing very well for herself as a professional director, publicly said that "LOST had been her university."

Besides all this, regular attendances were to be made at Edinburgh Festival largely thanks to the tireless work of people like Paddy, Mark, Steve, Antony and Julian, besides one or two others.

The under sixteen's was started and run by Mike who was more than excellent with them. I remember at one time saying to Mike that I felt the standard of the work needed to be higher. After entering a nationwide competition and promptly winning it, I promptly shut up realizing Mike's incredible ability at working with teenagers, one or two of those teenagers are now doing very well on the professional stage and screen Charlie Condau for instance.

Unfortunately Mike moved to Ireland where I believe he is now very successful with kids' drama. The group was very unsuccessfully taken over by one of our own members. She gave up and Jenny Runnacre then took over. The group now ticked over comfortably, but I still put it down as one of my failures. I was never successful working with that age group and desperately tried to find another Mike as I felt that the future of LOST lay in the youngsters. Other groups like *The Chicken Shed* and Anna Scher did so well with that age, we ought to be able to do the same.

At the other end of the scale was *LOST On The Road*. The dream was a company that could take members right from the start through to professional theatre. *Lost On The Road* led on by Pat Wilde and Steve Quinn, now organised a group of the older members to do professional TIE work and school tours and also to do straight professional productions in the theatre. The idea being, that members could hire the LOST Theatre at half the price of outside lets, also doing a series of Sunday night improvisation shows in the workshop theatre. All this met with some success but did not make enough money to keep it going.

This was another disappointment for me but still left something to be worked on.

We now had

1. The main full length productions
2. The annual pantomime
3. The annual musical

4. The One Act festival
5. The Opus shows
6. The under sixteen's
7. LOST On The Road
8. The student group
9. The workshop productions.
10. Edinburgh Festival

…….. and… Oh yes….a park bench.

Criticism for not having a definite artistic policy was frequently raised. I'm afraid my mind did not take in "artistic policies." Yes, I wanted a high standard, but mostly I wanted to give young people the opportunity to experience all the openings that theatre could offer. I still believe that with all the chaos, LOST really did achieve this, especially when I heard that RADA were recommending one or two of their unsuccessful applicants to join LOST for a year to get some experience and then re-audition. However the feeling that we should just be aiming at the best of the best still remained among some members whereas with me I thrilled at the thought of being able to accommodate both, people like Ralph, super talented right from day one through to people like Moroula who had to be begged even to try to audition as a student at Southgate and only agreed if everyone left the room. Moroula ended up playing many leads at both Southgate and LOST including giving an outstanding performance of Sally Bowles in *Cabaret*. I also have a soft spot for those who tried sometimes many times, and failed. At least there was the opportunity to try.

Money..... I never did understand where it came from or how we got it. But as previously stated, Steve, Mark, Nick, Matt, and others in the office through lettings to outside companies and to LAMDA, plus the takings from the stalls on the forecourt added to the pittance of door takings and sponsored efforts by the members (such as a sponsored walk to all the West End theatres at which we were met by Joseph Fiennes, plus a parachute jump which I was too nervous to even watch) somehow pulled us through. Though we repeatedly applied to Hammersmith Council for help we were always turned down. This was surprising as the Common Stock Theatre, a not very successful group in Fulham run by two young lads who had started with me way back at the Arts Centre, received eighty thousand a year from the council. I asked them how they managed it and was told that a friend or relative of theirs was a councillor.

We found out via Chris Watford why we were turned down.

1. We were elitist. (We performed Shakespeare!).
2. We were doing very well without a grant so there was no need to give us one.
3. We did not specifically cater for gays or blacks or minority groups.

The last one hurt as the entire aim was to open opportunities to all who came through the door.

Yes, there were one or two very high standard and/or memorable productions. Among my favourites were

Five Finger Exercise with Ralph Fiennes and Paddy O'Connor. (*Romeo And Juliet* with Ralph Fiennes, except for his performance where his potential was very obvious, was very spectacular, but a poor production). Certainly *Operation Elvis* done with the under sixteen's, where a very young, Daniel Torres, now a successful pro, showed his potential; *West*, which received such high praise from the papers and public at Edinburgh Festival; *Equus* which again did so well in Edinburgh; *What's Wrong With Angry?* written by Pat Wilde at LOST which transferred to the West and is now a cult film in America renamed *Get Real*. Mention too of *Little Shop Of Horrors* and *Sell Out*, which did sell out both here and in Edinburgh. Again *Hamlet* was a pretty competent production with Jamie Ballard as Hamlet, who later went on to play Hamlet at the Bristol Tobacco Factory, and of course we were fortunate enough to have Pat Wilde directing many memorable productions. (Apologies if I have omitted your favourite).

.......and at Southgate. This is difficult as, to the present I had been the only director. I will mention one or two of my favourites. *Tales Of Hofmann*, where Ros Mc Cutchion stood motionless as a statue for a solid twenty minutes convincing the audience (with quite some success) that she was indeed a statue, before slowly turning to sing. High on my list is *Candide* to which one or two cast members objected. *Mephistopheles...* unfortunately despite the brilliant performances of John and Lee, the singer playing Mephistopheles was unable to deliver the fun or energy demanded from this part so the production never reached the heights it should have.

Probably at the top of my list would still be the first *Faust* where a young actor, Duncan, played the young Faust while the older Faust, Bill Bailey, simultaneously shadowed him. I am also greatly indebted to Terry for having the courage to forward operas such as *Der Freischutz*, *Golden Cockerel* and *Christmas Eve* .... operas which no other amateur companies ever tackle, besides the extremely successful musicals written by him with parts specifically written for members of the company. They are greatly missed.

Of course I won't go on to mention the ones we would like to forget in both companies.

Bars, restaurants and making ends meet

Neither company was permitted to run a bar and sell alcohol at interval, a great drawback for any theatre company, both socially and financially. Being in the basement of the Methodist church meant no alcohol. Questors Theatre had built their entire new wing from the takings from their bar. A bar also served as a meeting place and encouraged patrons. I was conscious of all the money spent by our own members after shows at the pubs and thought that could all be spent in our own theatre IF there was a bar.

Space was available for a restaurant but no one seemed to want to run it which meant for every show I had to go to Cash and Carry to buy tea, coffee and snacks for interval and would end up washing coffee cups at two in the morning after everyone had left UNTIL... along came Soirai.

Soirai was a young girl who joined us to do theatre but Nick soon found out she was interested in catering. Before long, Soirai had completely redecorated and converted the front into a workable restaurant, open to the public, giving a boost to the feel of the whole theatre.

Unfortunately, after a year or two Soirai left us to tour the world. The restaurant then went through one or two different hands before eventually being run profession-ally by Claudio........ but he could not sell alcohol.

The theatre was below ground and next door to a derelict building also with a basement. I tried to find out who the premises belonged to but the council would not tell me. Breaking a door through from our restaurant to their basement would enable a bar which would not be on Methodist premises but would appear to be part in the theatre. Wishful thinking. Although the church in the main seemed to be helpful when they could, we were still having disagreements. There were long periods when we were able to set build on Sundays providing we did not interrupt the services. Sadly this rule was broken by many members, and so we were banned from using the theatre at all on Sundays which was essential for set building let alone rehearsals.

Once more I became determined to get our own theatre. Martin Stevens was still supporting us so I phoned him up.

"I want to build a purpose made youth theatre in Fulham but I don't know how to go about it."

"This is the wrong time to ask Cecil, as there is no money in the country at the moment."

"Well then this is the correct time as it will take at least ten years to get going. Money should then be available and we will be top of the list because we asked ten years ago."

"Good thinking. Come and see me and we'll talk it over."

Martin booked an appointment for me to see him at the Houses of Parliament the next week. Somehow this was a dream world. How could I be meeting an MP in the Houses of Parliament? Wasn't this meant for world affairs and not for people like me?

On the day I arrived still not believing that this was happening, I felt very important just walking straight past the queues of tourists waiting. Met by a man who apologized that Martin was held up but he would entertain me until Martin arrived.

"Would I like to see round the building?"

WOW!!!! A privately conducted tour.

"Yes I would like that," I said, trying to act as though it was just a normal occurrence.

Parliament was not sitting so I was taken round every-where including all the places that tourists don't reach.

Martin arrived. I had already been shown a long corridor full of desks, each with its own telephone.

Apparently MPs didn't all have their own private offices but just used any of the desks that happened to be unoccupied at the time.

"We won't use a desk," said Martin, "We'll have tea instead."

We went into a very large lounge with beautiful leather seating and wooden panels overlooking the Thames. Tea and sandwiches were ordered.

"Martin, I'm not asking for money. I'm asking how to raise it. People do build theatres so it must be possible."
"Yes it is." said Martin.

The tea and cucumber sandwiches arrived. Of course, it had to be cucumber!

"Now the first thing we do is find where there is some large complex to be built."

The cucumber sandwiches were very thin. One had lodged itself on the roof of my mouth and would not budge.

"We then approach the owners and give them planning permission if they agree to build a theatre for you in their basement."

The sandwich was still lodged but I tried to speak trying to just look excited.

"Well, there is this empty building next to us."

I explained my idea of the break through to the basement next door where we could have a pub which would then not be on Methodist premises.

"That's what I call good lateral thinking," said Martin, "But we could possibly get you an entire theatre."

My heart skipped a beat. That bloody sandwich! Martin arranged to meet me the following week at the Hammersmith town hall to trace the developers of the property.

As I walked out I thought 'This can't be happening. It's all too easy and was that really me in the Houses of Parliament having tea with an MP?' As arranged we met the following week. We sailed through all doors marked 'PRIVATE' straight to a set of filing cabinets. Martin knew his way and everyone obviously knew him. He soon found what he was looking for; the names of the owners. A very large development was being planned. On afterthought, Martin must have known in advance and that explained the quick finding of documents.

I seem to remember that this was all on a Thursday as Martin told me he was off to Paris for the weekend, but as soon as he got back we could get on with writing to the developers to set things in motion. Over the weekend I was ecstatic trying hard to believe that there was a possibility of our own theatre or at least the bar led through from the restaurant.

Came the Monday or perhaps the Tuesday, it's hard to remember details, I heard on the news that Martin

Stevens had been visiting Paris and while there he was stung by a bee and had died.

Martin had a huge funeral. All the papers remarked how he had been such an exceptional MP in that it did not matter to him being Labour or Conservative or any other party. Like Patience Mostyn, if he believed in the work being done he would support the cause. Apparently his funeral was attended by members of all parties. I now remembered and felt guilty about my original feelings about him when he first phoned me and I was so left wing looking down my nose at big fat conservative MPs.

The third disappointment

A third major disappointment, the first being the double cross by X when we lost the grant of twenty five thousand and therefore the building in Cassidy Road. The second...the closing of the Arts Centre and now this.

At least this wasn't another double-cross. My heart was still set on the next door premises. We now had the address of the owners of the building and asked if we could use them in the interim for rehearsal space. I had no idea even how to start any of the procedures Martin had talked of. Still there would be another MP and I could approach him. The new MP was voted in. It was ....X. No way would I trust him again.

Our chairman at the time was Nick Kapica. Nick had of course invited X down to the theatre hoping he could convince Hammersmith council to support us. Nick Kapika had not been double crossed and still had hope. X was due to arrive at about 7 pm, I think to talk and see a show. We received a phone call from Kapica to say he would

"Be a bit late and for God's sake don't let Cecil anywhere near X."

Kapica eventually arrived and in his own words.....

"There was Cecil at X's throat."

Kapica tactfully managed to separate us. I retired somewhere and left them to it. X was apparently won over and promised that since Commonstock were still getting their eighty thousand a year, he would try to get us the same.

An answer arrived from the council. We were to get a one off grant of £500. That was all.

I had recently had a heart attack and was not long out of hospital having had a bypass. As I had been put off all work I was expected to go to the dole office across the road from the theatre to collect dole. I sat in the queue completely embarrassed and feeling pretty grim over recent events and who should walk in but X. There was no hello from me. I confronted him straight and said:

"Why five hundred?"
"Cecil... Come into my office."

"WHY Five hundred?"
"Come into the office."
"WHY FIVE HUNDRED?" He turned and walked away.

We never heard from or contacted X again. He had visited us once and got his publicity with his picture in the paper at LOST "Supporting and helping the local youth company." Things went on as usual. I won't say that the five hundred we received was not welcome but at this time we really did hope for more. But then I should have not expected any help from X after my last dealings with him.

Suffice it to say that we continued to struggle for money, we continued to approach the council and charities for help and got none. We had a few visits from celebrities just coming to see shows that interested them. None of them offered us any real help although they were very encouraging. Actually this is not true. One year we were booked to go to Edinburgh Festival and despite all our efforts at fund raising, after paying all accommodation fees and the fees for the booking of the venue, we were still two thousand short which if we did not find we would not be able to go and would lose everything. We were doing a sponsored 24 hour impro with two weeks to go. At about two in the morning a gentleman walked in and said:

"How is the impro going?"

We told him very well and he went in to see a bit of it.

After not too long a time he came into the office and said,

"How much do you still need to go to Edinburgh?"
"Just under two thousand."

He took out his cheque book and wrote out a cheque for two thousand, and said,

"Now you should be able to go."

When we had got our breath back and thanked him we did ask if we could tell this to the papers. He asked us to please say it was an anonymous donor.

The shows continue

Southgate was going from strength to strength and while professional singers were very happy to sing for us, a number of home grown singers were beginning to branch out. Shirley, the little girl I first heard singing in Donald's office, had blossomed out, been to the Royal Academy of Music and was now singing Helena in Britten's *Midsummer Night's Dream* at Glyndebourne. I had first heard of Glyndebourne way back in South Africa when one of our stage managers at the Lyric had previously stage managed at Glyndebourne and told me all about it. Mentioning a new young singer there who Anne said was one day bound to be famous....Joan Sutherland.

Shirley phoned me and invited me to a performance of the *Dream*. I was very excited and had to go out to buy some presentable clothes with a collar and tie for the occasion. It was a Saturday. David, Shirley's husband, and I arrived early in the afternoon. Shirley took me on a conducted tour through the workshops, backstage, dressing rooms, etc. On the names on the dressing room doors I noticed a number of people who had previously sung for me either at Southgate or for one or two other companies I had worked with. I felt very important.

What's Wrong with Angry? Pat Wilde had written the show and wanted to present it as a professional production as per *LOST On The Road* which he and Steve had been running. In order to get the critics in, any show had to run for at least three weeks. Pat was given a three week slot. The opening night was good with a large audience. The next night or two were very thin but by the end of the week it was almost full houses. The following week was completely sold out and by the third week there were queues in the street that had to be turned away with a huge waiting list.

No critics had been to see the show so it got no write-up even after we had told them about the audience response. Unfortunately our theatre was booked for the following week so we could not extend the run. A transfer to the Oval theatre was made and with no publicity it again sold out for the week. The critics STILL did not come. It then transferred to the Battersea Arts Centre with the same results. At last the Evening Standard expressed an interest but too late for Battersea.

Pat then brought it back to LOST for two nights only....a Sunday and Monday as that was the only opening we had. The Standard reviewed it. As mentioned earlier this was the show that than transferred to the West End and then became the film *Get Real.*

The fights continue

After X, the new MP was Carrington. I met him and mentioned all the plans I had had. He was very sympathetic and said he would do all he could to help but like every other politician, bar Martin Stevens, he did nothing.

A phone call from Hammersmith Council to inform us.......

...... "you will be receiving an application form for an eighty thousand pounds grant for the arts from the Arts Council of Great Britain (GLC). As the only eligible Arts organization in Fulham you are sure to get it so please don't ignore it."

It seemed an odd call. Was it possible that after all these years Hammersmith council were at last trying to help us????

A second call, this time from the Citizens advice bureau......repeating the same story ....

"...... you will be receiving an application form for an eighty thousand grant for the arts from the GLC. As the only eligible Arts organization in Fulham you are sure to get it so please don't ignore it."

This must be true.

A third call ….this time from the GLC......

"...... you will be receiving an application form.............." etc. this time adding......

"this is a special one off grant and you are the only group eligible for it."

I can't quite describe my feelings about this. I was elated that we MIGHT actually get this grant but cynicism was setting in and I somehow did not trust anything. However the forms arrived. I went to great lengths to get quotes from Strand Electric for a good lighting system. Another for a good sound system, even for carpets for the Foyer. I had to say exactly what the money would be spent on. This all took the best part of two weeks but I had been given a time limit and this was well in time.

In the meantime, full colour brochures were arriving, one at the theatre for LOST, another at the home of our chairman Gabby, and one personally for me at my home address. I wondered how our private addresses had been obtained. These brochures stated that since we would be receiving a grant from the GLC they were sure we would get together a petition to save the GLC which the government were talking about abolishing.

I submitted the application. A few days later I received a call from GLC saying that they were very sorry but they had sent me the wrong forms and would I fill in the new set they were sending me. I gladly agreed. More brochures arrived. I wished they would just give us the money they were spending on printing! I filled in the second lot.

After that had been submitted I received a letter saying that the grant had been considered but we were not central enough so it had been turned down. I phoned back in amazement to say that the LOST Theatre was straight across the road from the Fulham Town Hall and right next to Fulham Broadway station. There was no way that it could be more central. They apologized and said something like 'clerical error' but the fact was that they had now printed some special forms for us as it was a one off thing which they would put in the post. The brochures kept coming.

I can't remember the exact date but the deadline was on the Tuesday. I had been assured that since the delay was their fault, it would not matter if our application was late. The new forms arrived on the Monday. Taking no chances I filled in the forms with speed as I was now an expert at filling in forms and took them down in person to the GLC. I believe the GLC building had seven miles of passages. I must have walked all seven of them, and more, being passed back and forward from department to department.

At last! The correct department and the correct man. He was a large man. He took the files from me glanced at them quickly then looked straight back at me and said,

"I'm sorry. These are the wrong forms".

A RED RAG.......I exploded.

"You now have four sets. Between the lot of them you must have all the information you need. Now if you don't accept them either you or I or both of us are going out that window!"

We were on the fourth or fifth floor.

"All right, all right! Calm down! We'll use these."

I left the building angry, confused, bewildered, thinking of all the brochures and thinking there was no chance that we would get that grant. But somehow, underneath I still hoped. Funny how hope refuses to die. We received a further letter saying our case had been reviewed but we had been turned down. No reason was submitted.

Later I found that this same trick had been pulled on other clubs in London, obviously in the hopes of more petitions signed to prevent the closure of the GLC. At the time Ken Livingstone was head of GLC, or at least I believed he was. I have never forgiven him and could never again trust any politician or council worker.

The LOST Theatre is threatened again

Somewhere around this time one of our founders, Seamus, a talented young lad, the budding young playwright who had written one or two shows for us, suddenly died; gas escaping from the bathroom heater. This was a great blow. Gabrielle, his girlfriend, was our chairman. She now understandably stepped down.

Steve now became chairman. Mark was now rapidly coming to the fore. Yes we still had the committee looking after shows etc. but it was now Steve and Mark who struggled with the finance, still applying to the council and whoever for grants, still getting turned down, still fighting with the church (or at least one man in the church who always seemed to find something to complain about) and still dealing with the store holders.

Then came the phone call. Next door's development was going ahead. The church was about to be pulled down. Would I come to a meeting with the developers to discuss? A bit hazy in my mind now as to why I asked Mark, and not Steve to come with me to the meeting. Perhaps both of them came - I don't remember. I do know I was grateful to have Mark there as he was so organized, even the way he dressed and carried a briefcase. I always looked like a tramp and felt I did not know how to handle high powered people. We didn't even know why they wished to talk to us.

They were doing this huge development including Fulham Broadway station, the derelict buildings next to us and the church. As such they were prepared to incorporate LOST into the scheme, so if we would supply them with plans of exactly what we wanted, they would pass them on to the architects to be incorporated into the scheme. Of course it would be an empty shell and we would have to equip it. There would be no rent to pay and central heating would naturally be part of the entire structure so therefore free as well.

I seem to remember going back to Fulham in a taxi, or was it in Mark's car? When we got back to the theatre Mark said,

"Come on. Let's go in and give everyone the news"
"I can't - I would just break down in tears. You tell them." I went home. My dream. It really was going to happen. I left it to Mark and Steve on their computers to draw up the proposed plans. The plans came, incorporating the theatre, dressing rooms, a studio theatre/rehearsal room and a bar restaurant. I was worried that this would be asking too much. There was another meeting with the owners (Jonathan) which I did not attend; my own fault. I was very conscious of the fact that the shoes I was wearing were falling off my feet and the clothes I was wearing were not what I thought would pass inspection in these quarters. I never cared about clothes nor did I have the money to buy them. I did go but sort of got lost and met Mark as he came out. I was told that they had accepted everything. Life was a whirl. Friends were congratulating me all round with "You deserve it. You've worked so hard."

I had recently done a production of *Midsummer Night's Dream* with LOST. A young lad had used Hamlet as an audition piece. His talent was exceptional. He played Lysander and I immediately offered to do Hamlet. At the auditions of Hamlet a young girl, again with an exceptional talent turned up, auditioning with Juliet. She played Ophelia and I then promised to do *Romeo and Juliet*.

Rehearsals for *Hamlet* were now well under way. Ralph Fiennes had just played Hamlet at the Hackney Empire and in New York so was getting a lot of publicity. In a weak moment at a rehearsal I said maybe I should ask Ralph to give us a master class. Jamie's eyes lit up and said,

"Could you?"

I was very fond of Ralph and he had already been down to LOST as our patron but he was now becoming world famous and I felt it may be an imposition.

On the other hand maybe the publicity would help. I phoned him. (I did have his private number). As usual he was away filming somewhere. I faxed and this was forwarded to his private secretary, Alix. "Yes he would be happy to do it."

I was now in contact with Alix and asked if I should invite newspapers. She immediately said no, she would do everything as there were certain newspapers that were only interested in scandal and who would not be invited.

The day arrived. There were T.V. cameras everywhere. There seems to be something sad that there should be any trepidation about meeting an old friend merely because the friend is now a world celebrity. I should not have been worried. Ralph walked straight in and gave me a big hug and was still the same friendly person I had known in the past.

He then gave a small speech, for the benefit of the T.V. and newspapers saying how sad it was that LOST was under threat and urged Hammersmith Council to help. This was all reported in newspapers and the news on T.V. But it fell on deaf ears in the Hammersmith council.

News reporters and T.V. personal then left. Ralph asked me to get the session started. Off stage, Ralph is very friendly but rather quiet and I suddenly thought, I know he's a brilliant actor but maybe he's not a good teacher. I started the cast with a warm up. Ralph sat silently and watched then suddenly sprang into life. His energy was amazing, sometimes sitting on the floor next to the actor he was working with, urging them on, other times standing back or following them, at times taking the hand of the actor but always willing them on. He was phenomenal and it was easy to see why he was at the very pinnacle of his profession. The boy playing Hamlet was Jamie Ballard.

Plans were all going ahead. Another meeting with Jonathan.

Jonathan put a proposal to us ....

"It's going to take at least two years that you will be out of the building and while we will pay for rehearsal space for you we don't want your company to go dead without a home. We are offering you a donation of six hundred and fifty thousand pounds to buy your own place instead of housing you as planned. There is no obligation. Think it over and let us know what you want to do."

I knew exactly what I wanted. A home of our own which belonged to us even if it was just a shack would be preferable to palatial premises belonging to someone else. We brought the proposition back to LOST. Steve was adamant that with a decision like this it should be put not just to the committee but open to all company members to discuss. On my own principals that the company must be run by the under twenty fives I had to agree. This worried me. I had now worked on building the company for twenty years. Was I going to allow people who had probably only been with us for a year or two, and who would leave in another year, decide its future? It was a big meeting. At the start I voiced my opinion very strongly and then left it open to discussion.

As Hannah our chairman at the time, was not available, Steve chaired the meeting. Steve was a very good chairman strongly encouraging view points from both sides. I kept thinking what would I do if it went against me. After a long discussion a vote was to be taken. Was it to be the money and our own home or a ready built theatre?

Steve put it to the vote. All those for the money? Every hand went up without hesitation. Afterwards Steve admitted that he knew that would be the outcome but we had to discuss it. As I said he was a very good and very wise chairman. I do miss him.

Time was drawing near to the final production. We decided to do a revue incorporating as many things from past performances as possible. It was to be called *Last Call*. Steve and Mark would do this together. I had on tape a lot of the past shows which had been videoed by Viola. I passed these on to Mark as reference to the past. The cast included as many people as possible.

It was sad, but a success.

Sadder still was clearing the hall. Getting rid of the chairs, the rostra, the front tabs, the tabs rail, the lighting .... remembering how we sweated to get them all. Anyone want a park bench?

After a very successful ten year stint and a very sad goodbye to the Methodist club, even though we had a bright future before us, the long and arduous search for premises began all over again, never realising that it would be a full seven years before we would move into a beautiful purpose theatre.

Southgate is threatened

The opera company had by now become, if not the foremost, at least among the top amateur companies in London. News reached us that the new principal of the college had decided to close down the opera section of the college. Apparently teaching English to foreign students earned more money. Much pleading and many letters to the headmaster but to no avail. Southgate Opera was now considered widely as, if not the best, certainly one of the foremost amateur opera companies in London and, therefore, maybe in the world, but instead of being used as a bastion of achievement for the college it was to be thrown out.

Of course there was no talk of closing down. New premises had to be found. I stopped to think. If I had lived in north London instead of south, would I have fought as hard to gain a home for the opera as much as

I had for LOST? But in the north of London, there was a strong adult committee, if not as dedicated, at least as keen, and before long future productions were destined to be presented at the Wyllyotts Theatre in Potters Bar.

The advantages of this were tremendous. It was a real theatre with raked seating, real dressing rooms, and a huge foyer with a bar licence. Of course the disadvantages were equally as great. No longer did we have a huge workshop to build scenery and it was so far from the centre of London.

The first opera to be presented there was *La Traviata*, a direct transfer from the college where it was to be the last. Despite the confusion caused to some members of the audience over the opening tableau, it proved a resounding success, boding well for future productions in the venue. Over the past few years at Wyllyotts the company has continued to present operas and musicals of a very high standard under the very competent baton of Neil Cloake.

It is now fifty years since Terry founded the company and a number of years since his retirement. Over these years the company has grown from a few borrowed singers, a scratchy orchestra and no scenery, costumes or props of its own. Singers have come and gone, some starting as children in the chorus and now singing big leads in this and other companies. Others moving on to the professional world even singing leads at Glyndebourne. Some passing through the company and retiring to become ardent supporters, and sadly, we have lost a number of strong members and friends who have now passed on.

Fondly remembered are events of the cabaret group, weekends at Theobalds Park, singing carols in the streets of Fulham to the accompaniment of a piano pushed on a trolley, the small variety performances mostly written by Terry and given in the octagon, an hilarious performance of *Lucia Di Lammemoor* in the Fulham Arts Centre, *Captain Noah And His Floating Zoo* in the Fulham Town Hall. All this besides the rapturously received performances of Terry's musicals such as *Italian Straw Hat* and others, and of course, above all, the not so much performed operas such as *Andre Chenier, Christmas Carol, Golden Cockerel* and *Mephistopheles* all rarely performed by other amateur companies and all this besides the standard war horses such as *Elixir Of Love, La Bohème, Carmen,* etc. Thank you Terry and Neil.

Searching for another venue for LOST

While in Fulham the latest search for a home had once more begun.

After seeing the first five to ten unsuitable premises, a beautiful building came up in Wandsworth Bridge Road called Bridge Studios, which was by coincidence very close to my home. It was huge, with space for a large theatre, a studio theatre (already there), dressing rooms, offices, rehearsal rooms and still space to hire out. Mark and Steve both approved. We got our architect friend in to look it over. He was satisfied that everything was possible. It was in the region of six hundred thousand. Within our budget but we would have to go to lottery for help. Lottery had always turned us down because we did not have our own premises.

Jonathan agreed. Again congrats all round. We were all very excited and an architect friend from Questors had inspected the building and drawn up plans for a conversion. Wow!!!! Our very own theatre - twenty years struggling but dreams do come true. It was all so easy. Only a few weeks after closing Fulham Road we were set to start the next one.

And then the council stepped in. No, we could not have the money. It had to be given to the council who would house us. This was under the same scheme that Martin was going to use for us but now it was being used against us. All our pleading did not help.

The council then put us in contact with a large school in Fulham where arrangements were made for us to move in and use their hall for performances. We had a meeting with the school. More out of politeness, we explained that we had come out of a school and were long past that stage. The council then met us and said that we could use the small concert hall in the town hall.

> "It is intended to build new toilets and refurbish the foyer of the town hall. The money you would have got from Jonathan would be used for that and would constitute your dowry, so you would not have to pay rent."

This would be impossible for us. We could only do one performance per week because of other things on in the main hall. Week end rehearsals would be out. All scenery would have to be brought up through the foyer. There would be continual fights with caretakers and unions. We turned it down.

We were now left with nothing. The council had let the newspapers know that they had offered us premises, and the town hall, and we had turned them down. I decided to meet the mayor/leader of the council head on and phoned for an interview. One week passed and I heard nothing. I phoned again; another week. I phoned again.

"Do I really have to go to the papers before I can get an answer?" An appointment was made for the next day.

I took Mark and Hanna, who was now our chairperson, with me. We put our case forward and asked again if we could have the money promised to us as we had found a very suitable building in Fulham. The mayor insisted that it was the developers who were withholding the money and that the council had nothing to do with it.

I thought of:

"The money promised to you would be your dowry" ????
"Are you really saying that you would rather have new toilets in the town hall than a tried and proved youth theatre?"

He asked where the building was. I replied that there was no way that I would tell him as I believed that the council would buy the building, put us in for a month or two and then throw us out. He still insisted that the council were not withholding the money from us. A deadlock was reached. At last ....

"If we do allow you this money you will have to tell us where the building is."

We parted. I was glad that I had had Mark and Hanna with me. We heard no more from the council.

Jonathan then contacted us to say that they were sorry that they had not been able to give us the full six hundred and fifty as this, and a great deal more, had already been given to the council to get their planning permission. They would as a matter of goodwill give us three hundred and fifty thousand instead.

We heard later that at a council meeting one councillor (I have forgotten her name) had said

"They're only a small company. They don't need that much money."

She had never ever put foot in the theatre to see what we were doing.

It was now that we had to get together a group of trustees and re-register with the charities commission. This was all work about which I knew nothing. Hanna's cousin (I think) was a solicitor and offered to help. I think too it was about now that Jamie started to come onto the scene -at first by stage managing for me at

Southgate Opera and then at Colchester. Marian, Jamie's mother and I had been friends from before Jamie was born so I had watched him grow up.

Another frantic search for premises. Steve had now made plans to emigrate to Australia. This was a big blow to me as although we had often disagreed Steve was always there to support me and of course he was a brilliant director of Shakespeare among other things. Everything now seemed to be left to Mark and me.

While we were considering this, another building came up. This one, also in Wandsworth was ideal with a hall on the first floor with a very high ceiling plus a smaller hall, and separate rooms downstairs - enough space for everything we needed plus restaurant, studio workshop, scenic workshop, dressing rooms etc., and even with space to spare.

It was absolutely ideal and, although the next door pub held a 28 year lease on the premises, it was for sale. Wandsworth Council seemed very keen to have us and not only keen but also indicated that if we took the place they would give us £50,000 towards refurbishing the building.

One problem.... The asking price was £600,000 and we only had £300,000. I really cursed Hammersmith Council. They appeared to have blocked everything I had attempted. The property had been found by a past member now in estate who claimed that he had a buyer who would be prepared to finance us. This seemed too good to be true and of course it was.

I was so keen on the premises that I decided to sell my house to make up the balance of the money. There was enough space in the building to incorporate a small flat for me to live in and I was quite excited at the thought of being able to live on the premises. The trustees flatly turned this down saying they would not let me risk my home.

The pub then offered us a 28 year lease. This we could afford and once again I was riding high. The owners agreed and asked us to make an offer in writing. The offer was submitted and once more I was telling all my friends about this marvellous new theatre we were about to get. I am still convinced that there was dirty work at the crossroads. Someone bought the building that week. How many more times could this happen?"

Again the search for suitable premises began. It is impossible to remember how many buildings I looked at. Mostly on my own but when anything remotely possible came up I asked Mark to come with me. Now whenever I travel around London, I keep remembering premises that were too big or too expensive or too small or just not suitable.

Desperation and despair

Time passed and despair began to settle in as nothing was forthcoming. The company had disbanded and members had obviously moved to other groups. I began to get very worried and was desperate to do something to pull LOST together again.

I decided that theatre or no theatre the only thing to do would be a production. At the auditions a young girl, Sarah, had done an excellent Juliet so I decided on Romeo and Juliet. I now had no-one to help, I mean no stage manager, designer or for that matter only one Juliet for a cast. An advert in Stage with a rehearsal room booked in a youth club, and I started. Slowly I got a few people together with a few phone calls. I had no suitable Romeo and could not forget my last Romeo, Ralph Fiennes.

As I had no theatre in which to perform I decided to try to present it to the schools. Sarah's mother turned out to be a school teacher and turned out to be a super, excellent promoter at selling to the schools. I had also met Nina while I was in St Petersburg and was still in contact with her. Nina had suggested that we try to present it in St Petersburg. Nina got us booked into the National Youth Theatre in St Petersburg which meant we would have to pay our air flights but we would be accommodated in a large hotel in St Petersburg. Although I did not wish to touch the money we had in the bank I knew it was there so I need take no financial risk on my part. We managed to present it to quite a number of schools which raised enough money to get it to both Russia and later, to Spain. This meant that we did not have to draw on funds in hand leaving our 300.000 intact

I now had the bulk of a cast together - mostly new members - and a number of schools had already booked us. Rehearsals were extremely difficult as we kept on having to change rehearsal space and sometimes ended in rehearsing with half a cast in the open. Still I pushed on and when our Friar Lawrence fell out Steve offered to play the part. At least this meant I now had three strong players in the Juliet, Friar Lawrence and Mercucio, a newcomer. Not that the rest were weak. At last we had to give our first performance at one of the schools. The production was vastly under-rehearsed so we announced it as a 'work in progress' performance. In the meantime I was busy getting together passports from everyone and on four occasions had to stand in the street in a very long cue outside the Russian Embassy to get visas. I had also had to stand in a cue to organize passports for one or two members of the cast. Apparently ex-members were all betting that we would never get to Russia, except Steve who claimed,

"Cecil has ramshackle luck and somehow things always happen."

The school tours had done very well and we had made enough money to pay all air fares. I had now taken on Jamie who had by now stage managed a big production of *Yeoman Of The Guard* at Essex University for me. Although Jamie was young he was a very organized and hard worker and was invaluable on the tour. It wasn't a good production and regretfully got really bad crits from the adjudication although the audience did seem to like it. I really did regret not having the time or organization to rehearse it properly, however we had got to Russia and it had given the company a kick start again.

We got back to London and with a few frantic changes of cast and virtually no rehearsal - I am grateful to

Julian, particularly, for taking on Capulet at such short notice. We decided to go to Spain and again with help from Jamie who grew up in Spain and spoke the language, we likewise got to play at the University in Granada, this time to a standing ovation.

It was next due to be performed in a fringe theatre in London where I had hoped to get in a rehearsal or two. Unfortunately I had not gone with them to Spain and now was in hospital (yet again) with heart problems so I never saw it there either.

I now cut short the following six years of again searching for premises and fighting the council.

Once again finding wonderful premises and at the last moment losing them. Hopes yet again raised and dashed....... but keep trying and something has to happen.

We still had about £300 000 odd pounds in the bank. I had insisted that this money not be touched and be held until we found suitable premises. Mark pointed out to me that as it was registered as charity money it could not be left standing idly. His idea was that we spend the money virtually being lavish on productions and try to get such a high standard and enough publicity to encourage some charity to finance us. (Grant) I reluctantly agreed. Mark had worked out that the money should last about ten years and if we hadn't made it by then, the chances were that we never would. I therefore agreed to Mark spending as much as he felt was necessary, hiring theatres and presenting shows.

I also agreed to facilitate matters by dropping my signature from the bank in signing cheques and change the signatures to that of Mark, and I think, Julian.

So for the next four to five years Mark, Jamie and Julian got casts together, hired theatres and presented plays, calling on me whenever needed to paint scenery or to transport props or even usher for shows. I received a card from them saying "Thanks for always being there when we needed you."

I went on searching for premises until at last...

Seven years after closing at Fulham a supremely beautiful theatre, fully refurbished and rent free for ten years, was made available to us - a converted lecture hall in the now Lambeth ex-university. After many more ups and downs the conversion is complete all papers are signed and sealed, there is enough money in the bank to keep us going for the ten years. Nothing can go wrong.

If life is a roller coaster I was now on the highest possible point. I was now 79 years old and naturally looking forward to taking it a little easier in the new theatre. There was enough money to keep us going for ten years, I was happy for Mark to take over the running of the theatre. I hoped to still work with whatever beginners came in and to be on the management committee. Although I never expected it, I have to admit a feeling of pride when two or three people had suggested that it should be named *The Cecil Hayter Theatre*.

A meeting between Mark, Jamie, Julian and myself was arranged in my house to start organization of the inauguration and opening production. Rather than being happily excited on their entrance the three of them seemed a bit subdued. I wondered why.

And then I was told. Without my knowing it, the inauguration meeting and the opening performances had already been arranged and directors for the opening production already contracted. Astounded that I had not been included in any of this, I asked why......

A short embarrassed silence while the three of them looked at each other.

I was informed that I was now too old to have anything to do with the running of the theatre and not good enough to be considered as a director.

Fulham Road...with bench

The Van

Playboy of the Western World

The Bartered Bride

Der Freischutz

Elixir...no right angles

Romeo and Juliet with Ralph Fiennes
and Fiona Egan

Sold Out...sold out at the Edinburgh Festival

LOST...at work

The Under 16's...are you here?

PART 2

Terry Hawes

Southgate Opera (Formerly Southgate Technical College Opera Group)

The Beginning

'The boss wants an opera group' I was told shortly after taking up the music post at the new Southgate Technical College (later Southgate College) in 1963. The 'boss' in question and the principal, a music lover and choral singer (a tenor!) and the bearer of the news was the head of drama, new like all of us, and of whom, more anon.

I replied that having had experience of such groups I doubted whether we'd get enough members considering that there were several such societies in the area, and especially as what was envisaged was a grand opera group of which there was already a successful one based in Enfield two miles away. In particular we'd have difficulty attracting enough male singers, knowing the difficulty of getting men to take part in anything of this sort.

However Mr M. had his eyes on elevating his lectureship to principle lectureship before retiring so in the prospectus for the next year an opera group was duly offered, and with hindsight grateful I am that it was, though full of foreboding at the time.

We intended to do a double bill of two short operas, Purcell's *Dido And Aeneas* (three acts but only about 80 minutes,) and Mascagni's one act *Cavelleria Rusticana* both powerful pieces of music theatre but in great contrast, one from the Baroque (late 17th c.) and one from the red-blooded 19th c. Italian verisimo.

The First Production.

Somehow we got a company together, short of male chorus (a theme to be referred to often), but with the performance date set at March to fit in with other uses of the college theatre we, with insufficient time to prepare such an ambitious double bill, had opted for a concert version of *Dido* and full stage performance of the *Mascagni*.

The *Dido* cast inevitably felt like the poor relations in this arrangement but to be honest they weren't very good. We'd had to scrape the barrel to find both casts from the enrolled class. I remember the first and second witches (In *Dido And Aeneas*). Every baroque opera had to have witches). Dear middle aged ladies, pleased as Punch to get even such small parts. One was short and plump, the other thin. When they sang their short duet 'Our plot has took the Queen's forsook' they reminded me of Laurel and Hardy.

I remember at the performance 'Laurel' turned up in a dress apparently made entirely of beads. Weird, yes. Appropriate…well…

The *Mascagni* had a somewhat more experienced cast but the Santuzza (leading soprano) walked out about a week before the date pleading vocal exhaustion. I still see her shopping in Sainsbury's occasionally, a sweet white haired lady who only recognises me after some prompting.

Fortunately a local singing teacher found us an advanced pupil who knew the part and did it for a small fee, and a few men from a light opera company I was directing came in and helped out with the male chorus, and yes! The music-loving principal himself took part in the chorus as a Sicilian peasant.

Cavelleria Rusticana takes place in a fishing village on Easter day, and calls for singers both off-stage (the congregation in the local church) and the 'overflow' of townspeople outside (on-stage). The principal conducted the off-stage chorus (who of course could not see me) using close-circuit television in order to follow my beat. Being first and foremost an engineer he was pleased as punch that his new technical college was using technology for an artistic purpose, and claimed that it was the first to do so.

'The Boss'

I should say a few words about Mr E at this juncture.

He was a rather tubby little man a bit like Harry Secombe, yes, a tenor also, with a degree in engineering which was his main reason for being principal of this college, originally set up primarily to service engineering students in the area who would then go on to the Enfield College of Arts and Technology though many other subjects were also offered. He was very informal and pleasant and took part in the choir, and several of the early opera productions. At school he had taken part in *Iolanthe*, as he himself said 'a fourteen stone Billy Bunter of a fairy.' Only on reading his obituary some years ago did I realise what an amazingly gifted and energetic man he was, and how much he had given to society over and above his official work. He certainly put music, drama and art firmly in a college where they were never intended to be, and, I know, aided by a few staunch allies on the committee, fought the good fight to keep them there

Men!

The great problem of every opera and musical comedy group outside the universities. Getting enough of them. Getting any! Especially tenors!

After *Cav* and *Dido* we started *Carmen* (surely, we thought, an attractive choice) with about twenty women and one man who disappeared quickly when he found he was the only one. A young couple who joined also disappointingly found a reason to leave quickly. In desperation we approached the singing teacher aforementioned who ran the nearby grand opera company. She declined the idea of a merger, but agreed to take on productions of ours, in which situation she was able to bring some of her then flourishing company to strengthen ours.

This of course, cut out Mr M whose job it was really to produce the opera but he made an excuse about 'too busy with other things' (which the principal swallowed quite willingly) and under Mrs B we produced quite creditably I think *Carmen, The Bartered Bride*, and *The Merry Wives of Windsor* although after the initial enthusiasm the number of men dropped again to almost nothing.

How did we manage in operas which to be credible needed male bodies on the stage whether they could sing or not..?

Well, one recourse was to use a few willing full-time students of the college.

A number of engineering apprentices were interested. 'Non-singing extras' one of the press critics called them. (But some could sing quite well).

I remember on one occasion in *The Merry Wives* Falstaff was being carried out in the linen basket by two engineering apprentices, one of whom suddenly looked at the audience and said quite loudly, "Christ, there's my mother!"

Pearl

Mrs B was another amazing personality. A one-time professional mezzo she had long been crippled by polio. Nevertheless she had a myriad of private pupils, some of whom became professionals. She taught in a number of schools (warning to potential trouble-makers. I walk on my arms!) produced opera with adults and with children (Gilbert and Sullivan). A tower of strength... and when she decided to leave after *Merry Wives* I was in despair, faced with the return of Mr M. who apart from other disadvantages did not, like Mrs B, have a pool of singing pupils to call on.

Enter Cecil Hayter. Shall I say 'and the rest is history'?

Cecil and I have often laughed looking back over the circumstances of his employment. He knew Mrs B had suggested him, an unknown producer from South Africa and could not believe his luck that he was appointed after a brief informal meeting with me in which we looked at the college theatre (really a large assembly hall with a stage and dressing rooms), and briefly discussed the opera society.

Mr M.

Cecil thought Mrs B must have done a wonderful job of promoting him for him to be appointed in such an informal manner.

"Cecil," I said, "I would have had a three-legged cow to block Mr M. We can get rid of Cecil Hayter without notice, we can't get rid of Mr M."

I was able to say to Mr M "Sorry Arthur, but we have already committed ourselves to this Hayter chap."

Mr M was senior to me then, so I thought at the time that I was lucky to get away with it, but to be fair,

I think he realised that I didn't want to work with him on this project, and was perhaps relieved rather than annoyed at being replaced.

Mr M's name sometimes crops up among those of us who were in the college when he was senior lecturer and we realise rather guiltily that it usually gets negative or at best jocular associations. Of course the man had good points, and did workman like productions of a number of straight plays. But he did make a lot of people unhappy and worried (perhaps unintentionally) at a time when they were trying to develop their careers in the college. 'A legend in his own lunch-time' as one colleague facetiously put it.

The man is long gone now, and one sometimes feels that one should have made more of an effort to accommodate what was basically his insecurity, but he didn't make it easy.

I'll just add that he had a long-suffering charming little wife who was an amateur actress and writer of poetry and plays. She did much to smooth his passage.

The Cecil Era Begins

For some reason Cecil and I decided for our first joint production on the relatively unknown Verdi opera *Louisa Miller* adapted from Schiller's *Leibe Und Kabal*. A story of true love tragically thwarted by class and rank prejudice. Although it's grouped with his 'early 'operas it is in fact his fourteenth, (no tyro's work then) and comes just before his blockbustering successes of

1853-4, *La Traviata*, *Il Trovatore* and *Rigoletto* and shares many outstanding features with those works.

At the group's first meeting with the new producer we were all amazed, aghast even by his knowledge of the opera and of Verdi. Only some time later did Cecil, confess that he was scared stiff of us and had mugged the whole subject up in the library.

For this production Cecil designed the best set the college had yet seen, and the story of this is told elsewhere by Cecil himself. It was a success in spite of only a shaky handful of men for the chorus (plenty of ladies).

Following this we did *La Bohème*, *The Elixir Of Love* and *Tales Of Hoffman*. One of the local paper's reviews expressed amazement that we could muster a complete double cast for this last opera with more than a dozen characters plus chorus. Some parts were doubled and singers were 'brought in' but the group was attracting talent by its achievements. Nevertheless the same local critic commented on too many 'non-singing extras' i.e. full time students drafted in to give us more male bodies. Same old male problem. They were supposed to have learned the music but often hadn't.

Cecil decided to set *La Bohème* in the 60's in swinging London (only the previous decade) partly to save money on period costumes, partly because the story fits the hippy framework very well.

Problem; the end of Act 2 demands a military procession watched by the on-stage characters and chorus. Military

uniforms we ain't got (and can't afford); an army of credible soldiers we (definitely) ain't got. What have we got?
Scruffy full-time students. Plenty of those, not exactly
scruffy perhaps, but certainly dressed casually enough.

The military procession became a protest march with
placards and banners (I rewrote the lyrics) which started
at the back of the auditorium and invaded the stage.

It worked very well. So well that apparently on the first
night some members of the audience hurriedly left,
thinking it was the real thing.

Or perhaps this is one of those endearing legends that
aren't true. Older member of the Opera Group go on
telling it. (You have to be pretty old to remember it.)

Cecil's method of working was refreshingly different
from that of most, in fact, any other producer we
encountered.

He allowed, in fact, encouraged the performers to think
for themselves and to find the motivation and emotion
in their own personalities. Of course he gave some
general directions about where to enter and the use of
the acting space but there was, for instance, no drilling
of the chorus (unless explicitly required by the script)
and everyone was supposed to bring their motivation.
Some members used to the traditional methods found
this hard at first but gradually it reaped rewards.

Cecil used to say jokingly, "I sit back and let you do all
the work then people say what a great producer I am."

A member of the company put it this way:

"He has the ability to release the creative energy in people and to guide it to make highly original performance."

Perhaps it's best summed up by an incident in the rehearsal, of *A Masked Ball.*

Baritone (Playing Riccardo.) "Shall I stand up here? Shall I raise my arm?"

Cecil: (With weary patience) "John, if you're thinking like the king anything you do will be right. If you're not thinking like the king, nothing I can say will help you."

A Landmark

After making quite a success of *The Elixir Of Love,* our fourth opera together, (but with still hardly any male chorus) we decided on Weber's *Der Freischutz* not well known in England, though popular in Germany. It requires some spooky effects which were right up Cecil's street, and it ends happily with a stage full of people, chorus and principals, a very important feature for a company trying to build itself up. (Only the villain is dead).

Another advantage, though containing only two leading female parts (plus short solos for four bridesmaids), it has six male leads, two tenors, three baritones and a bass and all these, save the bass, can be onstage during the choruses. Not only that but from the start the company had doubled the principal parts playing alternate nights and everyone sang chorus on their off nights.

Even without a male chorus as such we had ten male singers onstage for all the chorus numbers, plus few extra men. (A sad fact of life; it's easier to get men along for even a small part than to join to do chorus only. The male ego!).

Southgate has enjoyed many triumphs, crossed many rubicons, but I always regard the moment when it really took off as that first company rehearsal of *Der Frieschutz* when I walked into the octagon and found about twenty women, and sixteen men! We had finally made it, I felt. For once the men were not heavily outnumbered by the women, there were enough to cope with the daunting all-male choruses, and in front of me was what looked like a flourishing opera society.

The title *Der Freischutz* is rather hard to explain in English. It means literally 'The Free Shoot', one who shoots with bullets that are 'free' in the sense of being free of natural laws. To get seven of these you have to sell your soul to the devil in The Wolfs' Glen at midnight. Six will unerringly hit whatever target you wish, the seventh is in the power of the devil. Not a good bargain, one would have thought.

Everyone loved *Der Freischutz*, a supernatural drama with just a touch of comedy and the feeling of being in a flourishing society which was going places that perhaps few other societies were.

The Society Grows

We followed with a revival of *The Bartered Bride* (first performed by us under Mrs B in 1967) with real water and real frogs in the village stream thanks to Cecil's ingenuity, and real birds in the rafters thanks to a hole in the roof. Phil and Barry whom Cecil has mentioned were very active young men and with some other youngsters who came into the company, made the circus scene a riot.

After the comparatively familiar *Bride* I wanted to do Rimsky Korsakov's *The Golden Cockerell* and Cecil gladly agreed. This opera had been banned by the tsarist government in 1906 because it appeared to make fun of authority in the character of the doddering king who falls for a voluptuous queen of magic.

In this production our much loved tenore robusto David agreed to forgo his usual romantic roles (there isn't one in this opera anyway) and perform the part of The Astrologer which lies cruelly high for the tenor voice. A very noble performance well outside his usual comfort zone. Thanks David. I don't know of any other amateur company that has attempted *The Golden Cockerel* or our other Rimsky production *Christmas Eve*.

Male Recruitment

From here the company seemed to go from strength to strength, though not without a lot of work behind the scenes by myself and the members to attract and keep good talent (Especially men!).

Where did we get them?

Well, as I like to say, we found some of them 'under stones.'

There was Bernard who came to enrol for football training, got in the wrong queue, and after a bit of chat found himself in the opera group (a tenor!) and another John who was a plumber, (baritone), and Stuart who worked at a garden centre, didn't read music and to whom I had to teach every note of the several major parts he did for us. These and others stayed with us for some years playing principal parts and chorus, even helping with things like sets and costumes.

By the seventies the company had settled into a yearly routine of an operetta or musical in the autumn. (I wrote, or co-wrote a number of them), a grand or 'proper' opera in the spring, and two informal concerts at which members who didn't get parts could 'have a go.'

The Company Develops

Which brings me to auditions. The least favourite part of the proceedings for most directors. We all hate disappointing people, specially ladies for whom there are fewer parts than for men and more competition. But there is no getting round the fact that there are only a certain number of parts and not everyone can have one. And, let's face it, some people just aren't good enough anyway however hard they try, over and over again...At least in Cecil's productions everyone is encouraged to be an individual and you don't have to get lost in the chorus.

By this part of my story the company is well-established with many members, including major principals, who are prepared to muck in in all sorts of ways, and who remain for a gratifying length of time. (Fifteen years and more in some cases).

This commitment included a 'cabaret group,' who raised considerable sums of money with series of entertainments. At a variety of places. About a dozen of our star performers played in this, directed with energy and originality by Phil and with musical direction by the ever reliable Maurice.

One of the long-serving secretaries who came to the group from the college choir once told me: "I used to enjoy the choir because it was something to look forward to each week. But the opera group is different. It just takes over your whole life."

We were lucky indeed that so many people were prepared to give a chunk of their lives to the society.

With our combination of both light shows and grand opera we were at that time almost unique. Even now I know of very few societies to equal this.

Fond Memories

I had directed the rarely heard *Moses In Egypt* (Rossini) for Mrs B's company and I suggested it to Cecil. It has the reputation of being more like an oratorio than an opera because of the amount of choral singing, and the antagonism of Assyrians and Israelites is expressed largely in choruses. It contains some striking music though, and is a 'great sing' for everybody. Having heard the CD and followed the score Cecil said to me "Terry, I turn over page after page and it's all 'Praise ye the Lord, Praise ye the Lord.'" Nevertheless we did it and it produced one of Cecil's best inspirations.

Waiving The Rules

People said to him "How are you going to do the crossing of the Red Sea on a small stage with no special equipment?" and Cecil would laugh and say "I don't know, I'll tell you when I've done it."

This is how.

In the final act the Israelites were all wearing blue cloaks that they did not have previously. Cast out into the desert in chains by order of Pharoah, their 'chains' were in fact rope painted with metallic paint and held together with Velcro.. When the great chorus begging deliverance finished, first Moses then the others raised their hands, pulled, and the 'chains' magically snapped.

"Cast yourselves into the Red Sea," sings Moses.

The chorus formed into three lines and they all turned away from the audience and held the cloak of the next person, so that the audience saw a sea of waving blue. The music depicted the heaving waters and the chorus parted so that there was a pathway through the waters lit by a golden spot. There was also a wavy effect in the lighting and I think, some dry ice.

With the chorus being the waves only a token group of Israelites walked along the path to safety, Moses, his wife, son and daughter.

Sounds simple, childish perhaps, but it worked wonderfully and was talked about long after (a case of 'In Palmer's Green they speak of little else!') Pharoah's army (another token group, two in fact,) were engulfed by the 'waves' which then dispersed.

Well done, Cecil, but I claim, credit for the final stroke (unappreciated I may say.)

In the oldest score of Moses, I've seen the opera ends at this point but most producers finding this too tame end with a "Praise Ye the Lord' chorus from some other Rossini work. This makes a good climax, but, I thought, why not do what Rossini originally wrote (or didn't write). So our production ended with the music gradually quietening down finally leaving an empty stage with just gently undulating waves (in the lighting) and a few quiet major chords. A peaceful, mysterious, rather than exultant ending. Wonderful. And perhaps unexpected in Rossini.

Tenors Again!

We had another problem with *Moses*. At the period when it was written (1818) coloratura writing was not confined to female voices as was the case later, and the leading tenor, Amenophe, has florid passages like the sopranos.

I was more than a little worried when our long-standing resident tenor David declined to audition. No doubt he was right; the vocal writing did not suit his warm romantic style. But where to find another. Anyone, willing to undertake this florid part? After some work with another tenor who also proved unsuitable, ("look Tony, we've made a mistake, this part is not you") I was relieved when a recent full time student of the college came on the scene who was interested in doing it. Tom was the son of the harpist Ossian Ellis for whom Britten wrote many of the harp parts in his operas and he had the necessary agility, not to mention (and singing teachers will know what I mean) a 'dry' top D flat which he showed off in one of the cadenzas.

So *Moses* went ahead, a wonderful sing for the chorus, enjoyed by everyone.

Thrills and Spills in Carmen

I feel rather over-exposed to *Carmen*, having directed it in 1966 and 1985 and been second horn in the orchestra at the Cambridge College of Arts and Technology when I had only been learning (self-taught!) for a few months.

Although it is outside the scope of this book I cannot resist the following anecdote of that production (in a make-shift rigged up acting space, not a proper stage with all sorts of loose ends, as we shall see).

At the end of the opera Don Jose sings something to the effect; "I have killed my beloved Carmen. Take me away and hang me!"

A final crashing chord of F sharp minor from the orchestra.

Blackout. Great, but no-one seemed to know that the stage lights and the orchestra lights were on the same circuit, (there had obviously been no lighting rehearsal) so the orchestra was plunged into darkness for their last note which became a discordant raspberry eliciting not a few laughs from the audience (and the orchestra).

To top it all, at that moment a scenery weight fell with a crash between the first horn and myself. Had it hit either of us it would have gone through our heads like eggshells.

Health and safety, what's that? (This was 1955).

Or there was the time Cecil told me about in another *Carmen* he did elsewhere when Don Jose forgot to bring on the knife with which he stabs Carmen. No way of retrieving this situation so he decided to strangle her instead. Imagine the real expression of horror on the prima donna's face at this unexpected change to the production!

I was very lucky during my thirty years in charge of music at Southgate College (as it was later called) in having a number of stage pieces that I had written and co-written produced by the opera group and by full time students, excellent productions with set and costumes, orchestra and first rate performers, some of whom went on to become professionals.

And because I was able largely to choose the shows myself I got to conduct some that I never thought I'd ever see, let alone direct.

These include *The Golden Cockerel* and *Christmas Eve* (Rimsky Korsakov), *Andrea Chenier* (Giordano), *Moses* (Rossini), *La Gioconda* (without the dancing hippos but with the 'Hello mother, hello father ballet), and *Little Me*.(Student musical).

Andrea Chenier (1980) was (in the words of one of the orchestra) 'a pig,' difficult to play, and although rather in the style of the later Verdi, the music does not flow as easily as his. Nevertheless a very powerful rewarding piece, worth sitting through if only for the last act which is virtually a long love duet for the two lovers in the condemned cell. Rapturous resignation, meet death together and the world well lost. Wonderful music. Giordano found true greatness here. Sadly he never found it quite so powerfully again in some fourteen other operas.

A Benign Dictatorship

The choice of operas. Once it got really going the group had a committee under a chairman who guided the company jointly, representing the members' wishes as far as possible. They met periodically and worked hard thrashing out problems, including the choice of future shows. I was not entirely joking when I said that in choice of shows at least what we had was a 'benign dictatorship.' 'We have a full and frank discussion, then I tell them what we're going to do'

Of course I always listened to suggestions but frankly I was the person best able to judge whether a piece was suitable for the company, for the cast likely to be available, whether too difficult for the orchestra, whether we could sell it publicity-wise.

There was also a 'Friends of Southgate Opera' run very well by a succession of devoted husband-and-wife teams.

When I retired in 1993 my colleague at the college, Neil Cloake, took over as musical director (we had been sharing the conducting of the double casts for some years). He expressed gratification at being able to step into the directorship of a flourishing company without any interview or audition. And he did indeed benefit from hard work, not to mention chicanery, deception and downright lying that I had to use in the earlier years of the College to establish the music courses and keep them going. If I ever seemed not to appreciate your work Neil, it was because you don't come from where I come from in this. At the back of my mind there was always the feeling that we were bloody lucky to be doing this kind of work (and paid for it) in a college where it was never intended it should take place, and where, the principal apart, many of the governors were at best indifferent to it.

ODD BINS

Lucia

Act 2 of Donizetti's *Lucia Di Lammermoor* which the group performed in 1972 requires two offstage horns to play some brief but vital fanfares to herald the arrival of the wedding party dreaded by Lucia, and she has to sing some emotional music over them with no other accompaniment. We had two horns in our specially reduced orchestra but certainly none to spare to play offstage. In more recent times we would have recorded the two horns and then superimposed the tracks to give four horns (they play different notes in harmony).

But in those days we (I) had neither the knowledge nor the equipment to do this. So, I recorded the relevant bit myself on the piano, rightly thinking that played on an indifferent tape recorder, and muffled by being offstage, no one in the audience would know or care whether they were hearing horns, kazookis or Congolese nose-flutes. And I was right. At least no-one commented that the bridal party must have been trundling a piano round the Highlands!

There's no such thing as bad publicity

Lucia also occasioned a glimpse of Cecil's tireless and sometimes indiscriminate enthusiasm. We took the opera to the adapted laundry in Fulham for one or two performances, minus of course, the set, the costumes, the orchestra and the lighting, and with just piano accompaniment. Not surprisingly there was not what you would call a rush for tickets so, on a wall over the road Cecil painted in white letters about two feet high: LUCIA DI LAMMERMOOR.

I don't know what the good people of that part of Fulham made of it. They probably thought it was done by aliens.

Otello

This reminds me of the time when we performed Verdi's Otello (the first time, when Neil and I shared the conducting, one cast each). A letter appeared in the local press from someone who said he had lived near the college for years and not been aware opera was done there. "When I saw the name *Otello* on the poster I thought it must be some pop group, but no, it was the real thing with orchestra, sets and some jolly good singers. I'll come again."

Home-grown shows

I have mentioned operettas and musicals that I have written for the company and others, including the Student Musical Theatre (a separate body comprising full time students, some studying music-drama, but most not.) These shows number about twenty and all have been performed, some quite widely, in the UK and on the continent by students, amateur and professionals.

An Italian Straw Hat 1975-6 based on the famous French farce was so successful that we revived it with virtually the same cast next year, thus challenging Bernard Levin's dictum: 'Never revive musicals.'

To The Woods (1978 and 88) was based on "*A Midsummer Night's Dream,* written previously for the student group, LOST took it to the Edinburgh fringe in 2005 and Theatre Set-up (professional) took it all over UK and parts of Europe.

The Secret Of Santa Vittoria 1979 was based on the novel and film and was sponsored by Cinzano (a few thick heads after the first night party), and *His Excellency* (1982) was a Gilbert and Sullivan opera that never was. I set a libretto to music that Sullivan had refused (it's a long story, told on the CD leaflet). With music that many thought had real Sullivan flavour, the CD sold in Canada, USA and Australia as well as the UK, but not as many as I'd have liked.

There were nine shows in all that I wrote or co-wrote for Southgate including two pantomimes.

EPILOGUE

Cecil and I worked together on and off for fifteen years at Southgate and some other venues including LOST.

We have done occasional shows together since. Our good relationship is probably helped by the fact that we live at opposite ends of London and see each other rarely outside rehearsals!

I don't know how the conductors at English National and Covent Garden get on with the producers allotted to them, some of whom seem to go out of their way to present travesties of what the composers intended in the name of 'relevance,' 'originality,' 'progress,' and to appeal to that mysterious entity 'the taste of the young.'

If Cecil and I did not see eye to eye about some feature we would discuss it and work things out amicably and creatively, and, I think we only had three what you might call rows in all the time we worked together. I don't even remember what they were about now. Unfortunately each of them was in front of the entire cast of that particular show, but each lasted seconds rather than minutes and each of them ended with Cecil putting an arm round me and saying "Terry, you were right and I was wrong."

At least, that's how I remember them!

Well done Cecil. You certainly 'fought the good fight' if anybody did.

It's a crime that you never received the wider recognition you deserved or the youth theatre you worked so hard and so long for. You were up against indifference, ignorance, local politics, and finally unexpected treachery from within.

But it must be some consolation that over the years you brought happiness and fulfilment to so many lives, not least that of your friend...

Terry

PART 3

Neil Cloake

The opera group along with a symphony orchestra and a choral society had begun in an era where adult evening classes were supported by generous subsidies from local authorities.

Furthermore, all three societies along with numerous other musical and dramatic initiatives were founded and heavily subsidized by the enlightened policy of the first principal of Southgate Technical College (later Southgate College) and the board of governors.

When Terry Hawes retired from his position of Director of Music, it was by no means certain that I would be appointed in his place. However, following a successful interview, I was appointed as Director of Music and Performing Arts. I took over as musical director of the opera group at the same time.

To begin with, the college (now led by Michael Blagdon following the retirement of Bill Easton) continued the music policy as before.

This was, however, a time when funding to colleges was constantly under review by central government and it became apparent that the college would find it increasingly difficult to subsidise the opera group in the way it had done.

A large hike in evening class fees, paid though not without protest by the membership, still went nowhere near to covering the costs and the continuance of the group as a part of Southgate College relied increasingly on the good will of the governors and senior management.

As the years went on, this good will became increasingly diluted partly due to various reorganizations of the college structure and I was frequently called upon to justify the opera group's existence.

There was a view that the group had no place in the type of college which Southgate had now become. It was seen as a kind of social club with little educational value.

I prepared a defence of the group in which I was able to show that the opera group was a class like any other in so far as it had a structured learning programme with learning outcomes and which over the years had offered progression into the profession.

The opera group was saved for the time being, but it became increasingly apparent that what little remained of goodwill was running out. This was a time when every college course was expected to pay for itself and of course the crucial difference between the opera group and other college courses was that it received no government funding at all. A small subsidy from the local authority was removed during this time.

The breaking point finally arrived after an unsuccessful college inspection by OFSTED led the college management to spend a considerable amount of its financial reserves. This left it in no position to continue subsidising the opera group. The evening class fee was to be increased enormously and it became clear that independence from the college was the only option.

The group benefited hugely at this point from the expertise of long term members, principally Lee and Colin Davis in managing the rebirth of Southgate Opera as an independent, self-funding society.

During the time since I took over responsibility for the music in Southgate Opera's productions, I have had the enormous pleasure and privilege of preparing and conducting some of the finest musical scores including:

Macbeth, Iolanthe, Yeoman Of The Guard, Fiddler On The Roof, Samson And Delilah, Cav And Pag, Turandot, Carmen, Merry Widow, Mephistopheles, Candide, La Traviata, Die Fledermaus, Faust, Otello, Carmen, A Masked Ball, HMS Pinafore, Pirates Of Penzance, The Geisha, The Elixir Of Love, Manon Lescaut, The Bartered Bride, La Bohème and more.

The choice of opera is made with very much the happiness of the members in mind and the first consideration is always to choose an opera with a substantial role for the chorus. On the one occasion when an opera

(La Bohème) was chosen with limited opportunities for the chorus, we rehearsed a gala concert at the same time to be performed a couple of weeks after the run of *Bohème*.

It remains an important principal of the group to provide opportunities for members to perform and to progress – in that, the group retains its educational commitment even after its split from Southgate College. For many years, the season ended with a specially devised summer concert which as well as providing opportunities for members to perform who might not otherwise be cast in main productions, provided a means of raising additional revenue to the opera group's bank account.

Since becoming independent of the College, the new pattern of performances during the season has meant that the summer concert is no longer possible, but its role in supporting members has been filled in two ways: an annual concert for the Friends Of Southgate Opera and a members' soiree which provides an opportunity for anyone who would like to stand up and perform.

For the most part, the operas have taken shape over the rehearsal period in a calm and steady fashion leading to artistically successful runs of between 3 and 6 perfor-mances. A curiosity of amateur rehearsals compared to professional ones is that whereas a professional opera chorus is paid to learn and rehearse their parts, an amateur chorus is expected to attend a limited number of music calls at the start of a new production and must then go off and learn their parts on their own and what's more they have to pay a subscription to the society. Various means have been devised to help members to learn their music including recordings of the musical director (myself) singing the individual chorus lines. The term "singing" is to be interpreted very generously in this context and I always suspect these recordings are more popular for the unintended hilarity they must provide for the listener, although people are kind enough to tell me they find them useful.

Another difference between amateur and professional rehearsal periods is that although the number of hours involved might be similar, a professional piece will be rehearsed and performed intensively within a relatively short time frame, whereas an amateur rehearsal schedule will stretch over several months with gaps of between 5 and 6 days between each rehearsal. It is perhaps not surprising therefore that rehearsals often get off to a slow start with the performance date seemingly far in the future, only to dramatically intensify in the final fortnight. Southgate Opera has always set aside a complete weekend shortly before performance week for taking stock and increasing the momentum as the first night approaches. This is a time to wake up to reality and appreciate what still needs to be done. This is the occasion too for a first complete run of the production which always concentrates minds wonderfully.

Occasionally, productions have stood out for good or less good reasons. In the very first opera for which I was solely responsible, we had had problems with one of the lead tenors who always seemed to have an excuse for missing rehearsals and never seemed to know his music when he was there. It became apparent that he could not be relied upon to fulfil his obligations to the society and the rest of the cast and we had to ask him to stand down. Fortunately, in those days, we double cast and as luck would have it the other tenor was available to take his place, though it did mean he had to sing two dress rehearsals and five performances on successive nights.

Principal parts are not always taken by members of the society as the audition process allows for open auditions. We had no idea when we cast Paul Potts as Des Grieux in *Manon Lescaut* that in a short time he would achieve international celebrity as the winner of the X factor.

Often our principals have been successful singers who have left the profession to go into other spheres of work but who retain their love of singing and performing. Increasingly in recent years, we have had the pleasure of having, as principals, young singers from the colleges and conservatoires who are happy to sing with us for the opportunities we can give them to perform roles which perhaps they will not do professionally until later in life. It is pleasing to note the names of singers with the well-known professional opera companies who have at one time or another appeared with Southgate Opera.

Many of the productions since I took over from Terry as musical director have been directed as before by Cecil Hayter. His ingenuity and ability to inspire performers to reach unexpected heights of expression is one of Southgate Opera's great strengths.

When we did a first sing-through of *Candide,* we were shocked to find the show we had chosen lasted only some 1½ hours. We seriously considered quickly finding another show to fill the evening. Perhaps unsurprisingly, by the time Cecil had finished with it, the work had expanded to more normal operatic lengths.

Cecil's sets are always masterpieces in themselves, but it was the set of another producer, Clive Bebee, which caused us musicians a big headache in *Fiddler On The Roof.* By no fault of the director, the stage crew had misread his measurements for an extension to the college stage which projected into the auditorium completely surrounding the orchestra. It was extremely fortunate that we had scaled down the orchestration for this particular production in order to suit the director's conception of the piece and there was just room to fit us all in. One more player or instrument would have been too much and vital notes would have been missing.

It is always necessary to reduce the size of the orchestra partly because of costs (as the members of the orchestra are paid a modest sum) and because of considerations of space in a small theatre.

These days, there are many reduced orchestrations of the standard repertoire which can be hired. In respect of lesser known pieces such as *Mephistopheles* and *Samson And Delilah,* however, there is no alternative but to roll up one's sleeves and set to work reallocating notes to different instruments so as to ensure that as much of the original score is heard as you can possibly manage.

In recent years, this process has been greatly improved by the advances in music score writing packages such as Sibelius so that it is possible to hear the results of one's tinkering in advance of the first orchestra rehearsal. The transcription can still take several months however to achieve. The notes can be entered fairly quickly, but it is the performance directions which take the time. *Cavalleria Rusticana* is absolutely the worst in this respect since every single note seems to have its own performance direction – often duplicated (i.e. a staccato dot and the word staccato, two accent signs on the same note and so on).

At least, I no longer have to take opera scores on holiday and drive my wife to distraction sitting round the pool making pencilled alterations instead of enjoying the sun.

The orchestra plays a large, though often unrecognised, role in the success of a production. Seldom do orchestral members receive a compliment on their playing, comments being reserved for those rare occasions when something goes wrong. They must achieve a satisfactory level of performance on one rehearsal of between 3 and 6 hours. This is followed by one dress rehearsal and then it is the opening night. Southgate Opera has indeed been fortunate in recent years in the support is has received from a loyal and talented group of players who return to provide the orchestra for each production.

A recent development has been the formation of an opera company for young singers under the auspices of Southgate Opera. There are a great many young singers who have appeared as children both nationally and internationally on the stages of the world's great opera houses in such roles as Miles, Flora, the three boys in *The Magic Flute,* the children in *Werther, Der Rosenkavalier, A Village, Romeo And Juliet, Carmen* and so on. As they move into their teens, these opportunities naturally dry up especially for boys whose voices have changed and Southgate Youth Opera was founded to provide opportunities for these young singers to continue performing. So far, there have been two highly successful productions, *The Magic Flute* directed by Lee Davis and *A Midsummer Night's Dream* directed by Cecil. At the time of writing, rehearsals are about to begin for *The Cunning Little Vixen.*

A glance at the programme for these productions shows a few names which would be familiar to Southgate members and audiences from years past. The children of Southgate Opera performers are now continuing the tradition set by their parents.

I continue to be grateful to Southgate Opera for the gifts it has given me and I should add not the least of these being my wife of 25 years, Jennifer Lilleystone.

PART 4

Contributions From Past Members

Much thought has gone into the order and positioning of where and how to present the writings of those of you who have been good enough to record your memories and thoughts of the past.

In the end I have decided to present them in the true spirit of both companies to give equal rank to all, so they now appear in strict alphabetical order.

ADRIAN BROWN

LOST Theatre – The Early Years

My first acquaintance with LOST began in 1978 when I was directing Gounod's opera *Faust* for the Holland Park Opera. Although the ruined façade of the Jacobean mansion would be an ideal setting for most of the action – which I had placed in the Roundheads and Cavaliers period of the seventeenth century – I needed a small and transportable area to represent Dr Faust's study, in which the ancient scholar receives the devil Mephistopheles who, at the price of his soul, transforms him into a young cavalier. I did not know who to ask to provide this setting, and then someone told me about an eccentric South African, who was running a theatre group for young people in and around the Fulham area, and who was allegedly a 'genius designer.' I approached Cecil Hayter - for this was he - who designed an excellent portable study set for me, and all was well. Through this encounter I discovered that Cecil's youth group were shortly to present *Romeo And Juliet* at the Brompton Oratory School, and this I was determined not to miss.

Cecil was always ambitious, yet to allow his teenagers to present a play by Shakespeare, when most of them had never trodden a board before was risking a high degree of incompetence. This he got, one very small part, played by a very small actress being completely incomprehensible, while one of the numerous O'Sullivan brothers (Tim, I think) got a great round of applause for falling off a chair. His brother Charlie however was rather good, as I recall, possibly as Tybalt. (?) But the great surprise was the young man who played Romeo. He spoke the verse beautifully, lived the hero's predicament, and bore himself valiantly despite the long hair covering a good propor-tion of his face. One had a feeling that this young man would go farther – his name was Ralph Fiennes, who subsequently performed at LOST the soulful German tutor in *Five Finger Exercise* and then a gloriously funny caricature Police Commissioner, "Tiger" Brown, in Brecht's *The Threepenny Opera*.

For the next Shakespeare tackled by the LOST company, *Othello* which Cecil invited me to direct, I was determined to raise the standard of verse speaking, so we held auditions, to which surprisingly and disappointingly few of the founder members came, so that the cast had to be pieced together from other sources. Charlie O'Sullivan played two roles, I recall – Desdemona's father Brabantio and also her uncle Leonato. This must have been confusing for the poor girl, unless of course they were twins. I myself played the Duke, not very well, while various odds and sods of all ages were pulled in to be the solemn Senators. I recall a strikingly-handsome black girl who came to the auditions, was cast as one of Othello's household and then disappeared. We saw no more of her until the opening night, when she turned up expecting to take her place on stage – she seemed to think that was how these things were done. Fortunately we had a spare and rather revealing costume, so we put her in that, told her to take off her very modern boots and to come on in all the crowd scenes to "Do what the others do." So she did and looked fine, adding variety to the ensemble. We had an excellent Desdemona while Teresa who had been a little wooden in the role, suddenly – after Cecil had taken her off somewhere for some private magic of his own – matured into a very moving Emilia.

It was fairly obvious that no-one in the company would have the maturity to play the title role, so Cecil had already recruited Jeremy Trafford, an English teacher from the Oratory School, who was excellent in the part once we had forced him to stop singing the lines and to play them as convincing dialogue. Paddy O'Connor was having a brave stab at Iago, although inclined to find him a good chap really and, underneath a rough veneer, fond of his little wife Emilia – surely not quite the author's intention. Then, out of nowhere, a young man named James blew in from the street who was somehow instinctively aware of all the complexities of Iago's character, his ruthlessness, his envy of the 'old-Etonian' type Cassio who had supplanted him as the general's second-in-command, his skill at devious plotting – everything. Well Paddy was already well into the role so we decided he and James should alternate the characters, playing the dupe Roderigo on the alternate nights; a scheme that worked very well and allowed each of them to play two characters.

Not long after this Cecil's company had the good fortune to be offered a space of its own at the Methodist Church on Fulham Broadway, where for twenty years or so they fulfilled Cecil's ambition to perform a different fully-mounted play every month, as well as special evenings devoted to sketches and satire. The original members mostly grew up and fell away, but their places were taken by a host of other aspiring actors, some very gifted and others, sadly, less so. Among the shows I particularly remember was one featuring, maybe even written by, the Beatles, in which various improbable and imaginatively portrayed adventures somehow involved a quartet of young persons, three boys and a girl. I was never sure why those in charge had not seen that the "girl" should have been played by a boy too, presumably representing Ringo Starr, with cross-dressing adding to the surreal absurdity of the whole affair. Although as the girl in question was one of the best actresses who ever graced those Methodist boards, the production generated its own fantasia, with Gerry O'Sullivan squeezing his way through a non-existent tunnel among other contrivances. I am not sure why she did not go into the acting profession, as I am sure that by now she would be a familiar television name playing character roles. Very soon a number of skilled younger directors were working on productions – and I think of Patrick Wilde and Stephen Quinn – who mounted very worthily several plays by Shakespeare, *Henry IV, Part One*, *The Taming Of The Shrew*, while Patrick gave us Tim Rice's wistful *Blondel*, and Stephen a remarkable *Noises Off*, in which the set, representing both front and back stage of a theatre, was built in the middle of the auditorium, with the audience moving to seats in front or behind according to whether the action took place on stage or in the wings. Highly original and successful.

Other delights I remember are Cecil's production of *Charlie's Aunt*, with the formidable Stephen Requena in the title role, his *Dark Of The Moon* with Paddy O'Connor as a magical Witchboy, and regular revivals of *Equus*, in which a succession of beautiful young men and women revealed their all for their art. Other productions were, as I recall, less successful; there was *The Cherry Orchard* which required us to think the desultory self-absorbed monologues going on in each character's head did in fact make up a rational conver-sation, and this made a nonsense of the whole affair. Then there was a piece by Moliere, *Le Misanthrope* I believe, when the cast seemed to be aiming at the style of seventeenth-century aristocrats although, as they'd never met any, they seldom hit the target. Tricky, Moliere. Genet's *The Maids* was tackled, to show how completely uninhibited we were, with Michael Bridgeland playing one of the two murderous 'domestiques.' Plays by Joe Orton, Goethe, Marlowe, a welter of Berkoff, and others of lesser note, including myself, were all tackled, some delightfully, some disastrously, and then we heard that LOST was presuming to tackle that apparently simple, but actually highly complex work about marital aridity *Who's Afraid Of Virginia Woolf?*, to be directed by Paddy O'Connor. "Well this is certain to be a disaster," I thought, a pre-empting judgement to prove – if proof were needed – that I am not infallible; because it was a triumph, one of the most intense evenings ever experienced at LOST. Paul Rogan, a tall thin actor whom I had not much admired in other things, was excellent as the desiccated husband, while Nolan was simply superb as the bitter disillusioned wife in the lethal party-games in which they involve their two lovey-dovey guests, played by the ubiquitous Charlie O'Sullivan with Sarah Ennis. I once told Sarah, with only slight exaggeration, that when theatregoers talked of "The Divine Sarah," some meaning Sarah Siddons and others Sarah Bernhardt, I always thought of Sarah Ennis, since she was always good, always accurate, always reliable; although I had to qualify this encomium a little when she appeared as the heroine Vivien in my own farcical comedy *Guerrilla Tactics*, when she had to discover an unexpected and suspicious flight bag somewhere and quickly replace it with another. Sarah could not find the first bag one night because David Hall as the mad police inspector had placed it slightly differently from usual, and I saw her desperately march towards the on-stage fridge where she knew a similar bag was concealed.

If, however, the fridge bag was moved at that point, I knew, the whole plot of the play would crumble, and we would have got into a complete tangle and been unable to continue. So despairingly but irrevocably I had to shout from the audience: "It's under the sofa, dear," a phrase which has gone down in LOST history.

After a time Cecil organised also an annual drama contest in which four different short plays would be performed every night for several nights, with a judgement being delivered upon them all at the end of the week and prizes awarded. Our first experience of this novelty involved an adjudicator supplied by N.O.D.A. (National Operatic and Drama Association), who was so dreadful, giving the award to *Look Back In Anger* simply because the entire cast, taking their cue from the title, had all performed the play in an absolute fury - never has so much anger been unleashed upon any stage - that I felt I must take judging the contest in hand myself. And so thereafter for several years I did. I am told that LOST members would flock in from miles around on adjudication night to listen to my judgemental remarks "Because I was so rude to everyone." To be rude and discouraging however was not my intention, as I was rather attempting to persuade tyro actors and directors to look below the surface of the text to discover what would have prompted the playwright to write it. I remember one playlet by Strindberg, set in an artistic colony in Jutland or somewhere, in which a rather cross painter is impatiently waiting for his wife/model to return from shopping, dabbing at his canvas the while. In comes the lady, laden with shopping, and then the pair of them stand glaring eye-ball to eye-ball for the next twenty minutes with no further movement or indication we were in an artist/s beach-hut studio. Did the lady not think of putting the shopping away, for instance? Did no-one think that as she was a painter's model she might do a little modelling and he a little painting? Some excitement might even have been added to their recital of their marital warfare had the model perhaps removed some, or even all, of her clothing. No, nothing. For another play, highly favoured to win, Joan of Arc is brought back to her prison cell just after she has been condemned by the High Court, and there in the cell awaiting her she finds a comedy-relief gaoler who implausibly obliges her to trundle through yet again the arguments which had not won her any remission in the judgement hall above. In reality Joan, a vigorous peasant girl, would have told this impertinent meddler to "Piss off!!" She was tired and needed a nap. Several times I was afraid of reprisals when I left the hall after giving a particularly searching judgement of something by an author who was highly regarded – especially by himself. I remember one short play where the floor was completely covered in crumpled newspapers – something to do with the ephemerality of current events, I think - as well as several "important" pieces of 'new' writing, which almost always seemed to consist of a mattress lying on the floor of a tatty bed-sit, while characters shout the 'f' word and the 'c' word at each other. I expect I told them that this kind of tedious stuff was not new writing at all, but old writing, because all groups of young theatricals in turn devise such a play and think it 'new' only because they themselves have never come across plays with rude words in them before and they're convinced they'll shock us oldies out of our senses with the audacity of it all. They seem to be unaware that last year's piece of shocking 'new writing' has by now disappeared without trace, so they fondly imagine they are discovering a new continent untrodden by the buskins of their seniors.

A number of the actors and actresses discovered at the LOST Theatre in Fulham have made their way into the professional theatre, and good luck to them, while others will have settled back into their quotidian lives, all the better for the confidence-raising and friendship-building experience, and blessing Cecil and all who sailed with him in his shaky but indomitable craft.

ALLAN GIRDLESTONE

- Jan 1969: *Luisa Miller*

I played Count Walter. I don't remember anything about it. Also that year I did *Yeoman*, *H.M.S. Pinafore* and *Old Tyme Music Hall*.

- *La Bohème*

We had a problem when the bed for Mimi collapsed. Also in act one, if you were not quick, and unmusical entree's, you sang nothing.

- 1973: *Der Freischultz*

We had a very good stuffed bird, quite large. I was SR urging the hero to fire a magic bullet at a bird high up SL. He fired and the stage hands, I think Derek Bashham had arranged this, threw the bird from SR right under our feet. The audience loved it!

I also had to make a witches brew on stage from ingredients that appeared from nowhere. Someone beside me was making dry ice fog everywhere and Dave Luck was in a back room with a tape recorder making extra noises and echoes. When I was doing it for him the tape spilled out all over the floor. Back on stage David Walters was doing his stuff and had a different light on him. I think you said at the time that you had never tried these two effects together. I presume it worked.

- 1975: *Golden Cockerel*

You had a piece of canvas representing a tent lowered down onto the stage and all the female chorus came out of it. I was down stage of it and still could not see how it worked!

- May 1976: *Lucia Di Lammermoor*

I will never forget the performance of Jean Aird. We were just standing upstage watching her madness scene.

It was from 1977 that we started doing 3 shows per year, plus Musical theatre Cabarets; up to 20 per year. So I had to stop my ELODS shows and my Madrigal Group shows. However it was worth it.

- May 1977: *Queen Of Spades*

I had to sing and dance on a coffee table. From the audience it looked quite big, but it was tapered and was very small.

- December 1977: *Comedy Of Errors*

David Luck and I were cast as the twins Antipholus. His face is nothing like mine but we had special wigs and looked so alike that when I see the photographs I have to look at the costumes, the green and red sections were alternated, to see who is who in the photos.

- May 1978: *Tales Of Hoffman*

Wonderful sets; I don't know how you thought them up.

- Nov 1978: *To The Woods*

Wonderful show no incidents on my behalf.

- May 1979: *Turandot*

You pointed out to me that a blind man never looks directly to the person he is addressing. We never do that anyway, on stage.

- Nov 1979: *The Secret Of Santa Vittoria*

Again a wonderful show. There was a problem with water running over the stage. But a lovely after show party with all that drink supplied free.

- May 1980: *Andrea Chenier*
- November 1980: *Princess Ida*
- May 1988: *Masked Ball*

Very good sets.

- May 1982: *Moses In Egypt*

I remember standing on stage with a dark cloth hooked to my costume.

We were in about 4 rows across the stage. We were to represent the Red Sea. We turned round, took hold of the cape in front of us, and then swayed, alternately in our rows. We said to each other: They, "the audience" will never accept this.

The Red Sea parted for the Israelites then swallowed up the Egyptians. The audience believed it!

- November 1982: *His Excellency*

I had invented a balletic drill for the soldiers. Then after a song and dance, a short ballet. You told us not to ham it up, and it worked. We all looked at each other to see who was the most out of breath. I was ok but had done my own song and dance immediately before. So I was very happy.

- May 1983: *Gianna Schicchi and Pagliacci*

Again Jean Aird singing this time 'Oh my beloved father'

- May 1984: *Otello*
- May 86: *Nabucco*

I remember the look of shock on your face when at the first rehearsal I killed the first victim using a retractable knife painted red on one side!

- May 1988: *Faust*
- November 1988: *To The Woods*

In the round

- November 1990: *Christmas Eve*
- May 1991: *Masked Ball*
- November 1991: *Italian Straw Hat*

Not so good for me as the first time.

- November 1992: *La Vie Parisienne*
- May 1993: *La Traviata*
- November 1993: *The Gondoliers*
- May 1995: *Carmen*, Neil Cloake
- January 1996: *Christmas Carol*
- May 1996: *Mefistofele*
- May 1997: *Cav And Pag*
- December 1997: *Candide*

Quite the best show. The only problem for me was that you wanted, at dress rehearsal, me to do a mime. Looking for a man to wear this dress to do a show.

One problem was that I had never done mime before. The other was that I had to get offstage, change and get on again in 5 seconds. Sometimes my "helper" was not there.

- May 98: *Samson And Delilah*

When Samson destroyed the temple some of the blocks bounced nearly to the orchestra.

- July 1998: *The Best Of British*
- May 1999: *Elixir Of Love*
- May 2001: *Macbeth*

I had a lot to do with the set because Derek Basham left.

- 2005: *La Traviata*

I left before act 3, when Violetta dies. Shirley Pilgrim was very cross about it. She didn't know that so shortly after my wife Daphne died I could not witness a death, I still can't.

June 2007: *Cav And Pag*

As usual you wanted to have the Easter Chorus in the church. So we went into the church, basses first, turned to come out and found a large space in the scenery.

So for the first time we did it as Mascagni had written it. In the square and then exited into the church.

AL MORROW

I wanted to write something about LOST and what a fabulous and special time of my life it was. I lived up the road in Fulham with a flat mate Harriet who was at London University. I had lasted 4 hours at University and really hadn't got a clue what to do with my life. Harriet and I turned up one day and I think we did a number of workshops before you cast *The Visit* and I played Clare. It was just the most fun I'd ever had. I did a really dodgy German accent and wore an old red wig of my Mums but it really was the beginning of everything for me. Other productions I was in were *Aladdin* (the baddie – I had to sing a Solo, I was so tone deaf Steve Lee made the rest of the cast join in) and *Hedda Gabler* – the old Aunt and *Noises Off*. I remember Emma Campbell's Dad who was and is a wonderful scenic artist lending us paint for Hedda which we wasted by painting too thickly over Flats and Floor and of course I remember the grief I felt at Get Outs when another production came to an end, it was like a bereavement. I literally use to skip down the road to the Theatre, It felt like home to me and I loved everyone who was there – it was the days of Emma Campbell, Clare Lubert, Dennis Kelly and Matt Kelly, I spent hours in the café sitting over a baked potato even when I didn't need to be in rehearsal, just to be near what felt like the centre of the universe.

After LOST I did become a (very bad) actor and Emma Campbell and I went on to set up Indelible Theatre where we did plays at venues like *Pentameters* and *The New End*. It was that which then got me into producing. For the last ten years I have been producing Theatrical Feature Documentaries, I work for Met Film Production at Ealing Studios and have now made over ten features which have done well – they play in Cinemas before showing on the BBC or C4 or Sky Atlantic. It really did all start at LOST when I learnt that cleaning the toilet was as important a job as waltzing around the stage feeling important – I cherish those memories and LOST really did give me the confidence to take those first steps into working life.

I still see Emma Campbell and Clare Lubert and whenever we start talking about LOST we end up just laughing at all those fabulous memories. Writing this really brings it all back, the dressing room and the dodgy heater, the steep rake of the auditorium, and the really talented directors that taught us so much and treated us like real professionals which was magic – you, Steve and Robin especially. Thank you for everything!

Love Alison Morrow

ANDREW SPRAGGS

I first heard of Southgate College Opera from my Mother's friend, Margaret Rush. They met in Whipps Cross Hospital while Margaret was awaiting the arrival of her youngest daughter, Katherine. I think I was about eight years old at the time and Margaret became, where music was concerned, probably the most influential person during my young life. Over the next few years, I would come to meet some of Margaret's friends from Southgate College Opera. I remember when I was 15, talking to David Luck while trying my very first glass of Mulled Wine at Margaret's 40th Birthday Party. I recall David being a very funny man, and the Mulled Wine, (sorry Auntie Margaret)... disgusting. It was around that time I decided that when I was old enough, I would like to go to Southgate Technical College so that I could join the opera company.

I began studying for my A Level's at Southgate Technical College in September 1985 and joined the opera company soon after that. The first production I was involved with was *Orpheus In The Underworld* by Jacques Offenbach. I regret that I do not remember who directed that production. However, I do remember having a wonderful time throughout the rehearsal period and during the run of the show. Being only small and of an athletic build, I was often thrown about like a rugby ball between Barry and Neville Golding, which was immense fun. Although, best of all, were some of the women who were clad in sexy lingerie and the simulated orgies. Please forgive my shallowness on this matter, but remember, I was only a 17 year old boy at the time, so for me... it was a dream come true! And of course, it was great to see Auntie Margaret more often.

During the course of the production I had my first experience of the traditional rehearsal weekend at Theobalds Park Hotel. To be truthful, I really do not remember much of my first time there. This is probably due to the fact that on my first night at Theobalds Park, I got so drunk on Gin and Lime that I spent the following two days throwing up and having the shakes. Gin and Lime... I have never touched the stuff since. The fondest memory of *Orpheus In The Underworld* for me though, has to be, getting to perform on the stage of the Gladys Child Theatre for the very first time. Finally I was no longer just a part of the audience.

The next big production was Verdi's *Nabucco* in May 1986. The company did a revue show between *Orpheus In The Underworld* and *Nabucco*, but sadly I cannot recall any of it. (No, I was not drunk on Gin and Lime or any other beverage). *Nabucco* was directed by Cecil Hayter, who was already a legend at Southgate College Opera by then. I had heard about how marvellous and wonderful he was, and today he is one of my dearest friends. However, our first meeting was anything but friendly. Let's just say it was …. A little bit frosty. I met Cecil for the first time while the company were rehearsing for *Nabucco* at a church hall in Winchmore Hill. For some reason, maybe because of my slight build, or maybe because of poor eyesight on Cecil's behalf; (Only joking Cecil) he was under the impression that I was a 12 year old child belonging to a member of the cast. Which, he addressed me as such. I cannot remember exactly how our first encounter played out, but it went something along the following lines:

The cast were about to rehearse a scene in which I had no involvement and before starting, Cecil turned to me and said "Try to be good little boy," or something very similar to that. As an eighteen year old East Ender, this affront was not going to be taken lying down. My true response is probably unprintable, but I remember thinking "Who does this scruffy tramp, in a 250 year old jumper, think he is, talking to me, like that!"

I could be a very stroppy teenager when I wanted to be back then. However, with his innate charm, patience and loving kindness; it wasn't too long before he won me over. Back then, and still to this day, apart from my Mother and Auntie Margaret, I had and have now, more respect and gratitude towards him, than any other human on the planet.

Soon after my first encounter with Cecil, the company were again at a weekend rehearsal at Theobalds Park. (No drinking to excess this time) Cecil had decided to cast me as a Hebrew slave boy, and wanted to take some photographs of me that he could use to help with his set design. He had me dress up in just a loincloth and took photographs on a piece of grass outside Theobalds Park Hotel. It was springtime, but to me, being as skinny as I was, it felt like the middle of winter. Sometime later, Cecil showed me a pencil drawing of me that he had done. I was amazed. It looked just like me and was almost the same size as I was. However, that amazement was soon surpassed when I saw the fifteen foot flat he had painted of me which was to be used as part of the set. I still have Cecil's pencil drawing; I wish I had the flat. He made me look good.

It was at that time, when during the actual run of the show, I started to stay at Anne and Barry Golding's house as it was difficult to get back to Forest Gate late at night, and I had to be back at college early in the morning. Anne looked after me so well, and she also had me modelling for her art class at the college; which helped me to earn a bit of much needed money. (Thanks Anne).

My last memory of *Nabucco* is being sacrificed by Alan "King Rat" Girdlestone and being thrown into a fiery pit through the trap door on the stage. Oh well, all good things come to an end.

In December 1986 the company put on a production of *Dick Whittington And His Cat*. This version was written by Terry Hawes who was also my Music Teacher at the college. He too, in his own aloof way, was kind and patient with me while I was at the college. The production, much to my joy, was directed by Cecil

Hayter. In it I played Dick's youngest brother. I can't remember who played the middle brother, but one of the baddies was played by my best friend at the time, Mark Bastide, who was a brilliant sidekick to Neville Golding. Dick himself was played by Duncan McMillan. Mark and Duncan were also students at the college and we had a great time doing this show. I must confess I had a bit of a crush on my stage mum who was played by the lovely Faith. One of my favourite memories of the show is seeing a very young Katie Rush playing the cutest rat in London.

Around this time, my stroppy teenage self, had a falling out with my Drama teacher who refused to let me in her class. I should have been really worried about this, but, I wasn't. I thank God I had Cecil who took on the role as my Drama Teacher. I would go to his house in Fulham and learn far more about Drama than I ever did at college. Eventually, just before the A Level exams I managed to patch things up with my Drama Teacher, and while I was studying at Middlesex, I came back to Southgate Tech and taught a couple of drama classes for her. This was obviously because I had been given such a good grounding in Drama by Cecil. So, All's well that ends well.

A few months after *Dick Whittington And His Cat* I left Southgate Technical College and the opera company and went to study Performing Arts at Middlesex University, which was a Polytechnic at the time. I was really sad to leave Southgate College Opera as I had had such an amazing time with them. Although, not everything was always bright and breezy. I am tinged with sadness when I think about some of the notorious parties and the arguments that ensued within some peoples' relationships. Furthermore, and more painful, I still mourn the loss of my best friend Mark who was killed not long after leaving Southgate. I remember crying in the arms of David Luck at Mark's funeral. Thanks for being there for me David.

That should be the end. But how unfair would it be to end with such a tragic waste of life?

Once I had gone to Middlesex, I thought my days with Southgate College Opera were over. However, In December 1988 I received a phone call from Terry Hawes asking if I would like to play Puck in *To The Woods*. The person that was originally cast as Puck had to drop out and there was only three weeks left until curtain up. I gladly accepted. How could I say no when it was being directed by none other than Cecil Hayter.

To The Woods was another Terry Hawes masterpiece. Again it demanded an athletic performance, and again I was thrown around like a rugby ball by Barry who played the part of Oberon. My costume barely covered my modesty. Being almost naked in the middle of December is not exactly a barrel of fun. My body was painted with freezing cold emulsion every night by Cecil except for one when it was done by Stuart. I loved the sword fight that I had with Lysander and Demetrius. Cecil had made this magical sword which split in two so that I could fight them both at once. *To The Woods* was performed in the round. I remember that whenever Puck was in trouble with Oberon, I would run into the audience and sit on a beautiful girl's lap for protection. Sometimes I would do this with tough looking men because I knew it would embarrass them and wind them up. It's amazing what you can get away with when you are in the theatre.

During the time *To The Woods* was being rehearsed I held my first ever dinner party in my tiny bedroom in my flat in Palmers Green. I was honoured to have as my guests, Sarah Smith, my girlfriend at the time; Peter Rush and Shirley and David Luck. Sadly my Mum, Aunty Margaret and Cecil couldn't make it due to illness and other engagements. Just as well really, as they would have ended up eating on my bed. I still can't believe Sarah told everyone that I had skived college all day in order to prepare the meal.

To The Woods was to be my last production with Southgate College Opera. I'm glad this was to be the case as it was my most enjoyable production with them. This was still not quite the end though. Many years later in 2001, I formed my own performing arts school called the Upminster School for Young Performers. We had very little money, but thanks to Cecil and Southgate College Opera we did have curtains, costumes and scenery for our productions of the *Wizard Of Oz* in 2004 and *Joseph And The Amazing Technicolor Dream Coat* in 2006.

All I can do now is give a huge heartfelt thank you to all at Southgate College Opera for the memories, encouragement and support throughout my years of involvement with you. Thank you all. Exit stage left... I said left.

ANNE GOLDING

The longest serving woman chorus member (apart from Jenny senior)

In 1971 I sat in the Southgate College Theatre watching the college opera group perform *Tales Of Hoffman*. I had never seen a gauze used so magically in an amateur production. I wanted to belong.

As part of my job as art teacher at the college, I painted scenery with students for whatever productions took place.

I just met Cecil standing up a ladder on the college stage one afternoon He smoked then, and I used to rush out of the back gate before it was locked to bring him his cigarettes to "keep him going" for the evening.

My first production as a chorus member was *Elixir Of Love*. A very pretty, authentic looking Italian set by Cecil and costumes organized by me. While my mother in Bournemouth (under my instructions) dyed bodices, Cecil's mother, over from South Africa, staying in Fulham, made paper flowers (Wisteria) for the set. Unfortunately, the fire officer from across the road insisted the flowers be made fireproof and they wilted from the spray solution but still looked pretty.

The first production of *Bartered Bride* was set in a very realistic village, painted (all night!) by Cecil. We had an actual pond on stage, with "borrowed" goldfish from the science lab.

When Cecil produced *Turandot* the first time we set it in traditional Chinese theatre style. A pagoda like structure with the "poor" chorus and children on floor level in drab grey blue, ascending to vivid pink and green worn with traditional Chinese make up, which took a while to apply every night.

For our second production of *Tales Of Hoffmann* (by now I was a full time chorus member, and resident organizer, designer and maker of costumes) I was delighted when Cecil agreed to my idea of costuming the doll scene entirely in shades of yellow.

My most difficult costume design problem was the chorus witches in *Macbeth*. Each woman was enclosed in a stretch jersey "sack" with a mask on the back of the head. As we moved backwards on stage the effect was deliberately eerie.

For the female chorus, when we posed dresses as angels ascending the stairs, front of the pros arch in *Mefistofele,* it was the nearest we got to heaven, heavenly chorus music.

Another time, some years before, Jean Aird, our lovely resident soprano lead wore a large pink pinafore dress to cover her twin pregnancy in *Giani Schicchi.* Many years later one of those twins, Stuart, became a soloist in *Otello* and *Yeoman Of The Guard.*

Our reluctant move from the college to Wyllyots Theatre, Potters Bar, now works in our favour. We have new audiences while still maintaining many of our original Southgate patrons. We endeavour to maintain the very high standards that were originally set out when Southgate Opera Company was an evening class at Southgate Technical College in the 1960s.

Through the internet and the website we now, more than ever, bring in new members, chorus and soloists. The success of Southgate Opera is due to the excellent foundations laid down by Terry Hawes and Cecil Hayter, director and set designer extrordinaire. Now with a dedicated committee and Neil Cloake continuing as enthusiastic, musical director, the company strives forward. Fifty years of remarkable achievement.

ANN THEATO

When I was 24 years old, I rode a blue Honda RS250cc motorbike and had great aspirations to be an actress. By day I was a grubby motorcycle courier. I weaved my way through the city streets, delivered parcels and thought I was really cool because I smoked Major cigarettes beneath my helmet without taking them out of my mouth. I remember having a pine air freshener strung from the handlebars and stuffing an old baby-gro with newspapers, leaving the legs to dangle outside above my handwritten hazard sign, "Baby in Top Box." Oh yeah, I was hilarious.

It was in this fashion, I first rocked up to the LOST Theatre, to see a production directed by Gregory Mandry of Nigel Williams' *Class Enemy*, which I'd seen advertised in The Stage.

I remember watching that show – I loved the writing – raw, anarchic, hilarious and reflective of my own poor education in an over-subscribed Colchester comprehensive. One abiding memory of the show was the lighting on the floor – the shadow of a skylight. Simple. Effective. I was hooked.

A few months later I read in the Stage that LOST were holding auditions for the Edinburgh Festival– they were taking up a 'Shakespeare.' I parked my bike outside the front wall of LOST and was met in the corridor by Steve Lee, who was incredibly friendly and welcoming. He took me into the darkened auditorium which reminded me of the little drama studio back at my comprehensive – the only place in the school I had ever felt really at home – and Steve watched patiently while I stumbled through my prepared speech - Lady Percy in *Henry IV Part 1*.

Tactfully swerving the issue of whether my speech was any good, Steve offered me instead, the part of Cynthia Muldoon in *The Real Inspector Hound* – also going to Edinburgh. Suddenly I was part of LOST and it was there that I began to make and keep some excellent friends for life.

Melanie Nunn was in *Hound*, and we became (and still are) great buddies. She was dating a lovely actor called Simon Da Costa at the time, and who has since gone on to be a successful West End playwright. Mel would always "Pnaaargh!" and make double entendres out of innocent comments, and we were soon as bad as each other, earning the nickname "The Thin Slags" (a thin version of The Flat Slags from Viz comic, which was oh so popular at the time). Melly drove a little Fiat 127, which she christened Fanny and she was often heard to call out to some hapless passing actor, "Oy! Do you wanna ride in my Fanny?"

The cast of *Hound* were fantastic – I can't remember all their names but Robin Chalmers played Hound, Julian England played Magnus, Mel played Felicity Cunningham, Neil Sills played Simon Gascoyne, a girl called Selina played the hilarious Mrs Drudge and a guy who for some reason called himself Rudi Parbar-foulla (his real name was James), played Moon. The play called for my character to kiss Neil's character and I remember Cecil was the Director initially (then Tony Conway) and Cecil said firmly, "Just get on with it." So we did. And we got on with it a bit outside of rehearsals too.

Edinburgh was a blast although we had to stop just 2 miles up the M1 as our props and set had started to fall off the roof rack. We had a brilliant time in Edinburgh, putting our make up on in the back of a white van and touting for business outside the Fringe Club.

A few months later at LOST, the Christmas panto was in full swing. One night I arrived at the theatre after work – it was completely empty –no-one around at all, except for Robin Chalmers, who was lying in the auditorium on a chaise longue. For some reason, he was attempting to explain to me the theory of Loop Quantum Gravity. Naturally, this resulted in me gaffa-taping him from head to foot to the chaise longue and I waited until his screaming reached fever pitch before fetching the scissors.

We always used to go to the pub after rehearsals for a couple of pints. Quite often we'd return to LOST and share a joint in the dressing room and play the guitar or have a singsong. The Vibe at the Dressing Room was the place to be! At Christmas we'd go into the auditorium late at night to play the panto band's drums and then we'd get told off by the Vicar upstairs, who would come down and hammer on the door and threaten us with all sorts. He was a miserable so and so.

I taught drama to kids at LOST for a long time. I had some brilliant students - I loved teaching and I loved the personalities of the kids who came. I'm still in touch with some of them... Ivan Sheppard, Matt Blair, Katrina Mayhew-Taibe. We'd do classes on Saturdays and every now and then we'd put on a show. We did lots of smaller shows as well as *Operation Elvis* and *Bugsy Malone*. A young lad called Daniel Torres played the lead in *Operation Elvis* – he was absolutely fantastic – a great singer and a great performer and he grew up to become a very successful singer/songwriter in Brazil. A young girl called Morgann Runacre-Temple was one of my tiny dancers in *Bugsy Malone* – she loved dancing and was brilliant at it. She grew up to become Choreographer-in-Residence for Ballet Ireland. Her sister Mariele Runacre-Temple was a great little actress – incredibly keen – never missed a class – totally dedicated - has gone on to create the fantastic, multi-award winning Wireless Theatre Company.

I have made so many good friends from my time with the LOST Theatre and I'm still in touch with a great bunch of people I met back then and whom I would deem to be amongst my closest friends.

LOST touched so many people's lives. Whether as a parent or performer, a musician or an audience member. Child or adult, professional or amateur, LOST was so many things to so many people:- Entertainment. Inspiration. Salvation. Opportunity. Risk. Reward. Peace. Excitement. Expression. Therapy. Proving ground. Failing ground (**insert Mark Kemp's piece *"Inside The Mind Of A Chimpanzee At The Zoo"* here**). Springboard. Resting place. Matchmaker. Heartbreaker. It was home for anyone who walked in. It was a friend. It was family.

When we reached 27 we were forbidden to perform there any longer – it was a place for under 27's only. I can't express the grief and loss of the place, once you were too old for it. We all trailed away. Great actors, great directors, great entertainers, great musicians & singers.... Mark Kemp, Deborah Wheatley, Steve Requena, Tony Conway, Patrick Wilde, Gerry O'Sullivan, Deborah Collister, Helen Bradbear, Andy Whipp, Kevin O'Sullivan, Greg Mandry, Tom Marty, Graham Machell, Paul Trussell, Maurizio Molino, Stephen Lee, Kevin O'Sullivan, Neil Sills, Dave Peat (what a hilarious guy!), Julian England, Justin Shevlin, Lisa Trundley, ... Cecil's explanation was that he had given us a springboard and now we had to spring. We were supposed to try and make it on our own now and not to be tied to LOST's apron strings. A good idea in theory – to make space for newcomers and give other young adults a chance. But we didn't have anywhere to go. There was nowhere to spring to. There was nowhere else like LOST. And for that I will always be sorry.

And what am I doing now? I gained my Equity card during my time at LOST by setting up a T.I.E. company and I went on to have a successful career as a voice over artist and actress. I have two children – both of whom are very keen actors – my son Jacob Théato – whom I used to bring to the LOST Theatre as a baby when I was teaching my Saturday classes.... has been very successful, with main roles in TV films *Einstein And Eddington* (starring Andy Serkis & David Tennant) and *Recovery* (starring David Tennant and Sarah Parish) and BBC's *Robin Hood* Series 3, as well as playing parts in several different radio plays for BBC Radio 4 including playing Paul Dombey in *Dombey & Son*.

I am currently working as Manager for The Ralph and Meriel Richardson Foundation – a theatrical charity who support established actors who are experiencing financial difficulties. I am just about to start work as a private PA to Lucy Parham, a concert pianist, whose recitals will often include pieces of drama performed by well-known actors.

I still work part-time as an actress and voice talent and best of all, I am still in contact with my lovely student, Mariele Runacre-Temple, who runs The Wireless Theatre Company and who now employs me! I am part of her fantastic team of actors/directors at Wireless, who go in to LAMDA and RADA, to teach their graduate students about the amazing world of radio drama and we help them to record and produce their first drama and commercial voice reels.

I also write plays for Mariele's company. Most recently I wrote a 3-part audio documentary series called *Life At Death's Door*. Episode One was narrated by Brian Blessed and went on to win Best Documentary Long Form at the British Public Radio Awards. Episode Two has been narrated by the wonderful Jo Brand and we have high hopes for its success - it will be available for download from The Wireless Theatre's website in 2014. And if Stephen Merchant would agree to narrate Episode Three – that would make us incredibly happy ex-LOSTies!

P.S. Best ever memory? – being on stage as Gerry O'Sullivan (with pursed lips) made his entrance as a Roman Soldier dressed in a tunic made from an inside-out carpet. I'm still laughing today!

BARRIE GOLDING

I think I first met Cecil in 1967 in circumstances (very chance) that he describes in his book. For me, as I wager for many others, this led to life changing and enhancing experiences involving initially dance, drama and music in various forms. Above all I would say it was working with and getting to know an endlessly creative, open and generous person who was always working/striving with a sense of mission. If this sounds like a bit of a testimonial, it's just the truth, still is!!

A Few Memories

Seeing him bring a piece of canvass alive with a bamboo forest for a small cabaret his first boss, Les Shakespeare, was wanting Cecil to put on at a Parsons Green social club where Cecil also got it to 'rain' on the stage for one item—magical! (1968?)

Being in a dance evening presentation on the stage in Fulham town hall which Cecil mainly choreographed and financially supported- *'Arcana'*....

Being asked by Cecil to stage manage his first production at Southgate College Opera- *Luisa Miller*- when he found out very late that the group didn't have anyone to do the job – he lent me his car so I could get over from Watford so I could do it. I did the job the next year as well when the opera was *La Bohème* with the student 'protest' intrusion/happening.

Being the part of the development of the opera group as performer in some very exciting and wide ranging productions where the group dynamic and drive/ sense of purpose owed much to the kind of ways of working/ acting etc. together that Cecil and Terry encouraged and in a way demanded.

Seeing work that Cecil did with others, for example, a production of *La Tableau* by Ionesco for Questors Theatre-Theatre of the Absurd which caught fire and was joyous.

Tricks of the Trade or Suspensions of Disbelief

The door through which Dr Coppeleus disappears and vice versa in *Tales of Hoffman* made out of wide elasticated vertical bands painted and stretched to look just like a closed door, magical tromp d' art.

Mirrors arranged in such a way in a large box so that it looked like the character standing in it had only a half a body in *Golden Cockerel.*

The village square set for *Elixir Of Love* with a huge tree in the middle solely (?) for Nemorino to sing his lovesick aria in towards the end of the opera. I felt like destroying a real place when it came to take it down at the end of the run.

The above memories might give a false sense of the overall striving for truth (emotional and physical) that Cecil's productions by and large strove for, I think – not so much naturalism but realism and truth to the spirit of work undertaken.

Although our paths haven't crossed that much in recent years, those experiences of working together as a team have been central to my development.

Life with Southgate (College) Opera

Terry Hawes had started the Opera group as an evening class earlier in the 1960s- a bold undertaking for a Technical College perhaps-but one with the vital support of Bill Easton, the Principal.

After *Luisa Miller* my involvement with the group under Terry and Cecil continued and grew - a really exciting and interesting passage of time. There was a wide repertoire with original shows written by Terry (often specifically for the group) along with some operas, which I think Terry chose to challenge the group. *The Golden Cockerel* and *Christmas Eve* by Rimsky Korsakov for instance.

For me (and I'm sure many others) there were many parts of the jigsaw which made up the continued development of the opera group and proved very fulfilling- it was teamwork, creative and giving full value to showing 'the sum of the parts' could really produce something worthwhile-egos had very little to do with it and a lot of what stemmed from Terry and Cecil's drive and teamwork. It was fun! A real journey of kindred spirits.

Highlights

The weekends at Theobalds College working on a production; with often a mini production of part of the show to participants in other courses being run there. October/November weekends would end up with fireworks against a backdrop of the Old City gate (now to be found in Pater Noater square by St Pauls cathedral).

Feydeau/Alan Aykbourne style farce situations as to who was in what room with whomever arose from time to time, so I am reliably informed!

Taking parts in other courses as an 'extra' as in a Murder Mystery weekend course where, as a likely suspect, was photographed by the course leader in bed with another suspect, soon to become a 'victim'....or Dave Luck crashing spectacularly into a trolley of utensils...over dinner, 'poisoned' by the murderer.

Or at the very first weekend taking part with the wine tasting group on a Saturday evening when one of the tasters had too much and fell backwards through the open window- luckily this was in the ballroom on the ground floor!

Lastly for the memoir, being the German army captain (?) in Terry's *The Secret Of Santa Victoria* (a Dora Basham production) when we realised the show had to be cut drastically in order not to keep the audience there towards midnight. So my part and parts of the dialogue had to be cut and I had to check with the revised script in the wings at the performance to make sure what my next line was.

BEVERLEY CHALMERS

From 'Alice' with Love

I first met Cecil about 50 years ago when my then school teacher, Janet Rowland, asked him to provide Chinese movement direction for our school's Eisteddfod play entry, *The Price of Perfection*. As a rather protected, excessively polite and 'well brought up' 12 year-old girl, I was aghast at this rather astounding, scruffily dressed, young man who leapt up and over the footlights onto the stage at the end of our first run through of the play to give us feedback. Didn't he use the stairs??? Who leaps up onto a four foot high stage? What followed was even more astounding. In a matter of hours he turned our stodgy, amateurish movements into a dynamic, graceful performance which went on to win the Eisteddfod. Even more remarkable was the invitation Cecil extended to me to audition a few days later for "Alice" in his forthcoming production of *Alice in Wonderland*. He cast me as Alice and so began a life-long relationship that persists to this day and that changed my life and – I hope and trust – his.

We came from and lived in different worlds but met and shared a lifetime love of theatre as well as – and more importantly – a need for and value of honesty, openness, tolerance of difference and genuineness. Cecil – who was shockingly stranger and different from anyone else I had ever met – taught me as a young child that people from all walks of life can meet these standards and that wealth was not a criterion with which to judge others. We both recall incidents from those days that amuse us now. One was his admonition to me to wear working jeans at rehearsals so as not to spoil my exquisite clothes and my response "Don't worry! They can be washed." Another was my father's presence (to ensure my safety) at the many rehearsals of "Alice" that I had with Cecil on his own: Alice was alone on stage for the first half hour of the two hour show, and one-to-one rehearsals for this section of the play were obviously necessary. Yet another was his playful instruction to me at the end of my first rehearsal to memorize the script for this first half-hour of monologue (which I took seriously), and his shock when I returned for the second rehearsal having done so.

Although he hated performing and preferred directing, he was sometimes called to stand in for an absent actor. One of my fondest memories of him was performing the song and dance trio of *Old Father William* with him in which Alice was sandwiched between the Old Man and the Young Man. Cecil had been forced to take over the role of the Old Man when we moved the show to a second city with a smaller stage. If he had not held on to me I would have stepped backwards off the smaller stage and into the orchestra pit.

Yet another memory was his trust in me. He did not cast an understudy for Alice but simply told me that it was up to me: if I did not turn up for the play there would be no play. I did not let him down, but more importantly, I learned to shoulder responsibility way beyond what is normally given to a 12 year-old and grew immensely from that experience. His trust, respect, affection, honesty, enthusiasm and energy provided me with a role model that stayed with me throughout my life. The fact that he lived in a room above someone's garage, seemed to always be untidy (I have a wonderful newspaper photo of him with his hair all over the place), was always covered in paint, and ate fish and chips wrapped in newspaper, added colour to my images of him but in no way detracted from my admiration of him and my ability to perceive the gold that lay beneath his surface.

We worked together on a number of other plays: He directed me as (one of two) "Dorothys" in the professional productions of *The Wizard Of Oz*, as well as *The Sound Of Music* (as "Louisa") and in a school production – as *Aladdin* in the production of that name. To my everlasting regret he left South Africa to move to the UK before he could direct me as *Heidi* in the professional production of that name. But the lessons I had learned about acting, theatre and the stage stayed with me for life.

Cecil's involvement in youth theatre obviously started years before his establishment of the LOST Theatre in London, but the same qualities that I had so admired, and from which I learned so many of life's lessons, shone through all his later "LOST" years. I met with him over the years in London, and rarely missed an opportunity to seek him out on my many visits to that city. I recall my first visit to London, some ten years or so after he started "LOST." I found his address in the telephone directory but had no idea where on the lengthy Wandsworth Road he lived. So I caught the tube to one end of the street and began walking. Of course he lived at the other end, and it was some hours later that I knocked on his door, bedraggled, tired and hot. He opened it only to exclaim "Alice!" He remained close to me always, insisting that he meet my husband Bernie to ensure he was OK for me and would look after me and love me. Fortunately, Bernie passed the test and as Cecil predicted we have shared over 40 wonderful years together. He later welcomed one of our daughters, Dana, into LOST when she, as a 17 year old, moved from Canada to live in London and enter the theatre world. I was grateful that she had Cecil as a mentor during her ensuing career in theatre and in the academic world, both in London and Canada.

I have watched his development of LOST with admiration, and with some envy that I could not participate and share this life with him fully. My world, and my family, had directed my activities elsewhere and I became an international health consultant and academic involved in perinatal health globally. The good part of this was that my many consultancies took me through London regularly and I was often able to spend a night at Cecil's home to catch up on our lives, or just to meet him at the airport for a quick meal while in transit from London on to eastern Europe, where I usually worked, or back to Canada where I live. Typical of Cecil, he would often meet me at one terminal just to drive me to the next so that we could have an hour together between my flights. If that isn't friendship and love then what is?

Cecil's numerous ups and downs with the establishment and maintenance of the LOST Theatre read like an unimaginable novel. At times heart-warming, at others tragic and disappointing, with betrayal and deceit dogging him frequently, but always imbued with his remarkable ability to turn adversity into good fortune in the end. His wisdom and gutsy determination to achieve his life's goals drives him on beyond anyone's ability to prevent him from doing so. I can only admire him, respect him and love him for everything he has given to youth for over more than a half century. His knowledge is immense, his ability to experience emotions deeply and fully is at times overwhelming for him, and his humility admirable but detrimental. He deserves immense thanks from the hundreds, if not thousands, of young people – like myself – whose lives he has touched and enriched. For myself, I remain forever grateful for our lifelong friendship, for our shared love of theatre, and for the guiding light he provided for me that taught me to respect people for who they truly are regardless of any exterior trappings they may display. Cecil, thank you.

Beverley Chalmers (DSc(Med); PhD)

Adj Full Prof, Dept of Obstetrics and Gynaecology

Affiliate Investigator, Ottawa Hospital Research Institute

University of Ottawa, Canada

CELIA WELLS

I joined the opera group in 1991, *The Italian Straw Hat* being the first production I took part in. Terry Hawes was the Musical Director, Cecil Hayter, Director.

From the first rehearsal, the professionalism in the group was impressive.

Terry has always been totally dedicated to Southgate, not being involved in anything else. Neil Cloake, Terry's assistant, wonderful with people, worked well with Cecil and I found him very approachable. Both were very good men and as far as I know worked well with Cecil. Cecil has a great way with people and could always manage to get the best out of them.

We put on some first class shows, creating a good atmosphere everywhere, and this still continues to this day.

COLIN DAVIS

It was a damp Saturday morning in Palmers Green. The poster in the newsagent was advertising a local performing group, Southgate College Opera. The year was 1982. The auditorium was packed, and I was lucky to get a seat. The show was *His Excellency*, words by WS Gilbert, music by some guy called Terry Hawes.

It had been some years since I had performed on stage. In the early 70's, whilst a student at Imperial College, I had loved indulging my over-acting capability in many G&S productions with IC Operatic Society, in London and on tour in Budleigh Salterton. I had missed performing. I could see that this was a group of high standard, and one I would love to join. I can't remember much about the production, apart from Allan Girdlestone's hair style, David Waters' splendid voice and economical acting style and Terry Hawes's white shirt with pink spots. Odd what sticks in your mind.

In 1984, I saw *Sleeping Beauty*. A stunning production, fantastically entertaining. I joined the company in 1985 as a performing member, and was pretty soon on the committee as membership secretary, where I have remained for 27 years in various roles including Chairman and Treasurer.

In 2005 the company was in crisis. In its early years under the leadership of its first Principal Bill Easton,

Southgate College had generously sponsored its opera company, orchestra and drama society. Southgate College Opera thrived. It had free use of the College theatre, MD and Director and Accompanist funded by the College, vast storage space for costumes and scenery, free rehearsal space, and much more. After Bill retired, the increasing financial pressures in the world of 'Further Education' saw these privileges being reduced and eliminated one by one. And in 2005, the evening class fee paid by performers was to be raised from £100 to £153, and the Music Department was to be closed. Southgate College Opera was no more. From its ashes, the phoenix of a new group was formed. The imaginatively named Southgate Opera was created, and it's new performing home of Wyllyotts Theatre in Potters Bar was acquired. In that year, its production of *La Traviata* was performed over two weeks both at the Gladys Child Theatre, and also at Wyllyotts.

And happily we still survive! Funds have been maintained, performances continue to be of very high standard, and we are all still having fun. A recent influx of enthusiastic and talented young performers has given us all a great lift. Thank you to all fellow performers, stage hands, and others, for a fantastically enjoyable 27 years.

DAMIAN SCOTT

Mt first memory of drama or acting of any kind goes way back before the LOST theatre, it was as one of Fagin's gang as a young 9 year old at the Brunswick Boys Club in *Oliver Twist*, from there we continued with productions of *Bye Bye Birdie* and my favourite part, that of Tobias Rag in *Sweeney Todd The Barber*. For which I won best in drama and was presented with a trophy that was stolen the next night from the club. I still have the photo somewhere of me dressed in 70s fashion which made me look a total pratt, but I suppose everybody dressed that way.

I left the boys club at the age of 15 but that's not where the story ends, I went to the London Oratory School and sat in the school youth club. One dark winter night you walked in and asked if I was interested in joining the drama group up, my initial reaction was no thanks very much as I thought, I wouldn't be interested in it, but to coin a phrase the itch needed scratching, so I joined and took part in the company's very first production as one of The Sharks In *West Side Story*. We then did various productions and quite a few Opus Productions. My favourite part without a shadow of a doubt was as Shakespeare in *A Comedy Of Errors*. Not only was it a lead role, I had three very attractive secretaries.

I was hooked once again, as well as acting with the company I took a very active role within the school drama department and was involved in various productions such as *A Comedy Of Errors*, and too many productions to remember. My favourite memory of that was playing Sir Toby Belch, for the run of five nights we had full houses every night, and we were all asked and invited to the end of show party at Jeremy Trafford's House. Just goes to show that John MacIntosh was human after all and not a demi-god as some thought.

Anyway back to LOST. I remember the company quite well. There are lots of people I remember: Paddy O Connor, Tom Marty, Gerry and Tim O Sullivan, Derek Fitzgerald, Jill Healey, Valerie Ball, Mandy Smith to name but a few, all these outstanding people made LOST the successful company that is, was, and looking at the web site, still is to this day.

Anyway after the company moved from the school I lost touch with some of the people who were with the company the same time that I was. I joined the Army straight from school and served In the Grenadier Guards for 22 years, left the Army and I now live with my wife and two children in Letchworth Hertfordshire

DANA LORI CHALMERS

Rejoicing in Imperfections:
Memories of a LOST Theatre

I grew up hearing about Cecil Hayter. My mother performed in a number of shows he directed when she was a child, so when I started studying acting at 6 years old, I would hear a lot of 'Cecil says' in her coaching. In my very young mind, I imagined Cecil as a sort of God of Directing somewhere out in England. The first time I met him, I was eleven years old with my family on a trip to England. I have no memory of the show we saw, but it was a LOST Theatre production and I do remember loving it. The whole time there, it was like meeting a celebrity – I got to meet Cecil Hayter!

Several years later, I was approaching the end of high school. I had rushed through the curriculum and finished a year and half early, allowing me six months to travel between finishing high school and starting university. I used this opportunity to move to England and work at LOST.

My time with LOST was extraordinary. I was 17 years old, so my memories are peppered with some truly cringe-worthy moments of teenage awkwardness, but they are also filled with some remarkable learning experiences. At LOST, I was offered the opportunity to try anything. I started out wanting to act, but discovered very quickly that I loved literally everything to do with the theatre. When offered the opportunity to stage-manage, I took it, discovering a passion and talent for the job that was entirely unexpected. I stumbled, like everyone will when starting something new, but at LOST I was allowed to learn from my mistakes, to grow and try again. I learned to operate a lighting board, paint scenery, build sets, work in a box office, make and design costumes, hunt for props and create a show with a minimal budget and infinite creativity. LOST was not only a place to develop theatre-specific techniques. When I was stage-managing, I was the youngest person working on the production, working with people who were older and more experienced than I. Their advice and occasional admonition, helped me to learn to 'manage up', and to develop an approach to management that I still use to this day. In fact, I have even adapted this approach to my teaching style, with rave reviews from my students.

While most of my time at LOST was spent stage managing and discovering the unfamiliar world of theatre off the stage, I also had some opportunities to perform. At the time, I was too self-conscious about my – as Cecil phrased it – Rubenesque body to be a particularly memorable actress, but my experience at LOST started me on the road to changing this. Cecil offered me one tremendous opportunity in this regard – and I wish I had recognised it as such at the time. Cecil also asked me to play one of the fairies in *A Midsummer Night's Dream*. At the time, the idea of playing a 'fairy' – creatures I imagined to be petite, sexy and beautiful – was unimaginable to me. It was only years later that I realised that he had given me a chance to create a character 'against type' that could have been hilarious! Cecil is one of those rare directors who genuinely encourages actors to explore the roles themselves, rather than pushing a preconceived image of the character onto the actor. In retrospect, this experience became tremendously valuable, not only in my future years as an actress, but also as a director.

The lessons I learned at LOST have stayed with me through my acting training, my transition into academics and my more recent excursions into directing. I find myself remembering pieces of advice offered by Steve Lee or Cecil and even quoting them on occasion. I want to emulate Cecil's daring and willingness to jump in the deep end of a situation and sink or swim. I remember Steve telling me that directing is the art of convincing the actors that everything they do is entirely their own idea. I frequently recall an actor who lost his temper with me when I was being too pushy as a stage manager, and have developed a completely different leadership style as a result. I did a lot of growing up during my time at LOST. It was a place where a socially awkward teenager could go and start to come out of her shell. The people there were kind to me and remarkably tolerant and my time there was a truly wonderful learning experience.

LOST helped to start me on a fantastic journey through the possibilities of Theatre. My experiences there reinforced my desire to perform, and helped me find the strength to complete my first degree in Theatre. I also discovered my skills as a stage manager and went on to work on numerous productions. The people at LOST even inspired me to work as a venue manager at the Edinburgh Fringe Festival. Mostly, however, LOST helped me discover that my interest in theatre transcended the limits of performing. I realised that every part of theatre was exciting, including its potential to have an impact on the world. Today, I have just completed a doctorate aimed at developing techniques to use popular entertainment - including mainstream theatre – to challenge the ideologies that lead to conflict and genocide.

I've stayed in touch with Cecil in the years since I left London and have come to love him very much. I loved LOST long before I learned to appreciate Cecil, and recognise now that to try to talk about LOST without talking about Cecil is simply impossible. LOST is Cecil's child – one that he put so much of himself into and which he helped grow into a genuinely incredible enterprise. So much of what made LOST special comes directly from Cecil. At LOST we were free to explore with no limits on creativity or imagination. This is a characteristic that comes directly from Cecil's willingness to do all those things; to leap blindly and to trust openly. He did exactly that when he created LOST and instilled the same adventurous spirit into the company itself. In recent years, as his involvement with LOST has waned, I think that spirit in LOST has also begun to die – and for this I am both tremendously sad and immensely sorry.

We like to look back and remember the successful productions and great performances (of which there were many), but LOST also provided a safe place in which to try, even occasionally less than successfully – something that is unbelievably rare and exceptionally valuable. LOST was never about being perfect. It was about rejoicing in the imperfections that occasionally make great art, and always make extraordinary learning experiences. I was lucky to have been part of it at its best.

Dana Lori Chalmers, PhD.

DAVE LA FAME

The 1983 LOST production *Grease* was my first significant introduction to theatre and it changed my life. It started a journey that saw me move across the Atlantic and pursue a career in entertainment that has lasted 25 years. And still going strong

Many of the other cast members of *Grease* also seemed new to LOST. So there was a lot of excitement, enthusiasm and much bonding going on. The fact that it's such a fun high energy show added to the overall exuberance. So everyone was involved in all the aspects of pulling the production together. Cast members helped with the set building, wardrobe and props. Parties were arranged to watch videos of John Travolta and Olivia Newton John, et al. in the movie version.

At some point the question of how to build a car for the 'Greased Lightning,' the drive-in and final scenes, were being discussed. The idea of a boxy car made out of wood didn't seem appealing. Surely guys as cool as Danny and Kenicke could not be seen dead in a large Lego car! Somebody wondered out loud if we could get a real car. Perhaps a Fiat 500 or a mini? This idea was mixed because of comparisons to Noddy and Big Ears.

The solution came in the form of an Mk2 Cortina located in Battersea that had been condemned to the scrap yard. It was immobile and would need picking up. Armed with a tow rope, a group of us set off across the Thames to bring it back to Fulham. The rope was too short, the brakes on the Cortina were dodgy. The journey taking us across Battersea Bridge, along the Embankment, Kings Road & Fulham Road. It took quite a while and there were a few bicycle clip moments. But at last, it was eventually pushed into the yard at the rear of the theatre. 'Greased Lightning' had arrived!

The next problem was that the car was too long. It needed to be hidden behind a flat that would drop as the car rolled out for the scenes. What we needed was the front half not the back. It also needed to resemble a convertible, so the roof would have to go. We came up with a plan to cut the car in half. Across the top of the wind shield. Through the door frame and at the bottom of the car behind the front seats.

I can't remember what happened to the engine and transmission. I think the stage manager Andrew and another volunteer or 3 removed those parts plus all the brake and fuel lines. Once that was done we were ready to cut it up.

The tool chosen for this feat was a humble angle grinder borrowed from my boss. I worked for an antique fireplace dealer at the time. The angle grinder was normally used to cut fire grates, light metal frames and supports. The cutting wheel was reduced to half its normal size by the time I'd cut through the frame!

The Cortina had to be rolled on to a trolley sideways to get it through the back door. Once inside and lifted onto the stage, a homemade trolley with wheels was fixed to the rear of the car which was attached to a manual hand built rope and pulley system.

This was all manually operated during the show by the Stage Manager. The flat concealing the car from the audience, was hinged from underneath. When the time came, it was pushed over. The car was then heaved out onto the stage. Stopping only because the stage manager held on to a rope and dug his heels in! After the scene, he hauled the car back into place and then yanked on ropes tied to the flat to lift it back in place.

'Greased Lightning,' with lights blazing, would roar towards the audience out of the darkness! It always got a round of applause. If it weren't for the stage manager's heels...they would have got a little too close to the action!

Yes I was hanging with a rough crowd at the time I got involved with LOST and no one had ever said anything complimentary or encouraging to me up until then. Anyway, after moving from the UK it took about 2 years before I did anything in the theatre here. But when I did it was a regular paying gig at a dinner theatre. The contacts I made resulted in union card gigs in theatre, TV and film. I detoured from performing and started my own DJ and karaoke business specializing in corporate market. I still own that business but around 12 years ago created a comedy music show for my corporate clients. Impersonating and sending up famous singers. Out of that show the Tom Jones impersonation was a stand out and an agent suggested I create a serious Tom Jones tribute. Armed with wig and tight trousers this now accounts for 75% of my work

DAVID LUCK

Southgate and The Fulham Arts Centre. Too many memories both good and bad. Assuming the reader has a working knowledge of both entities by now, I shall concentrate on a few memories of those early days. Being of the age where I am more likely to be asked to write the obituary for a long standing member, use it or lose it comes to mind! Cecil's idea to perform a semi-staged version of *Lucia* at The Fulham Laundry where the performers outnumbered the audience, which included a dog, by ten to one, was probably marginally better than his idea of *No Named City* (a Wild West type review) coupled with *Pagliacci* at the Brunswick Boys Club in Fulham. I suspect the combination of Hawes and Hayter left an indelible mark on many. A highlight of the Southgate Opera year was probably the residential weekends spent at Theobalds; an intensive rehearsal weekend of work and play! These weekends were shared with unsuspecting courses of painters, yoga enthusiasts or historians. The latter having little sense of humour! The bar remaining open into the small hours, little or no sleep was likely. Smuggled bottles to provide afters ensured a continuous supply of alcohol. That is unless one dropped ones bag on registration resulting in what looked like incontinence as the liquid spread across the marble floor. Looking back, perhaps crawling along a second floor parapet to surprise female members would not strictly meet current Health and Safety regulations! To find one's bedding and mattress thrown from the second floor and being locked out during recovery all part of the weekend.

DERECK FITZGERALD

Where do I start?

When Paddy O'Connor walked up to me in the London Oratory Youth Centre at 17 years young and asked if I would like to be on the stage, little did I know of the adventure which would play a major part of my life over the following decade and indeed for the rest of my life.

"Can you sing, act or dance?" says Paddy, "We are putting on a musical called West Side Story."

"No" says I.

"There are about 30 Girls and 6 Guys at the moment," proclaims Paddy.

"Well I can dance and sing a bit," says I and the rest is as they say history.

A few months later I had the privilege to call myself a founder member of the LOST Theatre Company and went on to perform some of the best roles any professional actor would give their right arm to play. I also had a chance to be directed by some truly inspirational people, Cecil Hayter of course, Paddy O'Connor, Seamus Martin, Paul Rogan and Theresa Drea who directed me to win the best Actor award for my role in *Gotcha*.

The Company also brought me lifelong friendships, which no matter how long the time span between meetings, always seems to go straight back into the banter as if it were last week, also and no means least during a workshop meeting one cold evening my now wife of 28 years, Linda, walked into my life. We have one son Ciaran, who is 26.

Highs

The MC in *Cabaret* seemed to suit me down to the ground, I must admit I enjoyed every minute of it

Les in *West* again, what a role from the magic that is Stephen Berkoff, in particular the opening scene, which I could probably repeat now some 20 years later if asked.

Playing the part of Joxer in *Juno And The Paycock* was another part which could have been written for me and was a chance to do something set in the place I call home, Dublin.

Performing Juno at the Irish Centre in Camden Town in front of my fellow exiles and getting away with it to a standing ovation was a fantastic feeling.

The dumb waiter alongside Tom Marty and Sean Murphy.

All the Musicals including *West Side Story, The Pyjama Game, Grease* and of course *Cabaret*.

Winning the one act festival with *Gotcha* and performing *A Night Out* directed by Paul Rogan on the same night.

Epsom Downs, I still had people walking up to me weeks later thinking I was from Glasgow, so I must have got away with it.

Immediately after the line "hey buddy dis ain't Poopsie "when the audience fell about laughing, just the feeling of you doing something right. And again in *West* with,

"So I said pal Do I look like a tin of Dog Food?"

"Not really chum."

Being able to make people laugh and cry (usually at my singing) in the same period of time.

Lows

Not many.

The sad loss of Seamus Martin at such a young age, Shay was great friend with such vision and truly one of the nicest individuals one could ever have hoped to meet. RIP.

Being told the company was taking *West* to Edinburgh only for it to be taken away by what can only be called internal politics. You know who you are!

Losing the part of Mercutio in *Romeo And Juliet* after missing one rehearsal due to a migraine attack. Sorry Cecil I had to get that one in, but I do understand the decision.

Funnies

Far too many to mention.

It seemed that every time the head of the London Oratory, John MacIntosh was showing fifty or so potential students around the school, half way through he seemed to stop in the theatre to show off LOST, always at this point John Simpson seemed to be either showing his arse to one and all or shouting some form of profanity as a part of the play. Classic.

Gerry O'Sullivan having burst through the door at one of the many of the after show parties pronouncing "I'm going to rape all the beer and drink all the women."

In rehearsals for *Juno And The Paycock*. Josephine Nolan, bless her, was right at the front of the stage singing when behind without her knowledge appeared an arm from the side curtain belonging to Colin Bachelard attached to a firearm for the duration of the song, all around were on their knees belly laughing and she had no idea why. Absolute classic.

Mick O'Connor and I during rehearsals for the *Pyjama Game* having both jumped in the direction of each other we suddenly realised that one of us was supposed to catch and the other jump then we both like a pair of pantomime fairy godmothers met in the middle.

Where am I now

Linda, whom I met at LOST and was also in *Epsom Downs*, *Cabaret*, various one act festivals and workshops and I live in Worcester Park with our son Ciaran (26).

I work in Kings Cross at a leading electrical and mechanical contractor as a senior electrical estimator responsible for projects worth between 1 and 50 million pounds

I still sing, albeit with two choirs and keep fit by cycling, mostly for charity and we both use the gym. I also still love to dance and look forward to our weekly Zumba lesson despite snapping my Achilles tendon in half doing it a year and a half ago, all that Rugby and Football and I end up in plaster doing Zumba, only me.

A while ago I did a charity bike ride for Leukaemia and Lymphoma. The route took me right past the old building in Fulham Broadway and although I was on a time trial I had to stop for a couple of minutes, pause and just take it all in.

Great memories.

Regrets

Not many.

Only that I did not carry on, the whole world is full of shoulda, coulda, woulders and I am one of them.

Every time I go to the theatre I always come out and think I could do that. I know sad.

DORA BASHAM

It seems that most of my memories are based on props and scenery, costumes and make up!! I remember lying on the floor to fan the dry ice in Der Freischutz, and making balls with streamers painted with fluorescent paint so that they looked like fire balls when thrown.

Then there was double casting of Italian Straw Hat, where I used to come into rehearsal to find Phil trying out yet another outragous dance step with Felicity, which was then passed on to me. And during another double casting, Comedy Of Errors, where faith and I played Adriana there was an ominous silence which I bravely jumped in with dialogue only to find it was my error in the first place. That was also the occasion that I missed one extra rehearsal where my scene was changed, and was it difficult to catch up!! How I hated double casting, I certainly never did it when I was directing.

La Bohème was the first I did. My first opera, we didn't have enough scores and I learnt every one's part so my cues were all right and Cecil and Terry came round with a bottle of brandy to thank me for taking on the costumes at two weeks' notice.

I started to go the Coliseum and the Royal Opera House, as I so enjoyed my first one! After being in a musical Am Dram Group I had to give up seeing those to see lots of Operas instead. What a joy.

Tales Of Hoffman, where Faith flew in as a wooden doll and Derek supplied lots of curly wood shavings to put on her costume.

Turandot was never to be forgotten. Derek played the executioner and had to shave off his beard for the Kabuki make up. What fun I had with that, training the girls to make up the chorus and making all the head dresses and beards.

We had a great back stage team led by Derek and so many of the company were involved in the stage work and costumes etc. It never seemed that the stage crew were apart from us as we were so involved.

I always made sure when I went on to directing that there wasn't a 'them and us' feeling about the backstage and the acting members. It made co-operation to get the show up so much better.

I remember taking time out when *Italian Straw Hat* was revived to help Tony Boother do the lighting as I was intrigued by what could be done and had gone to some classes up in town. I had to climb up the ladder and the lights were on large grips which one pulled up and down according to the plan. Tony became aware that I was always tweaking it up as I thought a farce should be well lit!! This was done, I thought, surreptitiously by pulling the grips up behind my back!! But he noticed after a bit!

I loved my time with the opera group and made some close friends to this day. I know it wasn't your scene but what parties we had and the weekends at Theobalds Park.

We did *Lucia Di Lammermoor* I think at LOST theatre. The dressing rooms were in the basement with no exit to the street so we sent Phil out [he climbed out the back] to get the beer, which was hauled down to us.

I went on to do 102 plays, operas, musicals, cabarets, weekend schools, etc. Only MS stopped me in my tracks..... now I am in a large community choir which performs three concerts a year. I still paint and go swimming once a week. And see as many local shows as I can and occasional go to the Opera House.

I also love my computer and do art work, and cards and leaflets with Photoshop. Thank you so much for all the fun and commitment to music and art.

FAITH STRETTON

Thank you Cecil. You were a big influence on my life. I send you my love.

FELICITY GOLDING

I always looked forward to the first rehearsal of a Southgate show when Cecil revealed to the company his set design for the new production. They were, I remember, always working scale models - three dimensional and accurately designed for the Southgate stage. Cecil would spend time, in that first rehearsal, showing how the set changes worked and how much, or little, space we had to play with. As we marked out our scenes in rehearsal, we knew which entrances, exits, doors and walls were represented by the masking tape, chairs and benches. The model was there in front of us. As a bonus, Terry had a better than average chance of knowing where his soloists were for musical cues.

Cecil always recognised that in Don, Derek and team he had craftsmen who could understand dimensions and perspective and would always try to accommodate his artistic and architectural eye. The only slight confusion I can remember for those charged with converting the model's 'flats' and 'revolves' into an actual stage set was when Cecil announced proudly to one and all, that he had finally "gone fully metric" in his scaled designs – "one centimetre to the foot". Cecil's mathematical technique was brilliantly matched at the time by U.S. scientists, who when working on sending the Hubble telescope into space mixed up their imperial and metric measurements this wasting millions of dollars-worth of equipment. Cecil sympathised, "Easily done"; Derek, less so "Pillock!"

Nevertheless, his wonderful trompe l'oeil stage painting gave depth to scenes and his stippling technique gave age, for example, to the tired and worn houses of Seville (*Carmen*), the ancient crumbling castle walls of Scotland (*Lucia Di Lammemoor*) and to various Italian and Balkan village squares (*L'Elisir d'Amore* and *A Bartered Bride*): memorable and exciting visual experiences matched only by Terry's musicality and inventiveness.

GILLIAN PORTER

First Impressions

I joined Southgate Opera in 1980. I was keen to join a local group to increase my stage experience having got the singing bug as a child as a result of appearing in *The Pirates Of Penzance* (directed by Pearl Butcher) at school. A friend of mine, Daryl Greene who was a professional singer, recommended Southgate Opera as she had seen some of their productions which she considered to be of a very high standard. So I followed her advice and joined up.

My first production with Southgate College Opera (as it was known then) was *Princess Ida*. I remember entering (in fear and trepidation) the rehearsal room at the College and being greeted by a smiling Julia Popple. Immediately I felt I was in the right place. Another new girl that night was Pauline Rawe with whom I became friends and later shared a flat with. The other person I remember from that first night was Jenny Lilleystone (Cloake) who was very helpful and friendly. She was one of the principals and I remember being impressed when she sang by the power and quality of her voice.

Both Pauline and I learnt a lot during our first year with Southgate and not just about performing in shows! Some of the things we learnt (particularly at the Theobalds Park rehearsal weekends) I can't talk about as they relate to personal relationships between members of the group. Let's just say that it was a bit of an eye opener!! The weekend rehearsals at Theobalds were great fun. Yes, we rehearsed, but there was a bar, meals to be shared, games to be played and an evening cabaret.

Another surprise was that we were expected to make some of our costumes. Not being a keen seamstress I struggled to make my outfits. With no sewing machine and little experience I still managed to create my costumes which looked fine from a distance, but were tacked together and would not have withstood rough treatment. Pauline and I did upset a few people when we were included in the photo the local press used to illustrate their review of *Princess Ida*. We just happened to be in the right place at the right time when the press photographer turned up.

As well as being in a show the other attraction of being part of Southgate was the social life! Besides going to the pub after a rehearsal or a performance, there was always a party or some event to attend including weddings. There have been quite a few of those through the years between members of the group. I might add at this point that I met my husband, Tom, via the group. I shared a house at one time with Roz McCutcheon who sang many principal mezzo-soprano roles with Southgate Opera. Tom lived next door and although not an opera lover – he prefers pop music – we still got on! But the most important and eagerly anticipated events were the after show parties. Held in someone's house, starting about midnight when the set had been struck and the theatre vacated and very often continuing till dawn.

Our second show that season was Verdi's *A Masked Ball*. An opera I had never seen, but was made memorable by the outstanding performance of David Waters as Riccardo. He had a wonderful voice and was a charming man. For the ball scene we wore empire style dresses. Mine was a blue velvet evening dress I had been given by my sister. The neckline was too high so I altered it. Some months after the production (you guessed it!) she asked for the dress back as she wanted to wear it. I hadn't realised it was on loan. She was quite philosophical about the change and wore it anyway.

I stayed with Southgate until 1985 and from those later years the most memorable production was Rossini's *Moses In Egypt*. A rarely performed opera, but I don't know why as the music is wonderful. It was brilliantly sung and acted by a stellar cast including David Luck and Shirley Pilgrim. Every performance was a joy to be in and every night I was moved to tears! Cecil directed (one of his best I believe) and his idea for the parting of the Red Sea is one of those things that cast members still talk about today. It was so inventive and clever. Mind you it took a lot of rehearsing and some people never quite got the hang of it!

After leaving Southgate in 1985 and 23 years in the wilderness I returned in 2008 for Gounod's *Faust*. Some of the same faces were still in the group including Anne Golding, Ann Bourne, Jenny Senior, Allan Girdlestone, John Hardy, Colin Davis, Monica Sculpher, Jane Lichtman and Neil Cloake. It felt like coming home that first night! In some ways still the same group, but times had changed and Southgate had changed with them. No longer part of the College it had shown that it could survive change and recession and still put on a first class production with limited means. But the main reason for its continued existence is the people who run it - unpaid volunteers and unsung heroes who spend hours of their time and energy organising everything from the rehearsal tea rota to the hire of the theatre. We will have reached our 50th year in 2015 and our 90th production will be *The Mikado* in May 2015. Not bad for an amateur group that doesn't receive any funding!

GREG MANDRY

In 1979 I started my secondary education at the London Oratory School in Fulham. In the first year I remember the school put on a production of *Ernie's Incredible Illusions*. I had always been interested in drama even at primary school and so got involved. That was the one and only theatre production I remember the school doing until the year I left.

At some point during the 1st /2nd year, my memory is not that great, a group of fellow students started an after school drama club. I'm not claiming any responsibility for starting this club but I was certainly a keen member. The club ran from around four o'clock for about an hour and again I have no memory as to how or why but the club was run by, what seemed to us to be, a mad punk rocker called Tom Marty. Tom had unlimited energy and passion for drama and to us he was a god like figure. One thing Tom was more than anything else was a passionate disciple of a new drama group called the LOST Theatre. Later when Tom went off to Drama School his role was taken over by Mike O'Connor. Completely different in style and certainly no punk rocker (in fact a physics teacher) Mike shared one thing in common with Tom, like him he was a disciple of this mystical entity the LOST Theatre. At this point I think it's worth adding I don't remember if we ever paid for these lessons, they seemed to run because everyone involved was passionate about one thing drama – something that I just cannot see happening today.

So the inevitable finally happened I turned thirteen, the parents relaxed a little on me being out after dark, LOST ran from about 7.30 until 9 or may have been 6 – 8 but either way you get the picture and I made the leap to join the LOST theatre. I don't remember Cecil much from these days. I didn't really get involved with the politics of the place, but I remember that Mike and Tom who had taught me drama were here as an equal and I mean I had held these guys in awe and here we were taking part in drama games and lessons with them. And no one ever said "you are 13 and we are 20 plus go away." they said "what a great idea," "let's do that again" again something I don't think would happen today. Then the plays began, *The Threepenny Opera*, *Othello*, opus sketches, 1 act festivals and then *Juno And The Paycock* - more on that later.

In those days LOST ran at the London Oratory School and used its main hall as its theatre. The school's smaller youth centre was used for Opus sketch shows. *Threepenny* also holds some of my first strong memories of Cecil Hayter phrases like "Cue the whores" shouted at the top of his voice and "Tits and teeth!" shouted out at the dancers from the back of the hall, my school hall! If Tom and Mike were the disciples this was the real deal, this man was from Mars or something, a whirling dervish of a man. Avuncular, scary, dangerous... a Father Christmas in leather drag, an unexploded bomb, a drama messiah!

One of the things that also really stands out at this time was the tours. When we put on *The Threepenny Opera*, with no less than Ralph Fiennes in the lead, it played at the school yes, but also at the Riverside Studios. Another show went to the Questors theatre in Ealing and *Juno* played at the Irish Centre in Camden. Already the energy from this group, from Cecil, from the LOST Theatre could not be contained.

Our Own Theatre The LOST Theatre.

One day we all turned up at a usual LOST session and it was announced that there was a youth club in Fulham Broadway that had been closed down and the owners, the Methodist church, were looking for something to replace it. It could be our very own theatre. I know we had been given access to the Castle Club just prior to this but this youth club felt different. In what seemed like an impromptu moment (although in reality it probably wasn't) everyone decamped and off we went, like our own little exodus. This crazy bunch of theatre disciples wandering through Fulham Broadway to the Promised Land.

When we arrived in the space, a giant cavernous sports hall, like any new arrivals in a foreign land there is always tension and fears, and this was no different. Inside there was fierce debate about what this would mean for LOST and what should be done, while outside the usurped youth club youth, banged on the doors shouting "we want our youth club back."

We moved into what became the LOST theatre, the embodiment of all that was LOST and with it came new problems, not least running a theatre venue on a shoestring. Like everything, I guess having this base had pros and cons.

The Castle club went on to become a great rehearsal studio and despite its distance from public transport and the general main swing of things there were some great, successful gigs, events, poetry nights, I even remember fire breathers at one event, all helped by the fact that unlike at the theatre alcoholic drinks could be served.

Although saying the theatre was "dry" is not strictly true. Certainly among my immediate group of friends who were all still underage, it became our little drinking club. We could turn up with a few beers, after hours, rig some lights for a show, drink a few beers, listen to music... invite girls.

With a new theatre there was plenty to do... in fact there was always so much housekeeping to do. A flurry of activity saw new toilets put in. I remember painting what became the LOST café during the school summer holidays, largely it has to be said because my friend fancied Maria who was going to run it. I also remember putting up the lighting rig in the main theatre. Drilling holes through the steal supports and bolting scaffolding poles to the ceiling. I should point out that we were not structural engineers but school kids, James Quigley, Maurizio Molino and me and a few bottles of Grolsh lager. In fact we never finished the lighting rig because we dropped the last pole on Maurizio's head at about 2 in the morning and gave up. But what we did put up stayed up until they pulled the place down. One day again on a school break we were moving the curtain rail, a job that involved ladders, ropes, height, heavy poles. We had a knock at the door. A chap had come down from the council to check the asbestos? Okay fine we let him in and went back to heaving the pole up into position. The man walked in having changed into a full body, chemical protection suit complete with respirator and boots. He said it was "best to get these things checked out as we would want to have audiences in." LOST had already put on about three shows in the building. I never heard what the results of his tests where.

It was obvious that LOST was a cauldron of political debate and fighting from the get go. But I think this was because people were passionate about the place, the artistic direction and god knows what else. All that passion caused friction and, only to be expected, occasionally sparks. I pretty much tried my best to keep out of the politics but my "wake-up call" as to how heated this could be was yet to come.

Plays came and went, great productions, and I had the amazing experience of acting in many of them with so many amazing actors, crews artists and directors. Directors like Paddy O'Connor and later Patrick Wilde. Paddy was the brother of Mike O'Connor who along with Tom had led me on this crazy journey in the first place. I don't know if Paddy was the first to come up through the ranks to direct other than Cecil. And it wasn't just that he was a great director, it was also what he directed and his attitude. Paddy had directed *Juno And The Paycock*, and later *West* by Steven Berkoff, a play that was not without its own political strife at LOST but that for me had been a revelation. For me if Cecil and LOST had been about the simple fact that drama was possible and accessible for everyone (and for a 13 year old, the fact that arsing about, having fun could be called drama and people seemed to think this was a healthy pursuit for a young kid), Paddy brought attitude and relevance, which was what a 16 year old needed.

1986 One Act Festival

It cannot be overstated how this simple format "one act festival" was such a force for finding new talent in every respect, writing, actors, and directors. If LOST was measured by one act festivals alone the record would be amazing enough.

One night I was sitting with Paddy in the pub (and Paddy was by this stage a legend, I honestly feel that at that stage if Paddy had said we would do a play that involved jumping off a cliff the response from me and quite a few others would have been how high do you want us to jump?) and we were talking about directing. I had been thinking about directing something in the one act festival. Paddy said direct something; he said something along the lines of it being a baptism of fire, but that we, Maurizio and I, should go for it.

I called Tom Marty who was by now writing a whole lot of plays, songs and shorts and spoke to him. Tom thought it was a great idea he had the very play *Gone Fishing*. I spoke to a couple of actors Graham Machell and an actress who I won't mention for reasons that will become clear and we had a reading around at Tom's flat. It was a great success we had the beginnings of something. Well we thought we did, then someone came knocking on the door, we were apparently having an illegal rehearsal whatever that is? Against the rules. Anyway while we all sat giggling inside, a row had broken out on the doorstep in the middle of the night as someone, who again shall remain nameless came around to stop us in our tracks. I didn't think much of it but it was enough to scare the actress off and we ended up casting Marulla (can't remember her surname sorry) for the actual production instead. She was great, Graham was great I was 17/18 years of age and we had won the One Act Festival, but we had also had our first run in with what could happen if others thought you were treading on their toes.

From East to East

Winning the One Act resulted in directing full-length productions. At least one a year for the next god knows how long, until 2002 anyways. Full-length production, each of which would present unique problems and if anything, the political shenanigans, at least initially, seemed to intensify.

The first full-length production I directed was *East* by Steven Berkoff, which was also the last show I directed for LOST at the Edinburgh Fringe Festival in 2002. Along the way there was: *Bouncers, Conquest Of The South Pole, Greek, Ice Cream, The Devils, Milligan's War*, two *Bugsy Malones*, Edinburgh and Dublin festivals and countless productions on the London fringe and a whole lot of other productions at various venues, churches and parks. I had the pleasure of working with great casts, artistic talent behind the scenes, artists, designers, lighting technicians and writers.

New Writing

Contemporary work was always important to me, and nothing could be more contemporary than new writers. I have a real passion for new writing, and if there was any theme running through my theatre work it was always the new writing. I worked with Tom Marty for a number of new productions; *Simon Smithers* and adapting *Fall Of The House Of Usher*. With the under 16s group I adapted Spike Milligan's *Puckoon* into a stage play. I had the pleasure of working with Dennis Kelly directing one of his short plays. Along the way there were many other new writers including Adrian Page, Bryan Ryder. In 1996, 10 years after winning the One Act Festival I adapted *Milligan's War* from Spike Milligan's war memoirs, toured it under numerous guises before being invited along to the Dublin Festival an invite only festival.

Talent

It is one thing to talk about the actors from LOST that have gone on to do great things. But, for every one that did there were hundreds that didn't and some of these were great talents in their own right. But I think I can leave the eulogy of LOST's greatest actors to others. I remember one ex-actress stopping her sports car in the street. She thanked me saying that "by being in one of my productions she had learnt that acting was not for her" she was now a high-powered exec for a NGO charity, travelling the world, saving the starving or some such and off she went.

I want to say a thing or two about who we had behind the scenes at LOST. Because there was some great talent there and during my time directing at LOST I came across the best. Admittedly some of this talent undoubtedly shone brightest during their time at LOST, but a very large percentage of them you will meet working in the industry today. People like Mark Magil who stage managed so many productions for me at LOST, Patrick Wilde who as a writer and director has seen his work made into films and put on TV, Jo Nolan ex chair of LOST who I bumped into at the Cannes Film Festival and now heads up Screen South. Make-up artists, lighting technicians, James Quigley who as I write is off to some other part of the world to do yet another lighting extravaganza for some production or other. It seems to me that so many of the people who made LOST possible behind the scenes have gone on to greater things and I think you can put this down to the unique conditions LOST produced and the unique way you had to problem solve to get things done there. For me this is the true legacy of what was achieved.

Problem Solving

Putting on plays is a problem solving exercise. Plays at LOST where there were no budgets and little resources could often produce huge distracting problems. Sets, costumes, props, sometimes just getting actors not to mention some of the politics, would often cause problems and usually all of them together. For me facing down these problems makes the achievements of those at LOST even more remarkable.

For the very first show *East* it was so cold we introduced a rule that anyone could stop the rehearsal and we would all bounce or play tag for a while to warm up. I remember a cast member stopping the rehearsal checking I was still alive at one point.

Certainly for me the ability to problem-solve LOST style is something I like to think I've taken on into my video and film work. The amount of times someone says that something or other may not be possible and I always think this is going to need that special LOST approach. Even last week directing a promo, when no one from the production company had sorted out some relatively small problem pretty much brought the whole shoot in jeopardy. Thousands of pounds worth of equipment and labour was pretty much shrugging its shoulders and preparing to drive home back down the motorway – Seek forgiveness (if anything) never permission and "it can't be done" is not an acceptable option.

Ghosts

Just before they pulled the old LOST theatre down I was looking for a location for a short film I was working on. LOST would have been ideal, but it was locked and abandoned and awaiting the bulldozers.

I tried a set of old keys (not strictly legitimate) but they worked. So I quickly scheduled the shoot for the next week. We filmed in the old dressing room.

After the shoot I took one last walk around the building. By the entrance that the youth clubbers had banged on, where the Police had arrested some stagehand after he had stolen a bench from the local park to use in a play. Where we had locked the doors and watched the Chelsea and Millwall fans riot outside.

In, past the front of house where someone had tried to set up a listings newspaper. Where one actor friend had dived through the opening to escape a very unhinged naked actress. Where so many people had cued. Where the cast of my show *Bouncers* would eject me from every night because "my name wasn't down so I couldn't come in" (even though I was operating the sound for the show).

Through the café, which at its height had become a speak-easy with alcohol served in teapots and live music, and that I had painted so long ago. Past the gent's toilets with the two urinals because the third had been dropped. Passed Tony Conway's recording studio and into the auditorium.

The theatre was strewn with old props and bits of costume, I walked under the lighting rig we had put up some many years before, where as children we would drink and rig lights and listen to music and kiss girls. Where I directed plays, made films, built sets, held auditions, rehearsed, acted. Where we would party into the small hours. Where I met my wife.

I walked through into the dressing room where we had just been filming. Where we had posed for photos after winning the one act festival. Where as children coming of age we would sit on so many Saturday nights, telling ghost stories and drink beer and listen to music, especially when the theatre was too cold to sit in. Where we had put on so many costumes and so much make-up. Where the young, naive stagehand had brought her 10 tubes of K.Y. Jelly for the actors hair, not understanding why she had got such strange looks in the chemist when buying it. Where so many people, boys and girls had crammed into such a small space to change for a Christmas Panto. Where committee meetings would boil away hours of debate. Where outside a tramp had set up residence and who in a confused drunken fit during *Cabaret* had lamented after his once glorious leader, Adolf Hitler, who he had served as a sign writer during the war, leaving us all with an all too real example of how to do a Nazi salute.

I walked out passed the old electric room, with the power box that had its seal broken so many years before, so that electricity could be taken raw from the grid for some power hungry lighting extravaganza. Past the boiler room that delivered such little heat. Up the stairs to the Methodist Church, strewn with old bibles and paper. The room we would use as an overflow dressing-room on big productions. Where, when we had been doing a lighting rehearsal one Sunday (a big "no no" as no work was allowed during the day on Sundays) my friend, Alan O'Rourke had fallen through a panel during a Sunday service to the shock and horror of the congregation, and we laughed until we cried.

I picked up a few keepsakes, mementos of a coming of age, knowing that we would never see the likes of this place again. I locked the door and walked away on so many memories and so many ghosts. The building was razed to the ground within a week.

I really could pretty much write a whole book on the place. I've tried to cover what the place was for me because it was so much more than an acting factory.

Didn't mention what I do now, but if you want to add this? I am the MD of the Big Yellow Feet Production Company. So far I have directed 1 movie worked on others, made loads of promos, the odd TV Commercial - who knows one day I should do LOST the movie, but god it would be long.

I didn't mention you much, a little at the beginning, I'm sure you don't need a hundred people telling you that what you started and achieved at LOST was a unique and remarkable feat. Anyway hopefully a different perspective.

GUY SHIRM

I joined South College Opera at the tender age of 16. As I had sung in choirs at school and enjoyed it a schoolmate invited me along to join him at the opera group then rehearsing *The Golden Cockerel*. After a couple of rehearsals, some benevolent encouragement from Terry Hawes ("we really need tenors in the chorus, you don't have to be very good!") and Anne Golding

("Well are you going to be in it or not – as I need to sort you out a costume?") - I was committed, and remained so for the next 10 years (meeting my wife and actually starting a new generation of Shirm tenors as son Nick is in training at Guildhall).

I have so many fond memories of my times with the Opera Group that it is hard to recount them all but two particularly remind me of Cecil's unique contribution to my social life for so many years.

After actually finding I enjoyed being dressed in what can only be described as a loosely converted bed sheet (Can't really see why Anne had made such a fuss – I could have brought one of my own from home) and undertaking some convoluted choreography whilst singing Rimsky Korsakov and holding a large painted sheet of hardboard, whilst standing on a very temporarily constructed (i.e. wobbly) staircase, I was completely hooked. After the success of *Golden Cockerel* the company just went from strength to strength and it was on to the next masterpiece.

Lucia Di Lamamoor is one of Donizetti's finest and after months of rehearsal it wasn't sounding too bad. So good in fact that Cecil decided it should be seen by a wider audience, not just the burghers of Southgate, but also the citizens of darkest Fulham should be treated to a performance. Of course, without costume and scenery, which would have proved too logistically challenging, it was decided that a concert performance – at the fledgling Fulham Arts Centre was appropriate. Appropriate that is, until we reached the venue and our producer felt that although Terry's musical direction was certainly worth listening to, the fact that months' of rehearsals had actually produced a fully formed opera, it would be churlish not to give a fully sung - and acted - performance.

As most of my fellow performers tended not to be members of choirs and choral societies we were generally not owners of finely tailored dinner suits (the proscribed dress code for the Fulham performance). In fact Donald MacDonald (who was resident technician at the college theatre at the time) had probably never owned a suit in his life. Certainly the one he was wearing (or rather walking around inside) was clearly meant for a larger man. The evening began and for quite a while things went very much according to plan however the absurdity of watching a staged performance (including at one point a mime of a sword fight) delivered by a variety of people (and truth to tell we were a motley selection in those days) all dressed as if they were attending a smart dinner party became increasingly absurd. A situation not helped by the words we were singing, to see a 'Chorus of Huntsmen' arriving onstage (in full evening attire) singing a chorus that began "Through the woods we gaily bounded" was the last straw! Of course the pressure not to laugh simply makes the challenge of not laughing all the more impossible.

By the time we reached the latter scenes nobody dared look at anybody else in the cast for fear of helpless giggles. There were huge choruses sung by an entire ensemble looking at their feet for fear of catching another's eye, and groups of the male chorus who simply had to turn 'upstage' (which sounds so much better than turning away from the audience) to sing through bitten lips (it helped - but not much) with shoulders jigging up and down in ill-fitting jackets quite helpless with laughter – to this day I don't know how we finally got through to the end. Of course the audience were either too polite or just could not see the funny side and applauded in all the right places and made sure that our soloists were given the approval they surely deserved. That was the only staged concert performance I was part of at Southgate, a pity really because I really can't remember laughing more than we did that evening.

My second tale, appropriately enough involves an early production of *The Tales Of Hoffman*. Of course Cecil was determined to create an authentically debauched scenario for one of the scenes. He was looking for lithe young men (in those days I ticked at least two of the three boxes) who would be naked bar a brief pair of undies and subsequently have our bodies painted with (as I recall) a spectacular serpent design. Knowing that Cecil was both a skilled artist and a much experienced man of the theatre I agreed confident in the knowledge that my body would be covered in body paint and I would be resplendent on stage. Being one of the two bodies to be painted afforded what can only be described as VIP treatment. Rather than having to fight over the mirrors in the men's changing room (there were just two small dressing rooms behind the stage), we were invited to Donald MacDonald's private office (trust me it sounds better than it was) where a heater had been provided (it took a while to get painted), Derek Basham had prepared the body paint and master artist Hayter created his works of art.

The effect was marvellous and we were much admired. Towards the end of the evening I noticed that the paint was starting to crack a little as it dried out. I was curious that a product designed to be painted on a flexible canvas such as the human skin should not have greater flexibility and mentioned this to Derek. "There's a good reason for that", he told me, "The cost of body paint was more than the budget could stand – so we used standard matt emulsion!!"

Yes, my abiding memory of that particular production of the *Tales Of Hoffman* was the hours spent in a bath after the performance trying to scrape off my cracked and rapidly degrading undercoat, only to have to have it re-applied every evening. The body painting was still quite a highlight and I am sure others will remember the particularly unique greeting that was added to another cast members body where 'Happy Birthday Faith!" (whose birthday coincided with the show week) was adorned onto a cast member's behind – 'FA' on one cheek and 'TH' on the other!

HEATHER SHARMA

Hi Cecil, sorry for the delay! Hope your project went well writing about 'LOST'. I don't have much to say about it apart from I had lost the will to live the day I walked into the LOST Theatre, but walked back out again having regained my lost spirit. Working with you and Nick and Dom and the team really turned my life around and set me on a career path that I truly loved. Thanks for everything.

JAMIE BALLARD

In my final year of university, my then girlfriend, Tanya, introduced me to LOST.

She lived just off the Fulham Road and had heard of this hive of theatrical activity. They were doing *A Midsummer Night's Dream* and she wondered if I would escort her to the open auditions. I willingly walked her the few minutes along the Fulham Road as she went over her speeches, then waited at the wooden table outside while she went in to hopefully nail Titania or Helena. She emerged to say that it had gone reasonably well, but also that she had mentioned me to the director, that I was outside and would make a great Lysander or Demetrius. She was incredibly generous like that.

I hadn't planned on auditioning and so had nothing prepared! I began to get into a bit of a flap.

> "Just go in and meet him. This is where Ralph Fiennes went before heading off to RADA!" she squealed.

I had tried to see Ralph's *Hamlet* at the Hackney Empire whilst I was at university, but had failed to get my hands on one of the hottest tickets in town. If I was to truly embark on this journey of an actor, however, what better starting place than the youth theatre once attended by one of my idols.....?

I ventured into the theatre's dark corridor and then into the director's office. There sat at his desk was this beaming pixie of a man, with really funky hair standing to attention. We read from the play, talked about his plans for the production and he gave a little history of the theatre. He also mentioned that he was thinking of doing *Hamlet* in the near future....

At university I had done some Chekhov, Schiller, Jim Cartwright.....but no Shakespeare. Being welcomed into the fold at LOST allowed me my first real engagement with the text as a fledgling actor. Sitting round Cecil's table with the other members of the cast, or getting stuck-in in the rehearsal room contributed hugely to my love affair with Shakespeare blossoming, a passion that has constituted the majority of my professional career.

After playing Lysander in *A Midsummer Night's Dream* and the Maniac in the *Accidental Death Of An Anarchist* (directed by the brilliant Hannah Eidinou), Cecil asked if I would take on *Hamlet* with him - an offer I simply couldn't refuse. It was also at this time that the theatre's future was in jeopardy. It's home next to Fulham Broadway station was being threatened with demolition to make way for the new shopping centre's car park. As a result, Cecil called in an old member of the company to come and do a masterclass on *Hamlet* to raise awareness for the theatre's plight. I was, therefore, unbelievably fortunate enough to spend a couple of hours watching, learning, attempting and failing with.......Ralph Fiennes. We worked on the nunnery scene and the closet scene. It was an inspiring session and what I learned that day has stayed with me.

What Ralph got me to focus on was Hamlet's NEED. By doing this, it unlocked the argument and helped gain clarity.

> "The argument is the phrasing and it is fuelled by, the engine is, the NEED."
>
> "The words are there to make clear your needs. So they don't get lost in the noise of emotion, but, like a canal, your need, your spirit - whatever you want to call it - it goes through the words. It is like water in a funnel. You pour water into a funnel and it is contained BY the funnel - the need is contained by the discipline of the words."

Ralph didn't like to use the word 'emotion' and the first exercise he got myself and Ophelia to do was to simply say the text without any emotion at all - to just hear the words, to give every word its space, and to experience how they resonated with you. It is very easy to look at a piece of a text, a speech, and think you know what it's all about and to very quickly *put* an emotion onto it. What I got from Ralph that afternoon was that emotion doesn't really help or serve the text - but if you understand, locate and play the character's *need*, then by simply saying the words, an emotion, is brought about.

> "The NEED will serve the clarity, because everything is so important. Hamlet has come across this terrible

moral rendering asunder of the world and so every word he utters, yes it's dense and it can be difficult, but it's fuelled by a really important need to find the answer."

I was extraordinarily lucky a few years later to play Hamlet again at The Tobacco Factory in Bristol, under the direction of Jonathan Miller. From the moment I picked up the text and started working on it, the voices of Ralph and Cecil were there in my mind, encouraging me, focusing me. I owe a great debt of gratitude to LOST for giving me such wonderful experiences, introducing me to lifelong friends and for instilling in me the confidence to pursue my dream of becoming a professional actor.

I'll leave you with a line that Stephen Lee, another director at LOST, said to me after he had just seen my *Hamlet*.

> Stephen: "The gentleman next to me compared you to Derek Jacobi."
> Jamie: "Really?"
> Stephen: "Yes. He said, 'Compared to Derek Jacobi, he's crap.'!!!"

Thank you Cecil and all my friends from LOST.

JEAN BOOTHER (nee AIRD)

I have so many happy memories working with Terry and Cecil. Terry was always patient with us singers and freely gave his time in his own home to take us through our parts over and over again until we were sure of them. Cecil taught me all I knew about acting. I did not know what to do with my hands to start with, so Cecil gave me dolls to cut out of paper while singing my aria. I have a photo to prove it. This was in my first show with the company in 1973. It was *Der Freischutz*. Terry needed a tenor for this opera, so he asked me "Do you know a good tenor?" The rest is history. Singing duets with David Waters for example in *Lucia Di Lammermore*, was among the most exciting experiences of my operatic career. His acting may not have been of the best, but his voice said it all. There were funny moments too, like when the blade did not retract properly, when he stabbed me at the end of *Pagliacci*. (Well, other people found it funny!). By the way, my first entry in this production of *Pagliacci* was on David's shoulders. I was a lot lighter then! Cecil had some wonderful production ideas. Does anyone remember the naked Faust? I do. I was one of the Margueritas! We weren't wearing much either! What I grew to love about working with Cecil was the way the productions evolved. It was not all cast in stone at the first production rehearsal. If he saw someone do something he liked, although he had not told them to do it, he would say, "Keep it in." Everything had to come from the heart. Every movement had to have meaning. I was with the company until the late 1990s, and I miss it still. It has been great to see people taking leading roles who were in the chorus as children when I was playing leads. (Lee and Shirley are two examples) now it is wonderful to see Lee's daughter Emma playing leads and wonder of wonders my son, Stuart Boother has worked with the company too and even played opposite Emma. The producer, Martyn Harrison, who has produced for Southgate, has also worked with Stuart, and used to sing with me many years ago.

JENNY LILLYSTONE

I had been a soloist at the Royal Opera House for 10 years, but very young and attracted to Southgate Opera in the early 70's as I had seen their operas and the standard was very high and gave opportunities to study and perform roles in a small theatre.

The first opera I performed with Cecil was *I Pagliacci*. Other leads in their operas were in *Turandot, Queen Of Spades, Andrea Chenier, A Masked Ball, Bartered Bride, Eugene Onegin, Tales Of Hoffmann, Faust* and Terry's shows including *Comedy Of Errors* and *To The Woods* etc.

It is and was perhaps the best amateur opera group in the country and highly respected and the social side and network of friends has always been very good.

I met both my second and third husbands at Southgate Opera and Neil has been the musical director for (blank) years.

There have always been plenty of dramatic and emotional situations – an on-going opera in itself. Southgate Opera Group has had the lot: affairs, marriages, divorces, deaths and births to name a few.

Theobalds weekends were always a big event in the calendar and we all stayed overnight. There were big parties and music-making all weekend and fireworks on the lawns, although it was an excellent opportunity to study the opera and commit it to memory.

I remember one year when April Fool's Day fell on a weekend. Lots of tricks were played, but mine was the best. I crept down before breakfast and swapped the salt pots and sugar bowls around. The effect was quite startling and very funny at breakfast. The management weren't too pleased but I didn't own up and things were very relaxed in those days.

My solo singing has now taken a back seat but I have a large singing practice and teach the Chapel Royal boys for the Queen at Buckingham Palace.

I am still heavily involved with Southgate Opera Group through my husband, teaching some of the members and also being on their audition panels for the opera.

JENNY RUNACRE

My first memory of the LOST Theatre was going down there one day with my two young children, after picking them up from primary school about 3.30 in the afternoon. I had heard there was a very good little youth theatre in Fulham Broadway and I wanted to take my two girls aged about 5 and 7 respectively, to join them in the classes there. At this point the LOST Theatre was in the crypt of a Church on Fulham

Broadway, and the first person we met as we entered was Cecil Hayter himself -the founder of the LOST theatre, which had originally been the London Oratory School Theatre. Cecil was enthusiastic, positive, cheerful and very welcoming. We started chatting and when he realised that I had worked quite a lot in the theatre myself he encouraged me to teach drama to the young children who came there, twice a week. I was totally thrilled because it meant that I could work in the theatre which I loved and also have my two kids with me.

My daughters, Mariele and Morgann were totally enthralled with the LOST and started a relationship with the theatre that has lasted one way or another until the present day. It was a great experience for all three of us - as twice a week after I had picked the girls up from school we headed off to the LOST theatre where I taught a class in which Mariele and Morgann occasionally joined, but generally they went off to their own classes taught by someone else, and I taught my classes to the kids aged about 10-12.

I found it very exciting, it was the first time I had taught Drama regularly and I loved the perfect little theatre space. They had everything to put on great Shows. And everything went on, there was a Pantomime every year, *Cinderella, Aladdin, Babes In The Wood* - every chaotic extravaganza you could think of. There was always tremendous over -the- top excitement surrounding each production with kids contributing in every way. The Christmas Pantos ran right over Christmas and were always sold out. They were Pantomimes in the truest sense with the audiences joining in and calling out and everyone having a great time.

They also put on a lot of musicals, *Bugsy Malone* was a great success and there was lots of inventive makeup, dressing up, comedy and singing.

I loved teaching there and I loved putting on productions and hireling them. I remember putting on *Mr Pepperoni's Pizza* - which was a great success, *Dream Jobs* which had a few dramas attached to it and my favourite of all was when I directed some older students in Caryl Churchill's *Top Girls*.

One of the great things about the LOST Theatre is that there were so many people, children and adults who were involved in it and who are still around and in contact today. Several of them have gone on to do very well indeed.

The LOST Theatre is now an established theatre In Vauxhall -which puts on very interesting work. I love the One Act Festival - in which I have both directed productions, and acted in productions. But the greatest achievement of the LOST is how it has given young people of all ages a love and understanding of the Theatre that has never really left them, and that is no mean achievement.

JOHN LANIGAN-O'KEEFE

Life was miserable after my wife died in January 2003, but then my daughter announced that she was going to London to live with her brother.

"You can't leave me alone. I'll go nuts."
"I'm going."

A few days later I rang her back.

"What if I go to London in the Australian summer and work as a supply? We could all be together for Christmas."
"Okay."

I needed an ancestral visa but my grandfather had three surnames and, by a clerical error, two birthplaces, so getting the paperwork from Ireland was difficult. When I got the visa I couldn't get a flight out of Australia until after mid-January.

"Christmas by myself. No way." So I crossed the continent to see Mum, a former professional contralto. Her comedian gave me the number of one of her sopranos who lived in London - Andrea Whittaker.

When I moved into Finchley with the kids the first thing I did was to ring Andrea.

"Are you in a show?"
"I'm in Eugene Onegin."

Salivating wildly, I asked, "Can I join the chorus?"

"Come and audition. Where do you live? I could give you a lift."

The A to Z revealed she lived in the next street - in the whole of London.

So Andrea gave me a lift, Neil Cloake auditioned me, I joined the chorus and thirty-five hours after I arrived in Britain I saw Anna. I was smitten.

Six weeks later I manoeuvred myself to be her partner in the floor rehearsals.

"How old are you?" she asked.
"I'm 54. How old are you."

I needed to know because she looked so young.

"I'm (information withheld). No, I'm (top secret). I had my birthday last Monday."
"The 23rd of February? That was my late wife's birthday."

Two weeks ago, three years after we married, Anna came to Australia again and what opera did we see in Adelaide? You guessed it. *The Force Of Destiny*.

JOY MATHER

Memories!

Some wonderful memories of Southgate Opera -

The Secret Of Santa Vittorio written by Terry Hawes, was my first Southgate show – what an incredible experience! Directed by Dora Basham, the first act finished with Alan Girdlestone and Ken Forbes riding a genuine German World War 2 motor bike onto the stage – they put up a ramp in the green room at the side – the noise was incredible, the audience absolutely stunned! This show deserves another outing – the music was memorable, based on a true story of an Italian village hiding its precious wine from the Germans; would love to see this performed again. Also remember that the makers of Cinzano gave us some sponsorship in the form of cases of wine – which meant a memorable first night party as well as a last-night one!

Nabucco – and singing the Slaves chorus with our arms strapped to large pieces of wood – making movement difficult and falling on one's knees a dangerous experience but what a wonderful 'Cecil production' as were all the other operas directed by him – bringing out performances and emotions in us that we did not know we had!

Privileged to have had one of the main roles in the premiere of Terry Hawes' *His Excellency* – based on a libretto by W S Gilbert, the music of which Terry composed in the style of Arthur Sullivan. Another great Terry show. I remember on the Saturday of the rehearsal weekend at Theobalds, Terry told Faith Stretton, Stan Wilson and myself that he had written a patter trio – we went through it at lunchtime and he persuaded us to perform it at the concert we gave that night!

Faust – with a naked young Faust whose modesty was meant to be covered by dry ice – this did not always work at the right moment and we had to stand in the wings frantically blowing it in the right direction!

And orgy scenes – in so many operas – we became very good at those!

One of my first directing experiences – *A Savoy Grill* for SO based on G&S operettas and some years later directing *The Gondoliers* a very happy show with such talented principals and a lovely chorus.

So many memories of a company renowned for its wonderful productions, a chorus so good that it was known as the 'Southgate sound' and inspired performances.

I then turned more to performing in plays with Hoddesdon Players; for Alan Ayckbourn's *A Chorus Of Disapproval* we needed a beggar man who could play the piano on stage. With some trepidation I asked Terry if he would consider doing this! He did, and after many years is now a Vice-President of the Players and directs and writes the music for our popular annual revues. I have been lucky with the Players in having memorable parts from Lady Bracknell to Miss Marple but am now 'the other side of the footlights' directing Thomas Ryan in his one-man version of *A Christmas Carol* this Christmas followed by Noel Coward's *Hay Fever* for the Players in the spring. The experience I gained from working with Cecil Hayter all those years with Southgate has stood me in good stead when I have my own Director's hat on. I have to say that while enjoying doing plays, I do miss the overture!

JULIA NUNN

I can say my mum made Ralph Fiennes a cup of tea.

JULIA NUNN

She never got over it.

LEE DAVIS

Thank you to everyone over the years that have given so generously of their time to make Southgate one of the leading amateur opera companies in London. The company has given me the opportunity to sing many wonderful roles and perform with all my family.

Little did I realise at the age of 15 when I joined the children's chorus of *The Queen Of Spades* that I would sing some of the greatest soprano roles in opera, as well as make many special friends, meet my future husband, direct productions, and then be a proud mother watching my own daughter perform.

I have more memories of shows, parties and people than I could ever have the time to write down, but one memory in particular started my love of opera and my determination to perform.

After *Queens Of Spades*, I went on to sing in the children's chorus of *Turandot*. To this day, I remember every word that Turandot and Liu sang. Every night, I would sit and watch Jenny Lilleystone, my singing teacher at the time and now a very dear friend, make herself up, and then I would stand at the side of the stage for the whole show when not on stage myself, watching every move and listening to every word, thinking that one day that would be me. I never sang the role of Turandot, but I did go on to perform one of my favourite roles in opera, Liu.

LEON BERGER

Thanks for your message, Cecil. I hope you realise that you are the reason I persevered with an operatic career early on. I owe a lot to your inspiration!

LINDA FITZGERALD

Having heard all about LOST from both Valerie Bridges and Jackie Dower, I was invited to come along and see for myself what happened at the rehearsals. Finally, I accepted in February 1981 and went along with Jackie to watch rehearsals for *Epsom Downs*. I was rather overwhelmed to say the least. I quickly decided that drama was not for me but as I found the evening to be compelling, so returned again. Within weeks, I was cast as a bunny girl in the said play and also dating Derek. What a change for me in such a short period of time.

I didn't audition for any major roles in the shows but was a Kit Kat girl in *Cabaret* and got involved in the Opuses, helping with costumes and set designing. I recall a one act festival where Helen Salthouse was cast in a role but her attendance at rehearsals was limited. I sat in and read her part to help the other cast members out. With a few days to go before the actual performance, Helen pulled out and I had to step in and take her role on. It was terrifying!

I remember the rehearsals for *Cabaret* being particularly gruelling but great fun. It never stopped us from running down to The Harwood Arms to get a few rounds in and Mike Brady always had a row of drinks lined up for us. I wasn't as dedicated or as talented as Derek when it came to drama so I became less and less involved, completely withdrawing when I got pregnant.

It was exciting to see so many couples come together through LOST and many went on to marry - Jackie and Neil Percival, Mike and Mary O'Connor, Paddy and Lynne O'Connor, Gabby and Graham Machell and of course, Derek and I.

I think Derek has pangs of regret that he did not pursue his acting career but despite this, LOST did allow us to meet some incredible people and it is great to see how well Ralph Fiennes has done. It is well deserved and we can all say we knew him before he was famous!

The worse time for me personally at LOST was the tragic and untimely death of Seamus Martin. He was a lovely young man who probably would have gone on to bigger and better things but of course, we will never know.

I have good memories of the parties at Paddy and Charlie's flat in Baron's Court, parties in the pub and I can even remember Paddy's 21st party at Beltran Road.

I also recall falling out with Paddy one night as I came to watch a show. The front of house was deserted and as there was no one there to sell the tickets, I decided to step in even though I was half way through eating my dinner. In between sales, I continued to eat and at this point Paddy arrived and promptly told me off for presenting such a poor image. I argued back with him pointing out that it was not my role and that I was thinking of the company and doing them a favour. He would not accept my explanation and we carried on arguing, which on reflection was an even poorer image. Eventually, we did sort it out and Paddy realised my intentions were good and I accepted the image angle on the food. I was better prepared the next time I helped out.

Now I am employed by Wandsworth Council as a Business Support Manager. This means that I manage and run two computer systems for my section. I have worked for the Council since leaving school, which is over 33 years.

I am grateful to LOST for introducing me to some lovely people and of course to Derek. Given the amount of rows and splits we had, I am sure it has astonished many that we are still together, including ourselves.

Those days at The London Oratory School, Broomhouse Lane and Fulham Broadway seem a very long time ago now but they still hold some very dear and fond memories.

MANDY SMITH

I went down to a LOST workshop one night with Theresa, after seeing Seamus, Bernadette, and Joanna et al in *Comedy Of Errors*. I think the first play I did was *Dark Of The Moon*, as Conjur Woman. Julian was Conjur Man, and I've got a lasting memory of him in the dressing room, during the show, zooming round on a skateboard in full costume, reciting his lines just for the fun of it.

I remember being in *Opus One*, which I think was around the same time. Ooh, this is different, I thought - very creative and exciting. And I loved being in *Jesus Saves*. What a fantastic, innovative piece of work that was from Seamus. I remember he worked closely with Riccardo to produce some brilliant musical pieces and I have wonderfully vivid memories of the whole thing. In fact, I remember being generally bowled over with the stuff Seamus produced - *Just Playing* was a joy to watch, and it was a hoot playing the old woman in *Temporary Faults*, when Shay so cleverly had the character telling a bittersweet joke while her husband (played by Graham and Charlie on separate occasions) acted it out. One of several strokes of genius from a very talented young playwright and much loved friend.

I often found myself playing "the old bird" - Kath in *Entertaining Mr Sloane*, Meg in *The Birthday Party*, Nurse in *Romeo And Juliet*, Mum in *West*. So it was a treat when we did *Cabaret* to be Frau Schneider one night - a fantastic part, loved it..... but also to be a Kit Kat Girl the next night and actually get to wear a sexy costume!!! The set was dead impressive - beer barrels for tables, 1930s style telephones and all those vintage lights on loan from a flash shop on the Kings Road. How did you manage that? And the audience got into the swing of things with the alcohol from the working bar!

I remember being in the audience for Richard's production of *Threepenny Opera* and thinking "cor, this is brilliant - wish I was in it!" There were fantastic performances all round. The school hall was fab for those big, ambitious shows - *Epsom Downs*, *Othello*, and *Romeo And Juliet*.

Some silly/funny memories. For *Loot*, we needed a "body" for the open coffin on stage. Someone mentioned trying to get hold of a "Resuss Annie", and I had what I thought was a brilliant idea - phone the local hospital, see if they've got one. On the cadge, so be chirpy, I thought. So, I called the UCH reception: "Can I help you?" "Yes," I said brightly "I'm looking for a body..." and without pausing went on to explain we were doing a play and needed a Resuss Annie doll......etc. etc. etc. After a while I stopped for the other person to speak. Silence. It took a few seconds before I realised they'd hung up after the opening line!

Another one - during *Juno And The Paycock* with Paddy directing. It was one of those long, tiring, Sunday rehearsals. It was a serious scene where Josie and Fiona had to sing an emotional ballad, and it just wasn't going right. People were getting frustrated and the atmosphere was a tad fraught. Suddenly, from the wings, the barrel of a pistol started to appear, very very VERY slowly and eventually, unbeknown to Josie and Fiona, came to rest in direct line with the back of their heads. Perfect timing from Colin. It broke the tension, we all collapsed laughing, Paddy called it a day and we all went down to the pub!

Ah - then there was the "gondola" I made for *Blondel*! I'd been doing a Scenic Carpentry course and offered to make the gondola. I was a bit ambitious about my skills and too late realised I didn't have the foggiest idea where to start. Then Liam said "why not use that coffin over there?" (A small stage coffin down in the Methodist Centre?? No, I don't know why either.) That was the base around which I fashioned the gondola. Which had to move. And carry a singing Maroulla plus a steering gondolier (Simon). And Steve had to jump into it from a high rostrum and declare his love for Maroulla. Your face dropped when you saw it, Cecil, but it was too late..... So, there we are with a "boat" built for a very small person, sitting on a board with castors with a mind of their own, a "no-one will notice it" pole attached for steering, with 3 people shuffling on stage in it trying to be serious. I was a bit put out when it got a laugh from the audience!

Then of course, there were all the Opus's (Opusii??!). They were always fun and stretched our imaginations and creativity. Confession time, though - one of my favourites was at the Methodist Centre. No idea what the theme was, but somehow every other sketch seemed to be a song from Dave and Sasha and, yes they could certainly sing, but the general feeling was it was getting a little monotonous. I was overcome by a feeling of mischievousness and jokingly suggested to Danny that we could liven one of the more sentimental numbers up with a little spontaneous interaction. I thought he'd say no, but he was up for it. So we found a couple of old macs and woolly hats, and half way through this particular number, we appeared at the back of the stage like a couple of old tramps and did an impromptu "pas de deux," ironically in keeping with the song, and completely unnoticed by Dave and Sasha. It was very brief, 30 second stint, but the audience absolutely loved it. Sorry Dave and Sasha - it just felt so right at the time!

There are so many memories springing to mind now - all those weekends spent working in the Methodist Centre and wondering if it would ever be warm down there! The endless committee meetings. The after show parties and the unavoidable get-outs the next day. Some incredible and some not-so-great shows - and some of those wonderful moments that make your spine tingle when you realise "yep, that was special"...... Gerry singing "Sit Down You're Rocking The Boat," Ralph's audition for *Romeo*, Theresa's dying bit in *Othello*, Sasha singing "Summertime," Derek as the MC and Sean singing "Fatherland" in *Cabaret*, Sarah's "breakdown" speech in *Absent Friends*. And I know I've missed loads out.

LOST was such a huge part of our lives, we spent a lot of time together on stage and off and we really did live in each other's pockets. Wouldn't have missed it for the world.

After LOST, I returned to Hopscotch, the drama group that I and the Nolans and Theresa had been part of as children, and which sort of reformed. We even roped Graham, Gerry and Sean in on occasions!

I'm still in North West London, and I now work with schools running events for their students.

Really hoping this isn't too late Cecil, and hope all's well with you. Must come and visit that shiny looking new theatre soon!

MARGARET RUSH

I began a brief, but very enjoyable, period of teaching at Southgate Technical College way back in 1968 as an assistant lecturer in the music department. One of my jobs was to play for the rehearsals of the Southgate College Opera Group and so it was that a very nervous (and cold, thanks to the draught from the emergency exit!) young teacher sat at the grand piano in the theatre waiting for the first rehearsal of Verdi's *Luisa Miller* to begin. A young teacher somewhat overawed by the incredibly talented conductor, Terry Hawes! People began arriving, the nervousness grew until a 'heavily sweatered' individual bounced through the door and down to the stage, announcing himself as the new producer. From then on there was no need to be nervous...Cecil Hayter shared my first night!

I spent quite a lot of time wishing I could be on stage as I sat at the keyboard and a good ten years, marriage and two children later, I made my stage debut as the back legs of a centipede in Terry's adaptation of *Midsummer Night's Dream, To The Woods*. In the next ten years, I trod the boards in numerous guises, the most moving being as a Hebrew slave in *Nabucco*. Strapped to a horizontal wooden board, apparently facing death, made quite an impression and I've often quoted that experience over the years. Other particularly moving moments included Shirley Pilgrim's singing of Liù's aria in *Turandot*...a real tear-jerker. On the other hand, the vivid face make-up we wore for *Turandot* caused some consternation to an unknown driver at traffic-lights on the way home as I turned to face him!

There are so many incidents to remember, some of which are embedded in our household traditions. Terry wrote a great piece in his *The Secret Of Santa Vittoria* called 'Pass them on' when we passed bottles of wine to one another to hide them. To this day at family gatherings if anything is passed along the table from one to another at least three family members will strike up in song! Similarly, if anyone is particularly down-hearted, there is a chance that someone will begin 'Think positive' from Dick Whittington. Both daughters enjoyed their moments on the Southgate stage...one as a very blond Italian peasant and the other as a rat in *Dick Whittington*. Alan Girdlestone is still known as 'King Rat' to our younger daughter!

There are few societies like Southgate, where there is the balance between the serious and the light-hearted and a real mix of people. Maybe that's why I have never been tempted to join any other drama or opera group...the Brass Band will have to suffice!

MARK WILSON

So how many people asked you NOT to include things in the book??????

MATTHEW HEBDEN

I think the phrase life changing moment is over used having said that it was an advert in Timeout for the LOST Youth Theatre Co. that lead me from a 6 year career in the city to the steps of the Royal Academy of Dramatic Art.

I remember dragging my somewhat reluctant flatmate to a cold Methodist church hall in Fulham where we agreed to be part of Cecil Hayter's student production of *Dr Faustus*. In an even colder rehearsal room Cecil explained his unique casting method. We would all stand in a circle and on his signal one of us would randomly jump and (hopefully) be caught by the others. The signal came, I jumped and thankfully was caught. This act of momentary lunacy lead to me being cast as *Dr Faustus* in Cecil's show and 2 and a half years as a member of LOST including 18 months running it. The grounding I gained at LOST in all aspects of Theatre including sound, lighting, and set building, have been invaluable in my professional career as have the lifelong friendships forged there. Many of my friends from LOST have also followed me into the profession some like me as actors others as directors and producers but we all have that cold draughty Methodist hall in common.

Some of my happiest memories are from my time at LOST, of course it's also responsible for me being an impoverished frustrated out of work actor!!!
Matt xxx

MATT IAN KELLY

LOST Theatre played a massive part in my development as an actor, director and playwright. Importantly it genuinely helped to stabilise and mature me as a human being! It gave me some of my dearest friends who have remained with me to this very day. Unlike some of my LOST contemporaries, I had already attended drama school (ALRA) when I arrived at LOST.

I left drama school feeling fairly disillusioned with the idea of being an actor. This was partially due to the fact that I was still coming to terms with who the 'grown up' me actually was and wouldn't be able to move on as an actor until that was clarified.

My journey began with an advert I noticed in The Stage for a production of *Another Country*, a piece I had admired in cinematic form with Rupert Everett and Colin Firth. My audition was one of the most friendly and fun I have ever experienced. It was with Robin Chalmers who was directing and Justin Shevlin, who had already been cast as Guy Bennett. I was keen to take on the role of Tommy Judd. I did a Berkoff monologue - as was my default setting at that point - and then read with Justin.

I instantly felt comfortable with the two of them, but there was something about the dusty old theatre - the smell of glue and sawn wood (Cecil was building a set at the time. Cecil was always building a set!). It felt right somehow. I was cast as Judd and had one of the most enjoyable rehearsal periods that I can ever recall.

My first foray into 'gay themed' theatre! With LOST being so close to Earl's Court, which at the time was still a hub of gay life, this allowed post-rehearsal exploration of the pubs and bars and cafes of the area with other cast members. The two went hand in hand. *Another Country* and Earl's Court evenings. My confidence was growing at a pace, both as an actor and a gay man.

This was just the tip of the iceberg. As I was finishing *Another Country* Cecil approached me with the proposition of taking on the role of Mephistopheles in Goethe's *Faust*. He had been let down by a previous actor and said there would only be two weeks to prepare the piece. How hard could it be? I agreed and was then presented with the script! It was a massive tome which consisted of page after page of monologue. I had never before taken on a role of this enormity at this stage and felt slightly overwhelmed by its sheer size - let alone character work! However with Cecil's guidance and encouragement I soon found the key to Meph and threw myself into the piece with full gusto.

Both *Another Country* and *Faust* later toured out to the Redgrave Theatre in Bristol where I reprised both Judd and Meph. Therefore I hold both of these productions with high regard when I look back at my LOST period.

LOST gave me my first Edinburgh - *Much Ado About Nothing* as Don Pedro. My first panto - Widow Twankey in *Aladdin* - both directed by Steve Lee. My first Chekhov - Dorn in *The Seagull*. My first Ibsen - Judge Brack in *Hedda Gabler* working with Julian England. It allowed me to tackle roles as diverse as Arnold Beckoff in *Torch Song Trilogy* to Eddie in *Stags And Hens* to even Dennis Wicksteed in *Habeas Corpus*.

It has also lead to on-going collaborations with two gentlemen which I class as great friends and associates. Mr Patrick Wilde - who I met at LOST whilst he was developing *What's Wrong With Angry*. When the show transferred from LOST to the Oval House Theatre, I was given the chance to step into one of the schoolboy roles (still getting away with playing schoolboys on stage at that time). This led to performing with the show at BAC.

In recent years, Patrick has directed my second piece as a playwright, *Lightning Strikes* in London and at the International Dublin Gay Theatre Festival to much acclaim. We currently are working together on a yearly, on-going new writers' initiative with Greenwich Theatre - *And The Band Plays On*. We are looking to develop new and exciting gay writing/writers.

Secondly Mr Peter Bramley and I collaborated last year on a promenade/site specific piece designed for children and adults with a young heart. This was commissioned by Greenwich Theatre and led to the formation of my current theatre company, Powderkeg.

Patrick, Peter, Anthony Green, Claire Lubert, Emma Campbell, Rachel Hughes and Ben Jarrett are all previous members of LOST Theatre who remain very dear to me and all with whom I reminisce about the good old days back in Fulham on a regular basis. I am so grateful to LOST Theatre and Cecil Hayter for helping me find my feet and for providing me with some of the biggest laughs and happiest times I have ever experienced

MIKE O'CONNOR

My time at LOST - in its early days - was the best and the busiest of times, an age of foolishness and incredulity, of fun and also of hard work. We were all of us jack of all trades (building sets, taking them down again, selling tickets... oh and acting too), and master of few (knowing all your lines by opening night seemed like a major achievement back then). We were multi-taskers before it was fashionable.

I remember the all-nighters, when we wondered how we could possibly get the show ready on time (we always did somehow). And then there were the all-nighters afterwards, held at someone's (anyone's) flat (the details here are a little fuzzy though).

It was great while it lasted, however I retired at the grand old age of 25 (as no longer youthful).

MORGAN RUNACER-TEMPLE

I really want to contribute as I know LOST was such an amazing influence on my life now.

I came to LOST from the age of about 6 to 7 with Mariele my sister and was in many of the Pantos and plays. I work as a choreographer and dancer now – I'm sure I caught the theatre bug whilst at LOST all those years ago.

Memories of LOST Theatre

An Aladdin's cave hidden behind a church front I was 6 or 7 when I first started going to LOST, maybe even younger – so my memories of it are all quite fractured and dreamlike but incredibly vivid.

I remember the characters Annie, Steve Lee, Cecil, Melanie and Mark who were so bright and vibrant. We all wanted to be like them. I remember laughing so much.

I remember the dressing room, the ultimate dressing up box, abundant fabrics in different colours and styles, the smell of the makeup. I always wanted to touch everything.

I have no idea how many pantomimes and plays I was involved in at LOST growing up. But I know that it was being a part of these that planted in me the dream to do it forever, to be part of the shows, part of the spirit and team that is involved in theatre. I loved every minute of it.

I work as a choreographer and dancer now and almost every show I do I can trace an influence back to the days at LOST. The sense of fun, the spirit of just getting up and doing it. A sense of involving so many elements of theatre together, we sang, danced, had live music but also the involvement of real quality of the writing, directing and acting. Everyone was there because they LOVED it. It brought people together and made us all realise that anything was possible.

- Having a script of my own and a highlighter pen to mark my lines. A very proud moment. Real responsibility.
- Watching the shows from the window in the room upstairs during the Pantos in between our scenes... remembering all the lines of the lead characters and singing along with the band.
- Rehearsing the song for *Babes In The Woods* with the band aged 9.... 'if my friends could see me now' I thought.
- Steve Lee coming on stage with a bucket of water during a Panto saying the theatre was on fire.
- Freeze tag.

The LOST office. Another treasure trove of scripts and writing and ideas and plans and casting and characters and plays and music and singing and fun. One big wondrous world I'm happy to have been a part of.

NINA KREIDICH

How I have gotten to know about the existence of LOST Youth.

It was in 1999 in Saint-Peters burg. My school-fellow came to me from Siberia, more precisely, from Krasnoyarsk, a big city on the Enissey River. She was a teacher of English in the secondary school, and I knew some English words too.

One day, we decided to go to the Village of Tsar to see the palaces and parks of this ensemble.

We were standing on the bus stop after arriving by electric train in the village, when my attention was drawn by two gentlemen, one of whom had in the hand some map or guide, and they were evidently perplexed.

Those, who learn a foreign language and entirely prevent to speak it, will understand me: I came nearer to them in hope that they are English speaking people. Usually we begin a conversation with strangers by the words: "Excuse me, please …" and then typical English phrase: "Can I help you?" I had a chance: these gentlemen happened to be English from London and they were ready to accept my help. It wasn't very difficult to guess that they came in the Tsar village to see the famous ensemble founded in the reign of Catherine the first in the 18th century. We had the same intention, and I proposed them to join us.

When these gentlemen return to London, and one of them was Mr Hayter, all town got to know that one

Russian woman "picked them up in the street." That's why I didn't know how to look in the eyes of acquaintances of these gentlemen, when I, in my turn, found myself in London. All the introductions began by: "This woman picked me up in St.-Petersburg..." Fortunately, by this time I have already known that Mr. Hayter likes very much to joke. (At the end of my staying in London, I had a long list of English jokes and proverbs, which I appreciate very much).

Don't remember exactly, when I met some members of "LOST Youth." It was in some library in Fulham, where they were training learning the lows and rules of the theatrical art. I can't say that it seemed to me very attractive that first time. Then, I saw the performance of this cast in same school in Fulham too, if I am not mistaken.

By this time, I knew the story of this company: when it appeared, by whom it was created, what aims persuaded the organizer, why they were without their premises, etc., etc., etc., etc. More than that: I knew their dream to have their own theatre. My God, how Mr Hayter aspired to it!

It passed some month. By chance I heard about the festival of theatres which had to take place in St.-Petersburg in May 2001. To tell the truth, now I myself hardly believe that I succeeded to organize the invitation of "LOST Youth" in St.-Petersburg. However it happened and a group of young Englishmen came to Russia. I don't how about them, but for me it was a great joy and holiday. The children were housed in the oldest hotel of the city: "Octobrskaya," in the centre, 6 minutes by foot from the main street of St. Petersburg – Nevsky Avenue. They decided to show their performance of *Romeo And Juliet*. The judges didn't give to them the first place in the competition, but the audience consider it unjust. I know it because after the performance, when we were standing in the hall of the theatre waiting for everybody, some young Russians approached us and said how highly they appreciated the work of young Londoners. It was a pleasure even to me.

I hope the children and some adults, who were in this group, were leaving our country with good sentiments and souvenirs. May be, for the majority of them it will be the only visit to Russia. But we would be always very glad to see English guests in our country.

To finish this little article, I wanted to send everybody of the "LOST Youth" my best regards and especially to the youngest boy in the company, whose name I don't remember. If he read this article, I could remind him my words at the moment of parting. I said:" Tell, please to your parents that they have a very good son!"

And the last remark: how lovely that in our world exist till now such persons as Cecil Hayter who is the kindness itself, who loves theatre more than anything else and who gives his time, talent and love to children and to all who love theatre.

THE NOLAN SISTERS

The Nolans were involved with LOST from the beginning as Bernadett, Helen and Josephine were in the 6th form at The London Oratory School. Joanna joined Bernadette in one of the first productions when Seamus Martin convinced her, over one of the many pints consumed at the Harwood Arms, to audition for *Comedy Of Errors*, where she played Adriana and Bernadette's part in a crowd scene stealer character of a char lady brilliantly upstaging the main characters in the play. That was the lovely thing about LOST it was always fun and open to all - not just the school pupils. Before too long Mary Anne had joined along with many of our old friends like Mandy Smith and Theresa Drea joining too – Fulham became our second home.

As founder members they were instrumental in the move to LOST's first home in the basement of the Methodist Church on Fulham Road and have vivid memories of painting walls to transform the old church basement into a theatre. The Nolans have also taken on various roles in the early days of the committee, including Chairman, Treasurer and Secretary.

The whole family were involved in many productions such as *Cabaret* which saw the School Hall of The London Oratory being transformed into the Kit Kat Club. Mr Luke Nolan, the girls' father ran the real bar! Bernadette played Sally Bowls, downing raw eggs and milk whilst being very ill and on medication! The show must go on!!

Early productions included the many Opus Shows where improvisation was always encouraged and became a regular part of the shows. New writing was also encouraged and these shows became a great stage to show case new ideas. The Fulham Broadway *Choo Choo* (sung to the tune of *The Chattanooga Choo Choo*) was written by members of the group for one of the Opus shows *LOST In London*.

We think the One Act Play Festival was introduced by the family and gave Josephine an opportunity to direct plays such as *The Trial* and *The Laundry Girls*.

The production of *Epsom Downs* was particularly memorable when Helen played the Queen of England; Cecil had asked if anyone could get hold of a real pig's head for one of the scenes. Mr Nolan somehow managed to get hold of a pig's head, which definitely gave the scene a certain "je ne sais quoi."

We remember fondly Seamus Martin and his unique and fantastic writing skills and engaging sense of humour. Writing plays such as *Jesus Saves* and *Just Playing*. The latter being performed at The East End Theatre Festival. The play explored the fantasies of children through young adults' eyes. Very thought provoking and very well received.

Juno And The Paycock, directed by Paddy O'Connor with Josephine playing the lead part of Juno, brings back some fond memories of a trip to Ireland. After rehearsals one night, enjoying a few drinks in the Harwood Arms, Paddy commented that the only way we were going to get the feel of the play and get the Irish accents right was to have a trip to Ireland. Josephine and Mary Anne were in the production and in the pub (of course!) at the time. On their way back home from Fulham to Wapping they talked about whether their parents would allow them to use the family holiday home in Ireland for a week and take the cast there to rehearse the play. Their parents were delighted to be asked and were very happy for them all to go over and enjoy the use of the house and local pubs! It was a great week with many laughs and some rehearsing! The play was a great success and the accents and bond of friendships certainly benefited from the trip. There followed a series of Irish plays with favourites by JM Synge and Sean O Casey, with productions being held in venues across London including The LOST Theatre, The Irish Centre in Camden Town, The production Village in Cricklewood, (where LOSTs' name was seen in lights) and the Irish Club in Hammersmith.

Mary Anne remembers being in Peter Shaffer's *Five Finger Exercise* where Ralph Fiennes played her German piano tutor whilst she played the 14 year old daughter. It was great acting with Ralph. She was also in the production of *Romeo And Juliet* and played Lady Capulet. She recalls how Ralph arrived at the first read through knowing most of the lines for the part he played; Romeo. He was great fun to act with and always the professional.

Joanna went away to Brighton to study Arts & Drama and watched the talented team of friends at LOST go from strength to strength – organically growing and becoming one of the best and most talented youth theatres in London. In particular Seamus Martin was turning into a wonderful new playwright – she was blown away by plays like *Jesus Saves* and *Just Playing*. When she returned Richard Handsom was undertaking his LOST Directing debut *Threepenny Opera*; playing Mrs Peachum with most of the old gang in it – Bernadette remembers this production being a real challenge that we all managed to successfully rise to. Having been used to performing musicals to make a production like this successful was definitely a team effort. We had help from a local voice coach to help us prepare for our roles and two chorographers tirelessly managed to whip us into shape... although we think we totally exhausted them! The result however was amazing. Bernadette's part of Low Dive Jenny got her to new heights or should we say depths!! She often seemed to perform the let's say...more interesting characters!! Bernadette remembers we were asked to perform this at the Riverside studios in Hammersmith and getting a head rush when told she had to walk along an incredibly high platform which towered above the audience. She could only walk on it once before the production... hey ho the guts of youth!! Ralph stole the show though... when he played the part of the High Constable coming in on horse-back to reprieve Mac the Knife... he somehow managed to get this make shift horse to work for him and bought the house down!! He had a lovely way of saying – "outer Azerbaijan."

Following on from the success at the theatre of *Up Against It* and *West* – there was a real buzz and confidence and – lots of parties and all night sessions and planning the next big thing. Joanna remembers going back into the empty theatre late one night after the pub and rehearsing their Opus comedy *Nun* play with Gabby Grills until - laughing out heads off - the early hours...

Joanna also had a great experience working with Paddy on *Whose Afraid Of Virginia Woolfe?* – in fact she so got into the gin soaked part that she really did feel drunk after every show and was in fact breathalysed 3 times one night even though she had not touched a drop... thankfully... just shows how passionate we were about what we were doing.

We remember the first time LOST took part in the Edinburgh Festival and being astounded at the money we would need to put on a production there. After much fundraising including a team Parachute jump... only one injury!! In hindsight probably not the best idea but it did raise a lot of money... as did an auction where we all worked fiercely hard to get some good prizes which included Phil Collins drum skin (signed of course.. no mean feat) and Eve Pollards earrings !! Ah and a 24 hour improvisation... We performed Steven Berkoff's play *West* in the festival. Bernadette played Sylv, the girlfriend of lead gang member Mike played brilliantly by Graham Machell. We felt we took on Edinburgh and won thanks to Gabby Grills (now Machell) producing and choreography and Paddy O'Connor's directing. The boys were promoting the show with a characteristic walk to music wearing smart suits. This certainly caught people's attention and we were ready with leaflets in hand and information on the venue. A fantastic experience for a young, youth theatre.

Cecil was amazing really, as he was passionate about directing and just stepped back and let all these young hopefuls take over – his amazing knitted jumpers just got a bit longer as he sometimes pulled at the edges trying to hide his anxiety. I think he saw that most of the young people working at LOST were not stardom seekers – they were serious and passionate about doing plays and having fun and taking risks with friends.

Other productions which come to mind are:

The Rape Of The Belt

Grease

The Pyjama Game

Riders To The Sea

Playboy Of The Western World

The Threepenny Opera directed by Richard Hansom (The Nolan's cousin)

Birthday Party also directed by Richard Hansom

Entertaining Mr Sloane

Shoe Makers Holiday

Just Playing

Up Against It

Today, some of us are still involved in the theatre world, acting in local drama groups.

Professionally, Joanna is involved in the film industry being the Managing Director of Screen South; a regional Screen Agency serving the South East of England. Bernadette runs her own property business, Helen is a primary school teacher, Josephine is a nursery school teacher, Mary Anne is a company secretary and owns a brewery in Norfolk with her husband and two friends and John is the Duke of Edinburgh Co-ordinator for Westminster. They are all married and between them have 12 children.

LOST always brings back fond memories for them all and have made some lasting friendships during the time being involved with the company. It's still great meeting up with old friends and recalling stories and times spent doing something that we all love.

PADDY O'CONNOR

Like most 15 year olds, I had my life mapped out; I was captain of the school's rugby B team and was going to read Oceanography at University. Then Mike Ford (Head of The London Oratory School Youth Centre) told me I was to be dropped from the rugby team if I didn't go to a "rehearsal"- a direct threat! I went, missed training and Judo, met the strangest man I ever saw and loads of girls (most of whom I fancied-I thought "I'm in." I got my gang: Paul Yallop, Neville Pereira and John Morris (R.I.P.) to come to the 2nd rehearsal. Word spread, at the 3rd rehearsal most of the A and B rugby teams were there. We had enough for the Sharks and Jets

The Strange Man wove his magic and had us all spellbound for over a year, he was our best mate; we defended him from the mickey takers. Then it was showtime - four of the best evenings I ever had! After the "last night" we (everyone except the Man) went to Dino's Diner in Fulham Broadway Station and walked around Hyde Park till dawn; all of us in a sort of trance of agony and ecstasy - ecstasy 'cause the show was brilliant and agony 'cause it was over-finished!

Now what...? *West Side Story Part 2*, obviously. Nothing came of it 'cause none of us could write a note of music, not even the Man. So we did *A Comedy Of Errors* instead, which was even better than *West Side Story Parts 1&2*.

The Strange Man knew his Bard, none of us did; we couldn't get the words off the page at school- the Man made sense of it, moved it, brought boring Shakespeare to life in us. We could do anything now - No Fear! We were "Cecilised."

We thought we better get organised, so the lads voted me chairman (1977?), at something called an A.G.M., and The London Oratory School Theatre (LOST) was born.

We drafted and published a water-tight Constitution, with the Man as permanent Artistic Director. The Constitution side-stepped every legal downfall and survived a couple of attempted mutinies. We could do anything and everything, so we did. In no time we were pushing out a play a month, with a budget of £50-a fortune in the early eighties (a pint in the Harwood Arms cost 45p).

The Man couldn't direct a show a month; he had operas and musicals to do elsewhere; so he thought up The One Act Festival, to encourage us kids to direct, so at 19(?) I directed my first play-it bombed. I tried again and with the help of Ralph Fiennes and an offer of a free pint to Ed Pitt (the adjudicator), I swung it - I won best director. The prize: to direct a full length play- I did *Juno And The Paycock*-it bombed. Then I did *Straight Up*-it bombed. Last chance, I thought I'd try something easier: *Who's Afraid Of Virginia Woolf?* -it worked!

Since then I've dropped acting and just direct. Thanks to the Man, I now run my own am/dram company in the foothills of Sierra Nevada in Andalucia. As Steve Lee remarked:" You're just the same as the Man." I took it as the highest praise-I always will.

Lately the LOST Company has taken a different direction (to move with the times, I think) and a couple of Johnny-come-lately's have changed the Constitution, put out the Man ("Too old and not good enough"). In June 2013 the Man directed Tchaikovsky's *Eugene Onegin*; he needed a Pushkin (as you do). I was the nearest one that he thought could do it; I flew over.

PAUL ROGAN

My first contact with LOST was seeing a production of *The Birthday Party* by Harold Pinter in 1982 at the London Oratory, which was my brother Michael's school, and it was directed by his girlfriend's cousin. It was a terrific production, funny and spare, and beautifully acted. Even now I think that the company as it was in those early days was fantastically suited to early Pinter and Orton. The performers had a matchless and authentic London-ness to them, could do menace and comedy brilliantly, and were talented and charismatic beyond their years.

I joined in 1983, and had a fantastic few years performing, writing and directing. I think my first experience was being thrown into the one-act festival, performing in a hysterical 15-Minute *Hamlet* by Tom Stoppard, in which I remember putting clouds of talcum powder on a wig to play a Polonius so elderly he could barely walk. In the same one act festival I took over directing *A Night Out* by Harold Pinter, which won the award for best production that year, the prize for which was getting to direct a full length play in the following season. I was very lucky to have Derek Fitzgerald in the lead, one of the presenceful young Londoners I mentioned earlier. For the party scene, I recorded all the voices and sound effects of the party and had him miming and reacting and dropping in his dialogue alone on stage, a tough thing to do, but he was very convincing.

My first full acting role was in *Straight Up* by Syd Cheatle, in which I played a creepy dad. The play is like a Joe Orton farce, but written by a straight guy. Directed by the calm and brilliant Paddy O'Connor, it was a pleasure to be in from beginning to end of the process. The rhythm of those monthly shows – three weeks of rehearsals, the fourth week being production week, and just four shows, and then on to the next one, seems bizarre to me now. We never really had a chance to build an audience for a show. But the sheer number of shows per year was a fantastic training.

My first full-length directorial debut was *Alfie* by Bill Naughton, my prize for winning the one-act. I remembered the film, with Michael Caine, being very swinging 60's. But reading the play I was struck by how late-50's it actually was, so I kept that feel. (It was originally a radio play in fact, from around 1958 I think.) There was no glamour in the play at all, just gritty London truth. Gerry O'Sullivan did a brilliant turn as Alfie, charming and real. The character is just like many guys you see, who shamelessly try it on with every woman they meet, usually get rebuffed, but often succeed. The play had 18 characters, 9 men and 9 women, so lots of actors had parts. We built a set with two revolving trucks which became all the various rooms and bars that the scenes were set in, including a hospital ward with beds, screens, furniture borrowed from a hospital my mum worked in. A couple of the boys tried to "borrow" a park bench, but were caught by police while they were trying to undo bolts. Two policemen came and gave us a firm talking-to, but that was all. Phew. I loved the experience of that show. A wonderful cast, and huge production, great memories.

The following year I decided to go the opposite way from *Alfie*, which had had so many sets and a large cast. I put up *Absent Friends* by Alan Ayckbourn. One set, and six actors. Usually it's done quite middle aged, but I had a youthful cast, and I realised that that was really suited to it. I think the characters are younger than they are normally played. It is such a good play – I remember setting aside a lot of rehearsal time for the end of act one climax, which was very busy, with lots of entrances and action. But when we came to do it, we found that the timing was so ingrained in the script that it took no time at all to stage. Therefore we arrived at opening night very rehearsed and slick, which is good news if you're doing a comedy. I have uploaded it to YouTube if anyone is interested in viewing it after all this time. *www.http://www.youtube.com/watch?v=BPJlwhpoPFk* I'm astounded to find that over 2,000 people have viewed it! Sarah Chevis, sadly no longer with us, was a wonderful lead – a disappointed, betrayed, desperate wife in the classic Ayckbourn mould. The rest of the cast – Steve Requena, astonishingly mature as her cynical husband, Giselle de Siun, very funny as the gum chewing wife of fidgety Ben (Ayrton) Wellstood, and Mandy Smith, simply brilliant. Mandy used to ask me for direction, which I never could do because she was always doing exactly what I needed. This frustrated us both. I always thought she would have a fantastic career as a comedy actor if people knew about her. Sean Murphy was a perfect Colin. Relentlessly upbeat yet incredibly sad. My friend Tony Conway came and did a terrific soundscape for the show, which led to him having a long and fruitful relationship with the company.

Needing a place to put on a production of *Rosencrantz And Guildenstern Are Dead* by Tom Stoppard, my school friends Pat Wilde and Steve Lee brought their company *Young Mavericks* (which grew out of our old school Salesian College) to LOST. Once again I found myself playing an elderly Polonius in a Stoppard version of Shakespeare. Of course Pat and Steve went on to contribute immeasurably to the growth of LOST. Later Pat would further unify London Oratory and Salesians by staging *What's Wrong With Angry?* at LOST – Pat's landmark play was inspired by his schooldays at Salesians. I remember when it was first being staged at LOST, and Pat afterward in earnest conversation with Ian McKellen.

By this point I had discovered improvisation, and reading Impro by Keith Johnstone on the recommendation of Jim Sweeney. I started organising sessions at LOST, while also taking classes at the Comedy Store. We did a 24 hour impro fund raising marathon, and then a small team including myself, Steve Lee and Steve Requena ran an impro show called *Make Up* at the Castle Club for a while – Cecil was keen to have shows there – but because few people wanted to go there, the shows fizzled out. However, it was part of the process which led to my career in comedy, and which now includes improvising full –length comedy plays in the style of authors like Jane Austen, Dickens and Tennessee Williams with the group Impro Theatre, in Los Angeles (www.improtheatre.com). In particular, I remember Steve Requena managing to fit goats into his *foreign translator* sketches whenever possible, and it was always funny.

So many other wonderful memories...

Nick Kapica casually risking death by leaning off a balcony to adjust lights hanging off the ceiling, and delivering beautiful lighting designs time after time...

Cecil's amazing sets – I remember watching *Charley's Aunt* and being astounded that three jaw-dropping full sets had been achieved on the standard LOST budget of fifty quid. The terrific support crew at LOST over the years –and...

Maddy Carberry, Mairead Carty, Isabelle Thomas, whose calmness as Stage Managers helped me direct things, and everyone who ever helped out on one of my shows....

Cabaret, with Maroulla and Giselle, and all the joy of that production;

City Sugar, with Pauline and Christine and David Gifford;

Trips to Edinburgh to do the wonderful *Twelfth Night*, and *Tongue In Cheek;*

Arsenic And Old Lace, which was just about the most fun I've ever had as a performer;

Cherry Orchard – having a chance to direct a great Chekhov classic;

Who's Afraid Of Virginia Woolf? – playing George, with Jo Nolan as Martha, directed by Paddy O'Connor; and most of all...

The time spent with friends at rehearsals and in the pub afterwards, and the parties after shows. Most of my social life was at LOST for that period of time.

If anyone knows where any of the videotapes are, please have them all digitised and uploaded. I'd love to see some of those shows again.

Thank you to all of you I worked with and played with. It was a fantastic time in my life. Thank you, Cecil, for making it possible.

After LOST

I started doing stand-up comedy, and did that professionally for about 15 years. I continued improvising, acting, and voice-over. I now live in the US, in Los Angeles with my wife Justin and two daughters, Amy and Nicole. I still improvise, doing full-length improvised plays in the style of various authors with Impro Theatre, and I've been lucky enough to appear in a number of TV shows and films over here. I'd love to hear from LOSTies, and I follow all the Facebook threads avidly. It was a wonderful time, and reading the reminiscences of Soirai and so many others has me pining to be back in Soirai's wonderful café or in the pub with the crowd after a rehearsal.

PAUL TRUSSEL

I remember the first time I visited LOST. It would have been in about 1986. At that time I had been a member of Group 64 Theatre in Putney and was about to play Dad in their production of Steven Berkoff's *East*. It turned out that LOST had a production of that same play on as we started to rehearse ours. So our cast trooped along to see their production. 'To shamelessly steal the good bits' was how the director of our show jokingly described the reason for our mission.

Well I don't really remember if we nicked anything from their production but from what I recall it was an extremely good one. I loved their theatre too. Hidden away under a church, it had a slightly cloak and dagger feeling about it and despite a slightly musty aroma the atmos of the place was cool and sexy. I loved the auditorium too. Essentially a big black box, the sort of venue with enough possibilities to excite even my cynical twenty one year old eye.

There was an audition call in the *East* programme for people to be in Berkoff's *West* (Berkoff popular in that year) which the company would take to The Edinburgh Festival the following year. I secretly auditioned (not wanting to upset any of my Group 64 colleagues) and was delighted to land the part of Ralph. My first one or two visits to rehearse at LOST were a bit scary because in common with other drama companies I have come across it felt a bit cliquey. However I found a way of coping with it that might be described as the let them come to you method. Rooted in shyness but fairly effective. New groups are generally a bit more available to you if you display a little reticence about letting it all hang out, I've found. I still try to remember that to this day. Anyway I pretty soon felt like one of the gang and got on well with all the other chaps and one girl in the cast. The director Paddy O'Connor had an amazingly clear idea of what he wanted and firm but fun ways to get the best out of us actors.

As far as I remember I drove the yellow Transit minibus the whole way to Edinburgh. Perhaps someone shared it with me? I can't remember. We had a fantastic three weeks. We stayed in a lovely flat and it all felt very grown up and professional. The truth is that even now I look back and think that that was an absolutely brilliant production. I mean we were amateurs but the level of commitment from every single person was faultless. Let it also not go unsaid that there was no lack of very committed partying.

The yellow minibus died on the return to London and we pulled up outside the theatre in the back of an AA tow truck. I think that may have been the last journey the yellow minibus ever made. RIP old friend.

Back in Blighty I had no job and not really a clue what to do with my life. I had been fired from my job at the damp proofing company when I told them I was off to The Edinburgh Festival for three weeks to be an actor. So what to do now? A small group of other LOST guys had got their Equity cards (tricky in them days) by forming a theatre in education company and performing in schools. So with guidance from one of this other group (the irrepressible Steve Lee) I joined with Simon Hull from *West*, his then girlfriend, later wife, Sarah Chevis and other LOSTie Stephanie Ormonde and formed a company through which we got our Equity cards.

Having got my card I went on to pursue a career as an actor and last year, having been at it for some 25 years I had the honour and joy of getting to be in a new play both written and directed by the great man himself; Steven Berkoff. It's funny to think and it makes me a little melancholic that I got to work with this hero of mine in the end. Of course I owe that in part at least to LOST and of course to Cecil who was always discreetly in the background, keeping things on track.

It was at LOST that I first started writing, in their back office, and LOST afforded me the space to put on a one man show that I had written. It went down well and in 2007 I returned to The Edinburgh Festival to perform there a second time. Another one man show, written by me. I suppose I knew I could do it because I'd done it before. Twenty years earlier when I had been just a boy.

West

Lysistrata

Cinderella

Abide With Me

In The City

PETER BRAMLEY

In 1989, at the age of 18, I left my hometown of Doncaster, and moved to London. Back then local councils only gave out a limited amount of grants for people to go to drama school. I had made it through to the waiting list at Central School of Speech and Drama, but when a place eventually did become available at the beginning of September, Doncaster's grants had already been given out, and it was impossible for me to fund it, so I had to turn it down. I moved to London anyway, fairly heartbroken.

I loved the excitement and rhythm of the city. I still find London exciting. I drifted for a couple of years from aimless job to job; an office junior in Mayfair, waiter in a hotel cocktail bar, Our Price records, Tie Rack in Victoria Station...Feeling knocked, I continued to audition for drama schools, but with confidence increasingly drained and without success, and my life became further and further removed from what had been the one true love in my life; theatre.

I have always been driven by an insatiable ambition. It is sometimes a bit of a curse, because I have been in an almost permanent state of restlessness since I was 12 years old. Now in my 40's, things are pretty much the same, though the ambition isn't met with the same amount of energy as it was in younger years. I have seen many of my friends become parents, and watched their focus naturally shift, but mine has always continued to burn away. As I hit my twenties it was strong, and despite wild adventures in the city, I was unhappy. I had lost any sense of direction. The notion of having any kind of talent had faded into a distant memory. When you are not acting, you forget that you can. But I still felt a deep sense of need, and didn't know what to do. I was lost.

LOST Theatre first came to my attention in 1991 when looking through the small ads in The Stage. I was just desperate to perform again. My memory of details is fuzzy, but I do remember my first impression of The LOST Theatre on the Fulham Road... I wanted to clean it! It was a great space, a converted sports hall underneath a Methodist church, with a lovely café. It was better than any fringe theatre I had been to in London, though it was in a fairly chaotic mess. I auditioned for Cecil Hayter and Stephen Lee in a dusty, crap-filled, low ceilinged dressing room to become a LOST company member.

The earliest performance opportunity was to join the next 'Student Group' production, which was going to be *Arsenic And Old Lace* by Joseph Kesselring. I remember the first reading in Cecil's flat, which looked a bit like a Greek temple: filled with sculptures and theatrical odds and ends. It all seemed so exotic to a boy from Doncaster! I remember the whole process being playful and so much fun. I played Doctor Einstein with a bit of a terrible Peter Lorre impersonation. But it didn't matter; I was flying and loving it. I delighted in playing Canon Throbbing in Alan Bennett's *Habeas Corpus*, directed by Justin Shevlin, where I met Claire Lubert and Matt Ian Kelly, both of whom I count as dear friends to this day. All of this reaffirmed my desire to pursue a life in the theatre. I had been lost, but now I was found (naff play on words completely intentional).

Though LOST was a relatively brief period in my life, it was a fundamental one. It offered a fantastic opportunity to immerse myself totally in theatre. I was very hands-on, developing my acting skills, and also fulfilling some of my obsessive desire to clean and organise the place! It was a unique, fantastic environment; a place for someone like me to become part of a creative community, full of young people, all equally driven, with lives in front of them, dreams and ambitions. We all felt a sense of real ownership and belonging at LOST. Matt and I had ambitions to turn the glass summerhouse rehearsal space into a studio theatre. We began to paint the insides black, but didn't have enough paint and even less sense of what we were doing. That idea fizzled out as we shifted our entrepreneurial focus to creating our own cleaning and ironing service, which we named 'Scrubbers.'

LOST was the place for several 'firsts' for me. I won my first ever award for a devised version of *The Bacchae* at the LOST One Act Festival. I directed for the very first time at LOST, something I now do for a living; a student production of *Love Of The Nightingale* by Timberlake Wertenbaker. My first Edinburgh Fringe experience was with LOST; Claudio in *Much Ado About Nothing*, directed by Stephen Lee. We were one of about 4 productions of the same play that year, and we were in an enormous venue. Even when we had a fair sized fringe audience, it still felt empty. Disappearing into insignificance among all of the other hundreds of shows that year didn't really matter. We were having a ball! The experience was one I will always cherish. These days, I'm a jaded fringe veteran, but will always remember my first time as mostly joyful.

Having gained focus, I eventually moved on from LOST to study Drama at Royal Holloway and I didn't go back to that part of London for some time. Years later, when taking a stroll down the Fulham Road, I was shocked by a strong sense of nostalgic sadness to see a shopping centre where the theatre had once stood.

I've noticed several of my contemporaries from those days go on to achieve great things. Dennis Kelly is now one of the country's leading playwrights and Loveday Ingram's directing career took off after assisting Phyllida Lloyd on mammoth hit *Mamma Mia*. I trained with Jacques Lecoq in Paris, and since then I have worked in theatre, teaching, directing and ploughing that insatiable drive into my own company Pants on Fire. I'm the Head of Movement at Rose Bruford College working with young actors who, like me back then, have their lives in front of them.

I ended up doing some teaching at Central so many years after what had felt like the end of the world. Funny how things come full circle. Claire Lubert collaborated with me a few years ago, (15 years after our time at LOST) on a *Pants on Fire* project, and last year, after 20 years, Matt Ian Kelly and I worked together creatively on a project with Greenwich Theatre. We talk about LOST all these years later with great and genuine fondness....and wine. It was a springboard and a wonderful chapter of my life.

PETER PADWICK

It was a Sunday after lunch in the 1980's and the group had spent the whole weekend at Theobalds College rehearsing and preparing for their next production.

The afternoon had been booked by *The Sealed Knot* and they were marching and parading on the field between the New River and the college.

The opera group were preparing to leave and packing their bags in the bedrooms overlooking the manoeuvres. As the first volley of shots rang out every window on the south side of the building sprouted white sheets, white pillow cases and towels as the whole of Southgate Opera surrendered. Typical shenanigans of their twice yearly visits - when I was delighted to be in charge (as far as they'd let me be) and on duty.

PIERRE KACARY

I attended the London Oratory School from 1975 to 1982 and was involved in school plays either as a member of the school choir or else doing small roles, in usually a Shakespeare play!

I remember the LOST theatre presence at the School during my last couple of years there and was aware that they had continued to operate under the Methodist church on the Fulham Road, after I left school and studied at North London polytechnic.

Whilst studying I would pop into the place occasionally, when I returned back to my familiar Chelsea/Fulham home area and in 1985 I decided to become a member at the LOST Theatre up till about 1988; although I did return to watch the odd production at the Theatre up until it's closure on the Fulham Road.

During my time at LOST I remember going for drama classes at the Castle class in Broom Lane, which were run by Stephen Lee and attending these with Rachel Kavanaugh who has since gone on to become a famous director!

As for LOST productions that I was involved in, my first appearance was in production of *See How They Run* where I played the Policeman and witnessed the emergence of Simon Mendes Da Costa who took to acting like a duck to water!

Another production I was involved in was *The Shoemakers Holiday*, where whilst rehearsing for this show we all went out on a fund raising walk in costume to raise money for a production of *West* for the Edinburgh Fringe Festival. I have fond memories of the yellow 2CV plastered in LOST posters during this outing :-).

It was during this period that I became friends with Tim Boorman and Julian England and was involved in productions with either or both of them in *Three Sisters* and *What The Butler Saw*.

My last involvement in a LOST production was *The Importance Of Being Ernest* and then Tim Boorman and myself set up an independent group called Lemon Soufflé Dramatics in 1987, that put on a production of the *Rocky Horror Show* at Charing Cross Hospital, that was well supported by LOST members and contained a cast of mainly LOST members or nurses from the hospital!

The same show was then performed at the Bull and Gate venue in Kentish Town, with again Tim Boorman and myself involved!

There were no further productions from Lemon Soufflé Dramatics and my continued involvement with LOST, was my regular attendances to see productions, like the excellent *Sell Out* and many other productions like *Equus* and many of Berkoff's plays.

RALPH FIENNES

I first became aware of the LOST company when I saw a flyer for a production of *Cabaret* on the notice board in the Chelsea School of Art Foundation Department in Fulham. This was in 1981. My thoughts of pursuing a further course in Fine Art were being diluted by a stronger impulse towards the theatre and acting. I went to see this production of *Cabaret* (a musical that I loved) and was inspired by the commitment and youthful energy of everybody in it. Afterwards I asked how I could join or participate and was invited to attend a workshop the following week. I turned up at a classroom of the London Oratory School and found myself welcomed by the LOST theatre group. But the principle welcoming and galvanising force was Cecil Hayter whose brio and directness really inspired me.

Cecil provoked a generosity and openness amongst everyone. And like many other people who were part of LOST, I think some special spirit in Cecil produced a sense of excitement about putting on a play, developing an act of theatre. Many of us had ambitions to audition for drama school and Cecil was supportive of us but also benignly reluctant to encourage us towards leaving. I know for sure that without being part of LOST - and learning from Cecil's unpretentious and ballsy direction, I would not have had the confidence to audition for any drama school.

SARAH LODGE

I joined SCO whilst at STC as a sweet 16 yr. old and have very fond if slightly shocked memories of David Luck, Guy Shirm and the Golding brothers being quite inappropriately flirtatious with those of us only just over the age of consent (me and Lina Feraro). Still, no harm done and I re-joined after graduating at 21, and had huge fun and lots of laughs at Theobalds and The Southgate pub - the singing wasn't bad either! The group had one of the best reputations in London and the standard of production and costumes was second to none - I'm still disappointed when I sing with other groups and my costume isn't made or fitted for me by Stevie!

My fondest memories are *The Mikado* with the wonderful Judge John, *Faust* with the naked lead and the disappearing dry ice, fabulous cast, *Tales Of Hoffman* when the chorus were all dressed as whores, all the cabarets with wonderful Faith Stretton and Dora Basham, and the fits of giggles with Fran Macura - happy days indeed. Xx

SIMON HULL

LOST, but found memories.

It was the autumn of 1983 that the world of LOST entered my active consciousness, I had walked past the theatre many times on my way from Fulham road tube station on my way home from studying ballet and contemporary mime under the expert tutelage of Adam Darius, as I wearily got nearer the welcoming hot bath that was and is the refuge of the student dancer. My mother had been to school with the mother of Ralph Fiennes, and had been nagging me to go and see what it was all about, she'd heard great things of this youth theatre project, and it only took two or three months before I gave in to the avalanche of prompting.

These things could never be rushed in the over confident drama school wannabe.

When I entered what, from the outside, looked like a small set of rooms under that Methodist church, I was greeted, not only by a host of like-minded souls, but a groundswell of electric creativity. The production of *Cabaret* had just finished, starring, among others, the unsurpassed Maroulla Nicolau (now Wilks) and Giselle. Jean Genet was about to be shown to his full in a lavishly decadent production too. I felt that this was a place full to the brim with excitement.

I had come to see about auditions of a production of *A Christmas Carol* written and directed by Stephen Quinn (now an Aussie called Stephen Lee - still writing and directing). He was foolish enough to cast me in many minor roles; from ghost of Christmas Yet To Come to Mr Freddie Scrooge's dinner guests. The wife of that guest was a ceasing actress called Sarah Chevis.

It was a spectacular production, full of fun, drama, and extreme bouncing snowballs, that not only came back on stage, but also rebounded rather than splattered in the intended Victorian way. This baptism into the creative well of LOST, converted me, from an excitable over energetic dancer into an actor. Drama school still stood there as a golden chair to seat myself in and learn the craft, but LOST was a place to hone in audition skills and gain, much needed, experience.

The repertory style of LOST's year fulfilled my dreams of being an actor, the plays segueing into each other, *Once A Catholic, Saved, Blondell, West Side Story, East, Twelfth Night, Hamlet, Much Ado About Nothing, Macbeth, Lysistrata*, and so many other plays gave an insight, not only to the dazzling joy of acting, but also the varying styles of superb directors that LOST had in its ranks and grasp. Helping with the stage management of plays you weren't in were as much a part of being a LOST player as was helping to raise funds for Edinburgh tours and the seemingly never ending battle for funding.

It was at LOST that I made many friends, some I still meet up with, and some I miss dearly. It was that production of *A Christmas Carol* that first introduced me to Sarah Chevis, and I owe the world of theatre an apology for taking her away from the limelight and applause that she should have earned on a wider stage. In fairness our (yes Stephen Quinn was prescient in his casting) children will carry that torch of dramatic skill forward to a wider audience as they too start on their own journey on the stages and lonely audition halls of the hardest profession in the world. They and I can share what she will miss; the success of a Hull-Chevis drama heritage. Her too early death has fuelled and given extra strength and depth to a talent that is more than the sum of its parental donations. Watch out for them, they are on their way.

Words are cheap, they are easy to type and say they cannot carry the import of what LOST has meant to so many, for so long (certainly not in my hands). Many who have trudged the hard path of drama do not make the standard that brings recognition from an harsh outside world, but so many of the people I was lucky to share a stage with, a dressing room with, a smelly van up the great north road with, deserved the plaudits of having tried, having done it. Those of us who tried and strived at LOST owe it all to one man - Cecil Hayter.

Thank you Cecil.

SIMON MENDES DA COSTA

I arrived at the door of the LOST theatre having been sent here by a man I met by chance whilst queuing for coffee and cake during the interval of show we both happened to be seeing at the Questors theatre, LOST's well-equipped older brother from Ealing.

This man had sent me here to join up for a twenty four improvisation to raise money to send a bunch of his young actors to Edinburgh. Not quite sure why I was here or if I was doing the right thing, I nervously entered the door and promptly forgot the man's name. Panic, I like to be in control. It was an unusual name, I remembered that, not of this time, it had an aristocratic fey quality. I had it. Oscar, I said. ... Who's he? Came a squeaky reply .... Oscar sent me. I want Oscar. ... There is no Oscar here I was informed, which was true even though I discovered later they all aspired to owning one. ... Do you mean Cecil? Another equally young voice piped up. ... That's it I said. Cecil sent me. Little did I know that Cecil had a reputation for meeting people in odd places, top of the bus became a euphemism for this, and inviting them to join his theatre, which he basically said was run by the people. The young people. A collective with a benevolent disembodied older head, though not always disembodied. So I wasn't entirely greeted with open arms and later I understood this, as when you get your feet under the desk the place becomes yours and then someone else walks in with the temerity to think they can have a piece of this action too. However I now realise that it was LOST's ability to accept this chaos which was in fact its lifeblood. I was young and desperate to be part of something and it didn't take me long to realise that for the moment this was it. The sequence of events from meeting Cecil in the queue for coffee and cake with a vague notion of wanting to act to arriving at Bristol Old Vic drama school three years later was a journey I can only look back on now with envy and appreciation of what LOST gave me.

A twenty four improvisation has the benefit, at some point, four in the morning probably, of dropping the ego and glimpsing a touch of reality below – probably took me another twenty years to get close to that again. And maybe it was from that glimpse that I somehow got cast in LOST Theatre's first student production. Student production was at the time not a term I relished hearing. I wanted to be considered a member of the main company proper not a student. I was twenty eight after all and surrounded by people often ten years my junior. The 'proper company' had now vanished up to the Edinburgh Festival, I'd never heard of the Edinburgh Festival, I was a computer programmer, I had never even been to see a play before, a couple of musicals, yes, but not a play with just talking. And here were these people, so young, getting in a van and going all the way to Scotland to perform *Twelfth Night* which not only was a play with only words (actually there is a song now that I recall) but it was by William Shakespeare, I had heard of him, I studied him for my 'O' level's. It struck me as odd, later on when I considered this, to realise I had passed my 'O' level on a play I had never seen only studied. This was a world I had no background in but somehow knew it was where I wanted to be. Twelfth Night was directed by a man who seemed at the time to be a rather formidable character, Patrick Wilde. Although Patrick is now one of my closest friends who not only do I share a birthday but a birth date too, at the time this future blood brother was the nearest thing to the professional world of theatre LOST had. He was the man! And now while he and the main company were away I had an opportunity to try and impress and luckily I couldn't have been helped more because I was not only cast to my strengths but was to be directed by Cecil himself in a farce and Cecil is excellent at farce, I loved working with him. The farce was *See How They Run* by Philip King. I add the author's name here as a joke to myself because at that time I couldn't have given a fig for who wrote it and being faithful to their vision. All I was interested in was my bit with my laughs and my moments. I find that ironic now as I now write plays for a living and I'm sure there are people with exactly the same view of my work. It helps to be young and ignorant sometimes, so as Alec Guinness wrote in his autobiography, 'Enter ego from the wings' straight to downstage centre – it was very crowded there.For the next four weeks we rehearsed. By day I was a computer programmer, by night a returning soldier from the Second World War. For years I trod the line between these two worlds, money versus passion. While we rehearsed LOST belonged to the Student

Company and by the time the proper actors returned from their triumphant Edinburgh success I was under the illusion that this theatre was mine. They very soon, though, re-established their hold on the place and came on mass to cast judgement on the new intake of would-be hopefuls. I remember the moment, all too well, when Stephen Requena, the nearest thing LOST had to Anthony Sher, took me aside to give me his stamp of approval. I was in, accepted and here I would be for the next three years.

From *See How They Run* I was then cast in *The Cherry Orchard* by Chekhov. Nobody told me there were different acting styles and one size does not fit all. I played Yepikhodov, the character who has squeaky shoes, I was obsessed with getting those shoes to squeak, that's all that mattered to me. Emotional truth was a phrase I had yet to encounter. So not a success would be a polite way of putting it. Luckily though it didn't prevent me getting into the Christmas musical, *Blondel*, directed by The Man! Patrick Wilde. My chance to impress, however, was going to be difficult as singing was not my forte and keeping time my nemesis. I had somehow ended up being given a solitary solo line to sing and this was a daunting proposition. The line, I still remember, 'Sir, he'll tell you nothing but lies.' For years people sang it to me then burst out laughing enjoying the fact that I never knew when to come in. Surely you can hear it, people would say, listen Simon, der der, in you come. But I could never hear it so when Pat approached me in rehearsals and asked for a quiet word I assumed the worst, I was to lose my line. But no, not a bit of it he asked me to sing another four, a little ditty as a cockney newspaper seller. 'Extra extra, read all about it...' you get the picture. A character singing now that was different, a character didn't need to have a wonderful voice, and this character didn't, simple.

After another year at LOST I heard that Patrick was setting up *LOST On The Road*, a professional company, I auditioned, got in, gave up my job in computers and embarked on the road that I have been on ever since. This, however, is not a book on my story it is a book about LOST's. As Patrick once told us all whilst rehearsing *Hamlet*, remember what the play's called, never lose sight of who the play's about.

SIRI SADHANA KAUR (DEBBIE COLLISTER)

I chanced upon The LOST theatre at a tender age of 17. I had ventured to London to get away from a drug ridden teenage life in a seaside resort. I was homeless in London at the beginning, but met Andrea Daniels who was also new to The LOST theatre. She let me share her bedroom along with 3 others in Willesden Green.

From the moment I entered The LOST theatre September 1987, I was cast in a 2 hander scene extract from a play *After Liverpool* with Greg Mandry it was part of the One act festival. From that moment on and for the next 3-4 years LOST theatre became my home and a hub for creative exploration, it was my University. As is the tendency in the arts, when deeply immersed in your art, you connect so profoundly with the others that share your journey and experience, the bonding makes you as a family, almost inseparable! Many important loves and relationships were formed and broken. Many waifs and strays that hung out there became lovers, deep friends, mentors and pillars of inspiration on this unique and creative journey. What was interesting to me was the bonding that occurred despite the massive difference in people's backgrounds and upbringings. Those that stayed and worked at their craft shared a love and passion to make magic together, we were apprentices that often chanced on brilliance.

This period of my life was an intense experiential learning, coming from a huge lack in education and study - LOST replaced this and became my educational playground. I learnt from the great texts I was discovering for the first time, I was fortunate to play Masha in *Three Sisters*, Ophelia in *Hamlet*, and a witch in *Macbeth*. I was lucky to have worked alongside some very talented and decent human beings that to this day have a very special place in my heart.

Some talent just passed by LOST theatre never quite seeing its potential, whilst others committed blood, sweat and tears contributing to some skilled and masterful productions. The LOST theatre was in the gallows of a Methodist church, it never got the sunlight but it buzzed and came alive at night time with intense rehearsals and experimentation as artists chiselled away awakening their immense potential. It provided a great opportunity for budding actors, directors, dancers, musicians, stage managers, lighting designers, set designers. The LOST café housed many managers over the years who all bought their spice and flare to both the cuisine and environment.

Cecil Hayter was at the helm of LOST Theatre and was a beam of light, he had an elevated sparkle in his eyes and always smiled. He truly welcomed anyone who wanted to try their hand at something either practical or creative, what was amazing was really you could create what you wanted there, everyone had a chance to do something good, to contribute to a well-crafted project or show. It was a large space, a blank canvas. It was a place that you could carve out an identity of someone you wanted to become and be.

The local Fulham pubs were an intense and focal part of the rehearsals as continued analysis would follow on late after rehearsals in various bars or people's houses. When we were lucky and friendly enough with the bar tenders this often extended into late night pub lock ins.

I had a remarkable chance to play classic roles whilst diving deeply into personal healing at LOST. I played Anita in *West Side Story*, which top in my life as one of my most fun and moving experiences. The music is still a favourite for me, my world opened, emotionally, physically and spiritually. My soul came alive and I profoundly changed when I sang, danced and inhabited that production.

I played Rita in *Educating Rita* which connected me to my father and huge Liverpudlian family whom I was separated from as a child through my parents' messy divorce. At the time of the show I had been attending

Method acting seminars, and in the scene where Rita decides to leave her husband, I decided to use my father's suitcase as this represented a deep and important emotional memory in my life that I could draw from and use for my character. Many of my long lost aunts, uncles and cousins descended from Liverpool in support of me playing this role and were in the audience that night. All I heard from the audience that night where cans of beer being popped by my family badly disguised by loud disturbing coughs (there was no alcohol allowed in the theatre). When I entered the stage with my father's suitcase, my uncle shouted loudly from the audience 'hey she's got Kenny's suitcase' my family all roared with endless hearty laughter. It was meant to be a very serious scene! My father had become blind by the time I had met with him, and during the production he kept loudly and passionately asking the rest of the family what was happening every time the audience laughed. Meanwhile I was on stage doing my best to block out all the chaos and disruption. Meeting my family was healing and I learnt foundational tools in continuing no matter what!

What fond memories! LOST was truly special.

SOIRAI NICHOLSON

I first walked into the LOST Theatre in the early summer of 1986. I was 20 years old and working as a cook for a vegetarian restaurant on Fulham road. I had decided I wanted to be a theatre designer, and a friend had given me Cecil Hayter's phone number on a slip of paper.

I found myself descending the steps of a blocky 1970's Methodist church into the subterranean warren of dressing rooms, offices, and the huge dark space of the LOST Theatre itself. Stacked with rostrum, vast black curtains dividing the room and a scaff tower in the middle of the floor, the theatre had a feeling of creativity and possibilities. Steve Quinn (now Stephen Lee) had agreed to give me a lesson in stage make-up, and in a grubby back room packed with clothes rails, costumes and wide mirrors, I picked up make-up basics for the first -and only - time. Next up, a brilliantly delivered tutorial from Nick Kapica in lighting, about six of us crammed into the impossibly small control booth which teetered high above the rostrum seating. I think I was the only one totally enthralled by the multitude of cables, and the importance of coloured gels.

Around then LOST held an Opus, and I saw Steve (Requena and Quinn), Sarah Chevis, Paul Rogan, Pauline Meikleham, Stephanie Ormonde, Maroulla, Pat, Graham, Debora Collister, Simon Hull, Alison, Colm Lagan, Liam, and so many other incredible talents perform for the first time. I was gob smacked. It never occurred to me that this was a 'youth' theatre, everyone seemed so skilled, gifted and dedicated, and the shows were hilarious. Patrick Wilde as one of the directors and a dynamic creative, formed a successful touring company with a troupe of LOST's finest.

I helped out on several sets, spending hours with Nick stretching mirror foil over angular frames for the *Merchant Of Venice*, and attempting to recreate Cecil's brilliance (without luck) when painting brick walls for

West Side Story. Much as I loved the excitement of working from the top of a scaff tower, I wasn't that good at it. So finally, one day whilst half asleep after my dawn shift, Nick asked if I would turn the large front dressing room into a café. I think I was too tired to refuse.

When I look back its hard to imagine how fast everything happened. But that was the way with LOST, everything always seemed possible. Cecil had cultivated a place where young people could grow their dreams, or create new ones, and I was young enough to have no idea how rare that was but I grabbed the opportunity with both hands. LOST went to Edinburgh for the festival, and in the quiet weeks they were gone I built a café. I had raised some money by catering to the shows and getting a bank loan, and I bought chairs, painted walls (and even built one) laid flooring and filled the space with plants. Simon Hull built me a counter made of tongue and groove, and I was ready to go. I made flyers and a sandwich board, and advertised in the local paper. By the time LOST returned there was a welcoming, bohemian (slightly ad hoc) café which looked exactly like my preparatory drawings.

This was the period in my life when I had butterflies of excitement going to 'work' each day. When I would drink myself silly each night at the pub with the rest of LOST and arrive hung over and happy and ready to cook at 7am. I shared a flat nearby with Dominic Tucker and Heather, a gifted costume designer from Glasgow, and LOST was the centre of our lives. During shows, the theatre was always packed, having a brilliant local reputation and in between shows actors would drop in for lunch or a coffee, and a good long gossip. I knew exactly who was doing what with whom at any given moment and my lips are still sealed! I fell in and out of love with numerous customers and had the whole of the *Fine Young Cannibals* in the café every day for a week while they recorded at studios next door.

A year and a half after opening I decided to leave my beloved café in the care of my friend and fellow LOSTite Rachel. My main supporters were not around- Nick having left for university and Cecil being unwell, and my lively Wednesday Jazz Nights, glamorised by the sassy, sexy, Pauline Meikleham crooning huskily to the old upright piano, were attracting so much attention that apparently the church were getting nervous. To be fair there may have been the odd teapot filled with gin, or so rumour had it, which was against every rule! I was asked not to advertise or put my board outside. Passing trade was dwindling, and I had fallen in love big time and dreamed of travelling the world. It was time to go.

Those two years were some of the best of my life, and for us all it was a time of so much fun, creativity and rich possibilities that we have never forgotten it. Many of us formed our future careers and relationships around our experience at LOST, and our lives are immeasurably enriched. Thanks Cecil, and LOST. I love you to bits!

I wrote something.... now of course I am thinking of all I didn't say- the hilarious events around the otherwise very, very serious production of *Masterpieces* (Not hilarious at the time)- the WAVAW (Women against violence against women) booking out the entire theatre so they didn't have to share it with men, booing the men onstage, poor Simon! Who they accepted being there as a necessary evil, but only since they showed men in their 'true' light!! And then holding a conference in my café afterwards, stubbing cigarettes out on my new floor, demanding free cake because they were 'sisters', and worrying over whether they ought to be castrating their sons. Maddy and Sarah were grilled, and tried desperately to hold onto some thread of equality since they adored the men in the show! I was so alarmed it put me off lesbians for years and I didn't get that one sorted out till my 30s!

(But when I did- well, I just went the whole hog so to speak!).

STEPHEN DUNNE

I don't expect that there is anything I can add to your tome as a very minor player in the very early life of the company. I do however look forward to reading it. I was never a star nor ever destined so to be but I treasure those memories. That said as far I was concerned LOST taught me a lot about life. I met and got to know a great many people of whom I would have just been aware and for me it was an important part of growing up from a scrawny adolescent to a not quite so scrawny young man. You unknowingly helped me fit in and helped my confidence immeasurably. Thank you.

STEPHEN LEE

The LOST years

The LOST theatre came into my life when I was just twenty five years old in 1983. It soon became so much a part of my day: my refuge, my church, my school, almost my home, my place of pleasure, pain, torment and escape for the next nineteen years. It was a fundamental part of making me what I am today. I am not sure I am able to put into words just what the experience meant to me. And judging by comments and postings online from others who were also a part of our group, I do not believe I am alone in what I gained from working at LOST. I cannot speak for them, but for myself I wish to pay tribute to the vision and influence of one man...its founder Cecil Hayter.

Now don't get me wrong here. I am not saying working with Cecil was always fun. He could be maddening, stubborn, unworldly and tactless. Though I learned enormously from him, I also found myself in total opposition to his ideas on dozens of occasions. I honour Cecil not just for what he did, but for the atmosphere and environment he set up. The hugely exciting thing about the LOST Theatre Company was the fact that if you turned up with any sort of ideas or visions, you were given a chance to put them into practise. Not after a year or two, or in a small way, but immediately and fully. It produced one of the most creative, thrilling, positive and nurturing places to work that I have ever known. It could also breed anger, resentment, bad feeling and risk...but you can't make omelettes without breaking eggs.

What I would like to do is give a brief overview of my almost twenty years with the company. It is a personal view, and written solely from memory. No doubt I will get names and dates wrong, leave out important events or people, and mess up chronology a little, but if I can impart even a small taste of the varied and incredible experience it was, then please allow me a little leeway.

1979 - 83 My Life Pre LOST

I am not really going to say much about the setting up of the LOST. I was not involved at this point and I leave it to Cecil and others who were there to document it. LOST was born at the London Oratory School and eventually broke away from there and by 1983 had just set itself up in the basement of the Methodist Church in Fulham Road. Myself, I had left University College London in 1976, where I had been bitten hard by the acting bug. Since the age of eleven I had wanted to be a teacher, and had done little acting of any kind. At Uni I learned what a fabulous life the theatre gave. I acted, directed and helped run the drama society; and went on two tours; coming down from college, I totally revised my life plan. This was helped in part by an abortive year at Teacher Training, where I discovered I was ill suited to teaching anyway. Instead I had set up a company of my own (The Young Mavericks) outside of Uni with my friend Patrick Wilde. I had auditioned for the two year Acting course at Questors Theatre and went on to work in several plays for them, plus acting and directing for the Mavericks.

In a sense I found both companies were opposite sides of a coin. The Questors was big, well organised and had great facilities. Its productions were slick and professional looking, but (to me at least) seemed to lack something that would move or excite me. Capable rather than inspiring. Also it was not easy to make a mark at the theatre, many people had worked there for years, and directors rarely took chances on younger actors. In the Mavericks we had huge amounts of control (being our own company) but only a small limited number of actors to work with. We mainly performed Shakespeare, and here began a lifetime love of his works. Pat had realised the limitations of such a small pool of actors, and started to draw on other students he had worked with at drama school to augment the numbers. By 1983 I had begun to think of myself as a potential professional actor. We had mounted a very good production of *Romeo And Juliet* and were looking for places to play it.

1983 - 86 the Two Sides of
the Coin Come Together

1983

A friend of mine, Paul Rogan, had worked with the LOST a few times, and told Pat and I that they might help staging the play. He told us that the company were on the verge of collecting an enormous grant from the council (I smile now. We seemed to spend so much time on that verge. A verge we never once crossed). He told me of Cecil Hayter, and what an inspiring man he was. Paul also said he was staging a Christmas sketch and carol show at the theatre and asked me to be a part of it. I accepted and arrived at the LOST in December 1983. The show was a weird mish mash of sketches prepared by Paul (sub Python, a bit irreverent) and carols prepared by a guy called Tim Godfrey (very old fashioned and folksy). It was like eating beef and chocolate. Tim and Paul had not seen each other's material and as the show went on, they began making veiled comments about the item we had just seen as they introduced their own. Eventually these comments became less and less veiled until they were almost making snide attacks on each other in front of the audience. The tension even before the show was running high. I was introduced to Cecil Hayter in the coffee bar before the show, just as he was dealing with Tim about something. He gave me just about as much attention as you'd give an annoying mosquito. As I walked away I remember thinking what a rude and ill-mannered man he was...

Although I was not taken with Cecil at first sight, I loved the LOST playing space. It is long gone now, but anyone who acted there will remember. Though it was just a large gymnasium painted black, sixty feet long, thirty wide and twenty high (in the early days not even permanent seating, it was delivered each month), but it had one outstanding quality. While it was large enough to stage some very large and showy set pieces, it strangely still managed to keep a feeling of intimacy... and had the most incredibly friendly acoustic that meant a whisper could be heard. When I first saw it, it was still set up for the last production, *Grease*, with half an actual car sitting on a platform. It was a unique playing area that was endlessly adaptable.

1984

Despite my misgiving about Cecil, the young Mavericks staged *Romeo And Juliet* at the LOST. It was an excellent production, directed by Pat Wilde. Pat was an astonishing director, with the ability and imagination to produce first class performances. In a way this was not really a Mavericks show...most of our long standing members had moved on, and we had a bunch of one-off performances from post drama school actors. I played Friar Lawrence. Apparently it was a bit of an eye opener to many at LOST. They realised that they were not the only youth group producing quality work. We later in the year produced a joint LOST/Mavericks version of *Rosencrantz And Guildenstern Are Dead* which was equally well received. I realised that the Mavericks was reaching the end of its use by date, and started moving across to the LOST. Paul offered me a role in *City Sugar* and Cecil (by now noticing me!) spoke to me about auditioning for *Entertaining Mr Sloane*. (I think Paddy O'Connor was to direct originally and there was a reshuffle that left him in the cast and needing an actor for the Dad). I remember chatting with Cecil and he (with his usual tact and people skills) told me I played too much to the audience in *Ros And Guil* and was not a truthful actor. He then offered me a role! I found I got on well with Cecil and had many long chats with him.

Chairman. 1984 - 5

As I said before, one of the amazing things about LOST, was its ability to offer chances to new members. With many companies it is a long slow road before you are able to be accepted on a par with longer-standing members. True, university drama societies offer this kind of chance, but then they have no "old guard" (since people move on after three years or so). I think it is a huge part of Cecil Hayter's achievement and influence that the company, despite having many long-established members, was always able to offer new people these chances. (Over the years this became a bit of a joke. Someone would suddenly turn up as a director or to do Publicity for a show. When asked, we discovered they had "met Cecil on a bus." Aggravating at times, but very exciting...).

Now at this time I was twenty six years old. I believed with a passionate zeal that my opinion was always the right one. I still do to some extent, but the difference is that I no longer feel the need to ram this opinion down everyone's throat till they agree with me. I was also quick, intelligent and eloquent. I had many long chats with Cecil (often for hours into the night) about our ideas for theatre. LOST was at that time (still is to some extent I believe) run by a committee of young people. Most of them had been at the company since its foundation five years earlier. A talented young member of the company had recently died in a tragic accident. Cecil told me that he worried that the committee were too focussed on honouring him and losing their way in considering a balanced program for the whole year. I, with my usual passion, made a big fuss over this lack of objectivity. With a short time Cecil had convinced me to come onto the committee and plead this case from within. I did so, won them over, and within a few months was elected chairmen of the company!

So there I was, barely six months at LOST and chairman (this was well before the days of political correctness when we have learnt to call it "the chair"). Cecil's instincts were right, what LOST needed was a shake up to break it out of the mould of a cosy club of friends. With a bit of diplomatic tact and adroitness I could slowly open the company up to new ideas. In a few years it could become a different place. But I had nether tact nor subtlety, I was an arrogant, rash, bull at a gate young firebrand. I think I got the company to this new outlook in half the time. But in the process I made few friends and a bag-load of enemies. The old guard resented (and rightly so) this interloper muscling in and telling them how to run their company. Many of them made real efforts to bring me into the fold as a friend. I was not interested in this...I was out to change the world. I was probably the right man in the right place. What it cost was purely in human terms. I was aware that I was not winning popularity contests and this did worry me a little. It was hard to explain this to Cecil, who really never worried much about this aspect of things. At the end of my year in office the company had a very different outlook, much more open and welcoming. I think this change in the mentality of the LOST was what I really achieved in my year in office. I did have one very concrete change though. We were still finding our feet in the new building, and I persuaded the company to have a door knocked through between our office and an old lumber room, giving us far more office space and a darkroom. This turned out to be such an important move, giving us an office which allowed space to work, but also space to sit in and chat. This sitting and chatting in the office became a crucial aspect of life in the LOST over the next fifteen years.

To The Woods 1984

Although my abrasive arrogance was clearly to blame for some of the lack of warmth, another real problem was in an artistic sphere. I had directed a play for the theatre's One Act Festival which was a cut down version of *The Taming Of The Shrew*. I believe I did an exceptional job, even though I did not win. Cecil thought so too, and offered me a chance to direct the big yearly musical (see how the man works) a semi operatic version of *A Midsummer Night's Dream* called *To The Woods*. I had been directing for only six years, but of course I thought I was the next Peter Hall. I decided to produce the play set in the Wild West with the fairies as Native American spirits. Many of the stalwart members of the company avoided this production. They did not like the piece, and did not really want to work with me. I had never seen a LOST musical, or directed anything like this myself, so I was aware that the standard was variable (I had a number of fabulous people, but a large group of far less talented ones) and I just assumed this is what a LOST musical was meant to be like. If I were directing it now, I would simply refuse to put on the play without further auditions. Several times I told Cecil that I was in big trouble and out of my depth. He just laughed. He later told me he thought I was being modest! He did at last come and see a late run through. He sat me down in the office, and I asked him what I might be able to do. He suggested that my best bet was to tell the cast to do the opposite of every note I had given them! It was a gutting, terrible moment, and even though the eventual production had some fabulous scenes, and excellent ideas, the execution of many parts of it was woeful, and it took years for my reputation at the company to recover from it.

As a little coda to this story, eighteen years later I was asked to direct a play for LOST at the Edinburgh Festival in 2002. This was to be my final production before emigrating to Australia. I chose to do *To The Woods* again, and produced it with exactly the same set of ideas - Wild West etc. I had an excellent cast, and a lot more experience. It was a resounding success. It is really impossible to explain just how much pleasure that gave me...

1985

Although I rather arrogantly compared myself to be Peter Hall earlier, it has to be admitted that my friend Patrick Wilde really was a young Peter Brook. His plays were exciting, daring, imaginative and powerful, and personally he has a charisma just a notch down from God's. Once I was established at LOST I tried to persuade him to come and direct for us (already it was "us"). He agreed, and produced a stunning version of *Henry IV Part One* with myself as Falstaff. History does tend to exaggerate both faults and successes, but in my opinion the company never produced a better production in all my time with them (and we produced quite a number of stunning plays).

It was an imaginative resetting of the story into World War Two, and unlike my *To The Woods* the execution and casting fully matched the ideas.

In fact 1985 became a something of a golden year for the company. Not only was it opening out in numbers, and laying down the roots for its future success, but it was also turning out a number of excellent productions. apart from Pat's *Henry IV* there was an excellent *Who's Afraid Of Virginia Wolfe?* directed by Paddy O'Connor (one of the earliest members of the company); Cecil directed a spirited and beautiful looking *Charley's Aunt*; *Absent Friends; The Boys In The Band*; Cecil's *Cabaret* and my own *A Christmas Carol* (variable performances but an astonishingly lovely setting). We also staged a world premiere of a Jo Orton screenplay, written for the Beatles but never used - *Up Against It*.

There was also Paddy's production of *West* by Steven Berkoff. For sheer technical slickness and style this was an amazing production. It is a play about gang fighting in west London performed in quasi Shakespearian dialogue. This was a riveting version, which though I thought it lacked warmth and heart, this really was the nature of Berkoff's play and did not in any way detract from the powerhouse playing Paddy gave it. This production led to a major row. It had been so well received that Paddy requested that LOST stage it again later in the year at another venue. This would probably have passed through committee without anyone questioning it. I put forward the argument that we already had a full year's programme and that staging a play away from LOST would put a strain on our limited pool of actors and technical staff. All good points, but I think today I would be less confrontational. All these matters could have been discussed with Paddy outside committee. The problem was that Paddy built a fierce loyalty to the production inside all his companies, and I think that sometimes grated against my desire to have us loyal to LOST above all else.

In any case we voted the idea down. Cecil had not been at the early part of the meeting. When he arrived he insisted we open it up for discussion again. We did so (to me, nothing decided at committee ever felt right unless Cecil was there). A second time it was voted down, and Cecil, to his huge credit, as he often did, went with the will of the company. At the close of the meeting we discussed going to the company's local pub. This was some distance away, near the London Oratory School, and had been the local of the old guard members for years. No one on the committee fancied facing up to the members of Paddy's company who would all be there. I felt that not to go would be cowardly and went alone. It was fairly horrible...a good deal of veiled hostility, but several people made the point that it was a committee decision and that I could not bear all the blame. In many ways it was a turning point for me. Not that everyone suddenly liked and respected me (life is not a Disney movie) but that after that evening, nothing I faced in the company could ever be harder or more challenging than walking into that pub. And anyway, slowly the composition of LOST was changing as new members arrived.

One final point about 1985. One night, as I was working late, alone in the theatre (I cannot for the life of me remember on what), I heard a sound of someone rattling the locked door to the street. As any of the many who spent late nights at LOST can attest, a deserted theatre is a creepy place (one group of costume sewers actually called in the police with sniffer dogs because they were sure someone was hiding in the theatre space). I left the office and walked through the foyer to the doors I unlocked them and looked out, just in time to see a girl vanishing up the stairs to the street. I ran after her and asked what she wanted. It was a young lady of eighteen or so, and she was interested in finding out about us. She was very shy, and I got the feeling she would have preferred it if I had not called her back. Her name was Tracy Sable, and she later went on to become a major part of the organisation of the company. I often wonder how her life, and LOST's too, might have differed if I had not taken the trouble to run after her. So much of what happens to us turns on such small chances as these.

In fact Cecil's policy of giving chances to anyone who was willing (and often if they weren't) meant that we had a large number of people in administrative capacities over the years. A list of names means little to anyone who cannot, as I can, remember the faces and the stories that went with them, but nods should go to the people, some chairmen, some just admin, who have steered the company over the years: Tracy; Tony Conway; Robin Chalmers; Frances; Karl and Mark; Maurizio Molino; Dominic Tucker; Anthony Green; Kevin O'Sullivan; Mark Magill; Julian England....and of course Nick Kapica.

Nick Kapica

My first memory of Nick is that it was he who helped in carrying out my plan of knocking a door into the inner office. He took over as chairman and hit the company like a whirlwind. He built a lighting gallery in the theatre and made dozens of minor changes. He dealt with the repercussions of the *West* affair brilliantly. When a letter arrived from some of the company, pointing out that under the constitution if they achieved a certain number of signatures they had a right to put forward a vote of no confidence in the committee. At this point I might have just taken them on and put it to the vote, Nick merely checked the records and pointed out that a large number of their signatories had not paid membership for ages and so were ineligible to send such a letter! It was largely due to Nick (and Dominic his assistant) that we started touring to the Edinburgh Festival and opened up our green room into a coffee bar. He also built my superb set for *A Christmas Carol*. This set had an upper platform of scaffolding, stairs running up to it, entrances under it, and a street lamp over it, and all covered with snow. To illustrate the direct way Nick dealt with problems, I remember several cast members complaining that the backstage entrances under the platform were too low and they hit their heads. I passed this on to Nick, but could not see how it could be solved...raising the whole platform would have meant major work. Nick said he'd deal with it, no problem. The next day we came in and the set was just the same...except for several big signs saying MIND YOUR HEAD. Genius.

For me, the biggest problem with Nick was actually nothing to do with him at all. When I say that I understood how the old guard of the company felt a bit put out when I came, I speak from experience. Cecil hailed

Nick as the new Golden Boy of the company. In fact he hailed him to a degree that left me (and a number of others) feeling very unappreciated for all the work we had done. It did not help that Nick, unlike me, was not in the least arrogant about himself. He always discussed and valued anyone's contribution. Which made it even harder to feel any resentment - except that I know I did. None of this is his fault. But when Cecil instituted the Nick Kapica award for services to LOST above and beyond the call of duty only to be awarded in exceptional cases (first winner Nick Kapica), I felt very much like leaving LOST for good. I am glad I didn't, and I later went on to win the Nick Kapica award myself. He got his through brilliance, mine through sheer persistence, but I am happy with that.

1986

This was another excellent year for the company with many fine productions: We had now got into the swing of a production at the end of each month (sometimes just a review show, which we called an Opus, one month each year, our One Act Festival). We now always had one show performing and a second in rehearsal at all times. Happy days:

The Maids by Genet. Very well performed but the director had this clever idea of having live "dummies' sitting in chairs throughout the performance. I agreed to do a couple of nights of this. After just twenty minutes sitting stock still I was in sheer hell. There was just one ten second blackout in the play. Utter torture. I made sure I never did the second show.

Once A Catholic by Mary O'Malley was a fine production by Pat Wilde. As happened a lot at LOST, I played a sixty year old man.

Guerrila Tactics directed by Adrian Brown. I was originally cast in this but had to pull out because of a professional play (yay!). This was the legendary play where the director realised an actress could not see a vital prop bag, and called out during the show "It's under the sofa, dear!"

When Did You Last See My Mother? Of course all these views are merely personal opinion. The very worst show put on by the LOST Theatre. Ever. At times laughably awful.

Twelfth Night. Pat Wilde again. We took this to the Edinburgh Festival. A very atmospheric beautiful version of the play. Even beat *West* for Best Production Award (Our awards - "The Cecils" as they were known - ran September to September)

Lysistrata. My own production. Again ideas great, execution lacking. I attempted to make the Athenians like posh Londoners, while the Spartans were more lower class. Did anyone pick up on this? Cecil's comment to me: "They were all a bit samey. You should have done something like making the Athenians posh and the Spartans lower class..."

Blondel. By Tim Rice and Stephen Oliver. Pat and I co-directed this musical set in mediaeval times.

Rice and Oliver came to see it. On that night our leading lady Maroulla got into the wrong key on the last song. Her attempts to put it right meant she changed keys several times, each time getting further away. At last the key was so low she had to speak her lines. Stephen Requena as Blondel, who had to sing verse two, just ignored everything she was doing, and brilliantly came in in the right key.

Our Day Out. The first production of our new Under 16 group. They were to become such a vital part of LOST in the future, particularly of our later pantomimes.

Also in this year: *The Shadow Of A Gunman; See How They Run; The Cherry Orchard* and *Masterpieces.*

The last is a very unsavoury play By Sarah Daniels. It deals with violence towards women and particularly snuff movies. Sadly the play appears to me to be just a hate filled diatribe against men. This caused another minor controversy. It was decided that one evening of its run, all men would be banned from the theatre and a group campaigning against Violence towards women would come to the play. I thought then (and still do) that this was a bad way to deal with the subject. But whereas now I would just shrug my shoulders and get on with it, then, I was determined to come to the theatre on that night and make a stand. I hope by now you are getting a good idea of the kind of guy I was then... In the end, Cecil talked me out of it.

What I hope that this overview of just a single year shows is how varied and busy our programme was. We always played twelve or so times each year, and kept up this pace for almost twenty years. Also all our plays tended to rehearse over seven weeks or so, with rehearsals usually four nights a week and Sunday. Compare this to many societies that rehearse two nights a week and present three plays a year. We were giving our plays the amount of rehearsal that any professional play gets (spread over a longer period of course). We attracted not the casual amateur actor but young people who took theatre very seriously and were prepared to give up most of their time to it. Rather than making productions dull, this actually served in focussing our energy. We were young. We worked hard, but had a bloody great time.

I have now gone through just three years of my nineteen with the company. I originally intended to give an overview of the whole period, full of funny anecdotes and interesting observations. Of course this would be impossible without a whole book to myself (Cecil of course tried to get me to write one, but I simply cannot spare the time. A pity). In the end of course, I doubt that any account can actually capture what this experience meant to me or the others who shared it with me.

All I can do is pick out a few highlights, when the great joy of LOST was that it was there day after day, week after week, year upon year. Also these highlights tend to focus on the conflicts, the problems (drama is conflict - lesson one of acting), what it cannot capture is the sheer sense of unity, friendship, even family - that this company engendered. I have often felt this in various other productions I have been involved in, but only in LOST was it a constant on-going thing, changing and growing with the seasons and the years. To know that a play would be performed EVERY month, and to turn up and sit in the office (past my knocked through door) and discuss, talk, share, being a part even when one was not in the play. It was truly a golden time.

More highlights 1987 - 2002

As I said I cannot go through my whole time in detail, but I would like to pick just three other topics to dip into over the later years of the company. I will talk about The Edinburgh Festival; the Pantomimes; and the Sit-in.

Edinburgh Festival

Originally set up as a fringe event to the main international Festival, this has become a major festival in its own right. Hundreds of halls, churches and rooms over pubs are turned into performance spaces and over the course of three or four weeks there are many, many performances (a thousand a day we were told once). In 1985 Paul Rogan was preparing to take a comedy sketch show there. Quite late on, we decided to revive our recent production of *Up Against It* for the Festival. This ought to have been the perfect choice for an Edinburgh play. Sadly we were new to the whole idea of this. It was too late to get an entry in the Fringe programme (a listing of all events playing) but we were assured that we could publicise the show by leaf-letting and word of mouth. Also our near midnight would not be a problem in Edinburgh. Both sadly, sadly wrong.

Playing to five people a night, with one often a drunk, was certainly an experience. Over the years we got so much better at organising this, and became quite a common fixture of the Fringe Festival. Around 1987, Pat Wilde and I worked together to form a sub-company called *LOST On The Road* which used the theatre during the day and was a professional wing of the company. There was much banter and fake rivalry (at least we always pretended it was fake) between the two sides. But for a few years LOST had a double presence at the Festival.

Going to the Festival was a useful experience on so many levels. It was tremendously bonding to have to find and select a venue to hire, organise and arrange accommodation, sort out transport and publicity. It was also very good for us as actors to present our shows to an audience not made up of friends and parents. Our first review, *Tongue In Cheek*, went down a storm at LOST but struggled a little more in the tougher playing field of the Festival. As the years went by our reputation for producing good plays rose considerably, and our reviews were generally either good or excellent. Also the sheer experience of having to raise funds for the project was very good for building company spirit. Although we rarely achieved major grant aid at LOST, the council were often able to help on special projects or arranging cheap minibus hire. We also tried several drama based ideas. Our first was the 24 hour improvisation. We started an ad libbed scene and kept it going for a whole day. Actors were sponsored for how long they stayed on the stage in fifteen minute increments (toilet breaks were allowed). This was a rather difficult undertaking.

I managed to last the whole 24 hours, but no one else did (though one LOST stalwart, Maurizio Molino, arrived two minutes late for the start and was docked fifteen minutes. He ended up with twenty three hours and forty-five minutes! Boy did that rankle with him...). In later years we arranged it so that the COMPANY was sponsored for the time completed rather than the individual actor. One year, we were fifteen hundred pounds short of our target, and this was mentioned in the evening paper, along with details of the 24 hour impro. According to reports (I had gone home for a break) someone turned up and stood watching for a while. He then went to the office and asked how fund raising was going. Told how much we were short, he asked if fifteen hundred was enough and wrote a cheque for two thousand dollars. It was a famous star of musical theatre who, since he specifically requested us to not publicise his deed, I will not name: but his help and generosity, with no thought of self-aggrandisement, is to this day an act I salute and admire.

The Pantomimes. 1988 - 98

Cecil had always wanted the LOST to focus on good theatre. We did not specialise in any one type of play but were ready to perform anything of sufficient quality - Ancient Greek authors, Chaucer and Shakespeare rubbed shoulders with Wilde, Orton or Steven Berkoff. This I think was a tremendously educating process. Though mainly a youth company (originally three quarters of each cast had to be under twenty six...later this became the whole of a cast), we in no way focussed on "youth" drama. Cecil also insisted, as part of this complete theatre idea, which we put on one musical a year. An excellent idea in principal, but we sometimes fell down badly on this. Productions of lighter shows like *Grease* or *Blondel* fared reasonably well. Even *Cabaret*, as much a serious play with songs, was within our means. For the more operatic songs of *To The Woods*, as I have said, we lacked at the time strength in depth, and we had similar problems with *West Side Story*. Even with *Cabaret* I recall an embarrassing note session (note sessions, for those not up with theatre jargon, occur after runs of the play close to the first performance: the director sits down with the cast and tells them all the things that need to be worked on or changed). I was playing Max, the non-singing club owner, so I was present as Cecil gave a spoke to one of the girls who sang which he thought was rather weakly performed. Now for obvious reasons I will not name her, but if she reads this I sadly have to say he was in my opinion totally right. But he merely said to her, in front of the rest of the cast, words to the effect: "you are having problems with that song aren't you my love.... let's give it to someone else," he then continued giving notes, apparently oblivious to the girl sobbing in front of him. I say "apparently" because I sometimes suspect Cecil would, so he could get his message across, be prepared to allow himself to appear tactless or thoughtless. He once spent a couple of hours explaining at length to me why I would never be a professional actor. I was determined to prove him wrong even though his arguments were logical and credible. And now I am a professional.....so was he wrong or just cleverly encouraging me?

But anyway, we often struggled with musical theatre. Eventually a new idea emerged. As we settled into the theatre, we had made several changes. The office door, and lighting box have been mentioned. We had a long narrow dressing room with two doors. We walled off one end of it, with one door, and built a small recording studio supervised by our leading musician and sound guy Tony Conway. He and I, along with Stephen Requena, put forward the idea of writing our own pantomimes. I wrote the book and Steve and Tony the original music and lyrics. They were an astonishing success. *Cinderella, Aladdin, Babes In The Wood* and *Dick Whittington* were performed and revived again and again. They allowed us one production a year with parts for the main company, the under 16 groups (now thriving) and the adult student actors. They were bright, colourful and fun, with humour specially tailored for our audiences. Many of our under 16's grew up with them from the age of five, and went on to act for the company proper ten or twelve years later. This more than anything captures the theme of LOST as a family. These shows also bridged the gap back to mainstream musicals as the company grew: in our last year in Fulham Road allowing us to stage very successfully *Little Shop Of Horrors* and *Oliver!* And in 2002 a ghost (for me at least) was laid to rest with our extremely successful revival of *To The Woods*.

The 1991 Sit-in

My final event I wish to talk about is the sit in at the Castle Club. Though only a few days in our history, this really captures the kind of relationship we had with the council or grant awarding bodies. Many theatre companies live and prosper on grants and council aided funding. LOST always seemed on the point of getting major help but never quite succeeding. This is not to say we were given nothing: although we had to pay rent to the Methodist Church, it was never full market price for the property (they had been given money to build the church, under the proviso they had a youth group on the premises - and their own attempts at running one had not worked out well). Rent and utilities therefore had to be paid each month, and we constantly needed to make a profit on the majority of our shows to keep our head above water. Cecil received a small payment as a youth leader, and once we had the coffee bar running, that was a small source of income. From the council we were delivered seating and rostra every month, eventually we were able to keep these permanently set up. We had occasional grants for projects such as Edinburgh Festival, and the use of the resource centre in Hammersmith. This was in the days before home computers and printers, where roneo and lettraset ruled. Basically the problem was that a Labour administration gave us nothing because we were too elitist (i.e. we did not care about colour creed or gender, just whether people could act), Conservatives politicians felt that we were a shining example of what could be done without hand-outs, and so gave us none.

One area where we did get help was in rehearsal space. In the theatre itself we only had a dressing room, office and coffee bar, no extra rehearsal room. But since we performed a new show each month, and as our shows needed six or seven weeks rehearsal, that meant we always had two shows in production at any time...one in its final weeks rehearsing and performing in the theatre itself, the other in its first four weeks of rehearsal had to have another space to rehearse in. When I first came, we used a building some twenty minutes' walk away, near Wandsworth Bridge, called the Castle Club (and yes...it did look very like a castle). But we had always been promised use of a scout hall next door to the Castle Club, and we had spent time clearing it all out. Eventually the council found other uses for the Club, and allowed us to move into the scout hall, which had a courtyard and storage shed. For a while we were in clover, not only using it for rehearsals but even setting it up as a small studio performance space. Then came the bombshell, a new council was in place and had earmarked this building for other uses. In vain we protested that it was promised to us....there was nothing in writing. Nor were the council even keen on discussing the matter. This would be a major problem. Nor was possible use of school halls at odd moments much of a solution...we needed somewhere we could access as and when we wanted.

We told the council of the work we had done on the space (setting up lighting rig, painting, masking) and the costumes stored by us in the shed. We were given a day to come and remove our stuff. Though I was not quite the confrontational young firebrand of the past, I suggested a possible plan of action. When we arrived late one Friday afternoon to collect our stuff, we set up camp in the shed and told the work men it was a sit in. This caused great hilarity. We had planned a sit in, just when they were heading off for two days anyway!

They wished us a happy weekend and departed chortling. This was not quite how we had envisaged it going, but we gritted our teeth and dug in. Here at least we were well organised...we had a trip to a local store and bought in camping stoves and torches etc. (all paid for out of his own pocket by Cecil). One of our technical people even brought lights and a portable generator. When the workmen came back on Monday morning they did not smile. They were greeted with the whole courtyard rigged with lights and chairs, and a roaring camp-fire. And by good luck their next job was to relay the floor of the courtyard. If they fell behind, penalties would apply.

At this point I will be frank and say that my memory of exactly how long the next events took is hazy (it was over twenty years ago). I know we kept it up for several more days, but could not be more precise. I do know that people from the council were informed and I was approached by the workmen and asked to ring them to discuss it. I found a phone box (no mobiles then!) and called. I was eventually asked to come to the council buildings to discuss it. I told them to come to us. And come they did. We put our case, and they went away. Some days later and we were losing heart...I would estimate that by the following day most of our troops would have given it all up (we were working a rota system of course, but it was still dull, cold, boring work, and the initial excitement was long gone). I phoned the council one last time and told them we were prepared to stay for another month. They caved. They did not give us back the scout hut, that would have been too much to hope for, but offered us 24/7 use of a greenhouse style building in the grounds of the castle club. This was not a perfect result, but it was a great deal better than we had been offered before. And in all truth another day would probably have seen us slinking away with nothing. We had saved face. The council too in part had saved face. It was a workable solution.

And in a small way it also demonstrated Cecil's almost legendary luck. And I don't mean with the sit in. Cecil was always arranging things that we warned him were impossible, we constantly used to tell him that we had no time, money or people to do it. And time and again it worked out - usually because we threw ourselves into the breach to make it so. Cecil had determined we would take *Equus* to the Edinburgh Festival a second year running. In vain we pointed out how late it was to organise this, and that such a thing needed a year's planning. Cecil was set on it. For once we all stood back and said: let it crash and burn, that will teach him. And then the sit in happened, and an Edinburgh Tour had to be postponed because of it. Cecil walked away convinced that but for the council he would have taken that play to Edinburgh. There was no way on earth it could have happened. And he will never believe a word of it.

A final word

I sit here today in Perth, Western Australia. I am working as a professional actor, director and teacher. I have just come home from performing in our yearly open air Shakespeare production in King's Park (we have the weather for it). Every single day I use talents, skills and techniques I learned at LOST. When I started to write this I hoped to convey some of the magic and wonder of the place. Of course it fails; all you get is a bunch of humorous anecdotes about people you don't know. But anyone who has acted will know the amazing camaraderie and closeness that can develop during some plays or drama courses. Usually this lasts for a few weeks, or months. Occasionally (such as in a university drama society) a year or two. LOST kept that amazing feeling of belonging going for twenty years (for me). Talk to many people who lived through it and you will hear the same story. What about the company this feeling so intense?

I believe in some ways I have given a less than balanced picture of Cecil Hayter in this article. I have pointed out the annoying, tactless, often brutal frankness he possessed, very clearly. It all makes more interesting reading. What I have left out is the thrilling intensity of a man who loved and lived for theatre. A man who you could phone at midnight and explain that a set needed painting to have him come with his brushes and work all night (while explaining to you in detail where you stuffed up). A man always willing to give lifts home to the most out of the way places. I do believe if you told Cecil you had missed a train to Aberdeen he would offer to drive you. And if ever while driving he took a wrong turn, and I said "this road doesn't go anywhere" he would reply: "all roads go somewhere; let's see where it takes us." An amazing philosophy to live by.

And when this man set up a theatre company, look at the way it was arranged: some theatre groups rehearse two days a week for three months - we rehearsed five days a week for six weeks. Some companies presented five or six productions a year - we regularly did twelve. Many companies rehearse for a couple of hours - we often did four, and sometimes pulled all-nighters. Every single decision made was in the direction of turning up the intensity of the working environment until one lived, breathed, ate and drank theatre. For many this would be far too much, or only endurable occasionally. Such people came, then moved on. But for the huge numbers who stayed, some like me for decades, this was heaven. We were part of a family created by this emotional, intense, dedicated man. And, sadly, as time went on, many of this family came to lose respect for a figure from an earlier generation to them, even while they profited from the world he had created. For some years I tried to hold back the tide. Circumstances took me half a world away: but had I stayed, eventually I would also have been drowned by it. Sadly it is sometimes the way of youth to wish to assert their individuality by rebelling against their upbringing.

I salute Cecil Hayter both for what he created, and what he is. All actors strive to create a character. Directors try to create a credible world for these characters to inhabit. Cecil went one better, he created a place where all these could live, grow and flourish in the purest intensity of their art. It is a truly astonishing feat, for which I honour him daily from my very soul.

Thank you Cecil.

Stephen Lee

Perth, Western Australia, 14th January 2014

THERESA SHORTLAND (THERESA DREA)

I remember joining the LOST gang for *Dark Of The Moon* after hearing about it from Bernadette and the rest of the Nolan's. I recall being in many other productions which the Nolan's have outlined. I do remember spending a lot of time travelling to Fulham from the east end with the Nolan's and Seamus.

I remember Josie, Gabby and I being in the 'committee' for a while. We held the meetings at your house!

I did enjoy doing *Threepenny Opera*, I played one of the whores with low dive Jenny played brilliantly by Bernie Nolan. I also remember Joanna and Gerry being fabulous as Mr and Mrs Peechum and of course Ralph as McKeith.

I also did *Othello* playing Emilia, with Cecily as Desdemona and Paddy's rather cunning role as Iago. I do have a smile when I think of Jeremy Trafford blacked up to play Othello! He loved playing that role. It was directed by Adrian Brown! He had also had a cameo role as the duke! I can still hear him saying to me during rehearsals 'iambic pentameter darling!'

I recall after this play doing a trip to Germany with Paddy, Frank, Kelly and Brigit to see Joanna perform in a touring version of *Hair* in Munich. We drove across Europe consuming much alcohol on route! My memory of that trip topped off with Brigit driving through the border control to Germany without stopping in Paddy's old car!

I also remember the one act festivals giving us a chance to direct. I directed Derek Fitzgerald playing the lead role in *Gotcha* a Barry Keefe one act play. Derek played a delinquent teenager and held his teacher hostage. The teacher was played by Tim O'Sullivan playing Ton and Josie Nolan playing Lynne.

The plays I enjoyed the most were the Irish ones in particular *Juno And The Paycock*. I played Maize Madigan and do recall on occasion real alcohol being put in the glass I had to down in one on stage! A stage prank of which there were a few!

I also remember playing Shibby in *The Pot Of Broth* (WB Yeats, I think) with storytelling workshops as part of the production. This was again with Paddy and Graham Machal. It took us to Irish centres all over London and even to Leicester. Paddy had a radio interview!

I do recall doing *Pound On Demand* by Sean O'Casey, directed by Paddy, at the King's Head during a fundraiser. This was with Gerry playing a very convincing drunk and Mandy Smith a post office girl and Charlie as the 'polis' man. We all had a few drinks before that show I recall a slapstick element creeping in!

There were lots if parties! Lots of hours spent in the pub and lots of time hanging out with each other.

As I was good with a sewing machine I often ended up being wardrobe mistress which I loved!

All in all I have such happy memories of The LOST theatre! Days full of friendship camaraderie and being part of something very special. We were a bunch of young people that just loved acting and theatre and had an opportunity to be creative and have fun as LOST!

I live in Surrey now and work for Reading Council in Education services. I carried on with amateur drama with Hopscotch players after LOST for many years doing plays in local festivals. I now enjoy watching my daughter nurture her love of theatre and acting!

Hope the book goes well.

Love

Theresa Drea. Now Theresa Shortland. Xxx

THOMAS MARTY

So there I was at the age of 15 interested in acting and going to watch some musical production the school youth club was putting on. Well it must have been good as the school was deluged with kids inspired by watching the show, wanting to join this group. The school could not ignore the call and got the man responsible for all the fuss to create a new theatre company and The LOST Youth Theatre was born. It was always different from other groups as Cecil Hayter (the Guv) wanted us to run it. Imagine that, a youth theatre run by young people? So, committees were formed and tried out, formulas came and went until the right people and the right jobs were successfully put into place. We did what the group became known for best, which was putting on shows. Not just the three big productions a year other groups did, but once a month the opus (workshop) shows came into being. These encouraged budding playwrights, actors and directors to learn and enjoy their trade. At least four major shows a year were produced and just to add a little flavour to the mix, the one act play competition came into being.

My particular interest was new writing and like many others enjoyed the fact that this was a theatre company that bent over backwards to help us out. A Monday night writing group was started and many shaky ideas grew with encouragement and support over tea and toast into important milestone poems, plays, songs and sketches for us new and budding writers. This was a magic place where we could talk art, create art and also perform our own and established work and there was never anyone telling us we shouldn't. Shows stood up on their own merit and a strange world was created for blooming artists in all the trades of the business; actors, writers, designers, lighting, directors, stage managers, poets, singers, musicians, singer songwriters, film directors and so on... If a member wanted to write a musical, Cecil was great at bringing people together and provided musical people to help out. He would always encourage us at every point and perhaps we didn't know how privileged we were. This man wanted us to succeed and backed us with a faith and trust you couldn't find anywhere else.

I was lucky and was the first member to swan off to drama school (The Webber Douglas Academy of

Dramatic Art) many others followed and spread out into the profession. Many times in the future I would meet old friends and make new ones who had tasted LOST`s unique experience and realise just how powerful and immense LOST was in the beginnings of our careers. In fact after leaving drama school there was a thriving fringe theatre element to the company made up of many of these old members and their new friends intent on making a name for themselves either as new writers, directors or actors.

I spent sixteen lovely years working in the profession and have managed to transfer all those skills into writing, directing and teaching young people in my own theatre in education company, Public Arena. Many times when running classes my thoughts go back to those Friday nights in the London Oratory School and then at the Methodist church in similar classes being led by Cecil. I always think about how many hundreds of young people have been inspired by him and in turn how they have inspired hundreds of others to have a creative element in their lives.

TONY CONWAY

Up Against It – in more ways than one..........

Unlike many of my contemporaries, I joined LOST not as an actor, an aspiring director, or back-stage supremo. I joined as music and costume consultant on the Opus *LOST In The Sixties*. How apt, I've been lost there ever since that day.

When my good friend Paul Rogan asked me to give a hand that day, I little realised the consequences it would have on my future, and Maurizio's fashion sense...

I accidentally tried directing in One Act Festival, bizarrely choosing the first act of John Osborne's *Look Back In Anger*. When the adjudicator, even more accidentally awarded us an.....award, I was given the chance to direct a full-length play the following year.

Joe Orton's screenplay for The Beatles, *Up Against It* had never been filmed, or more importantly, adapted for the stage. So, along with musical colleague Ed Ball of The Times, we decided to perform it at The LOST Theatre in 1985. An extraordinary cast nursed us through and we achieved the ultimate establishment recognition - a good review in the London Times.

The show, at very short notice went to the Edinburgh Fringe Festival, where a great time was had by all, and we also put on the play.

And we staged it in the Edinburgh Masonic Lodge! Orton would have loved it....

We thankfully did plenty of Orton, and Berkoff, and Shakespeare, amongst others – most memorably Steve Reqena's *Hamlet* in Patrick Wilde's production, every-one in Paddy O'Connor's *West* by Berkoff, and Gerry O'Sullivan as Bill Naughton's *Alfie* in Paul Rogan's staging, stained with a Senior Service authenticity.

Other random personal highlights, for many reasons, would include most of the Opus shows, the Synge and

O'Casey productions, going to Edinburgh, *Henry IV Pt I*, Curved Air's *Sonja Kristina* at the excellent LOST Cafe. Mike Kelly's Youth shows, the panto writing sessions, The Harwood Arms, The LOST Newsletter, *Entertaining Mr Sloane*, late -night lively political discussions with Cecil, Steve Lee, Patrick, Julian, Robin et al in the 80's, rigging with Nick and Dom, an anonymous donor turning up one day with 1500 pounds to save us from extinction, *Doctor Faustus*, late-night chats etc. in the dressing room, *Sell Out!*, the Beatles favourite brand of tea, *Lark Rise To Candleford*, the Celebrity Items Auction, *Rags To Riches*, recording with Tom Marty, *Twelfth Night*, the Panto bands, The 24 Hour impro, *What's Wrong With Angry?* And the LOST parties, especially Charlie's............

And the gigs – amongst others, *Tom And Gerry, The Direct Hits, The Perfect Strangers, Bad Karma Beckons, The Faith Brothers, Mood Six,* and of course, *The LOST All-Stars*.......(I warn you, as we speak, there is footage waiting to be uploaded onto YouTube).

Then there were the Pantomimes - Stephen Lee, Steve Requena and myself, along with the superb casts and musicians, took the traditional Pantomime format and added a mash-up of Carry-On, Marx Brothers & British Music Hall humour, topped off with musical pastiches of every style ranging from Lionel Bart to Deep Purple and from Gilbert and Sullivan to The Beatles.........all fuelled by copious amounts of the Beatles favourite brand of tea...and just in case, in a parallel universe one day, we re-open at 450 Fulham Road...I've still got the full set of keys, in one sense, anyway...another tea, Steve?

EPILOGUE

I am now eighty years young and, although I profess to having retired from theatre, I cannot resist returning, when invited, to do the occasional opera with my beloved Southgate Opera company. As to the LOST theatre... suffice it to say that no parent is capable of 'getting over' the loss of a child.

Besides bringing back many joyful memories, your writings have brought me much joy, at times moving me to tears, and at times embarrassing me greatly by reminding me that I could be so unthinkingly cruel. I heartily apologise to the young girl (whoever you are) to whom I so rudely told she couldn't sing. Also to those of you, like Stephen Lee, I told would never be professionals. With the exception of one or two with obviously super talents (i.e. Ralph) it was usual for me not to encourage young people into a very difficult and competitive career. I felt that if you ignored me and still went for it, you may have a chance, if you took my advice, and if you didn't, you would never have made it anyhow. So a very big congratulations to those of you who did ignore me and have ended up in very successful careers, and there appear to be many of you.

I think back and remember the very first musical I attempted when, in all my ignorance, I adapted *Alice In Wonderland*, got my piano teacher, Gwen Vickers to write the music, and designed and painted the sets. I wouldn't dare do that today, even though at the time the show appeared to be very successful. But I think in the same way that Ralph, with one or two other talented actors, carried the day with Romeo and Juliet, so did a very talented little twelve year old girl called Beverley, playing the part of Alice, with again one or two talented actors to support her, do likewise, both of them turning up at the first rehearsal knowing all their lines. We know what Ralph did. Beverley went on to earn two doctoral degrees. Both also, never lost touch with me and have always supported me.

So, when I was young and ignorant, I felt I was the real thing. Now that I am old and a little wiser I feel a complete fraud and can only thank, from the bottom of my heart all those numbers of you who have so solidly supported me through thick and thin.

Lightning Source UK Ltd.
Milton Keynes UK
UKOW04f2229080714

234819UK00001B/66/P